Praise for David Armitage's

CIVIL WARS

"Compact and intensely thought-provoking. . . . Densely researched and smoothly written, [*Civil Wars*] is a pointed attempt to understand the nature of civil war by understanding its history. . . . 'Civil war is an inheritance humanity may not be able to escape,' he writes at the end of his account, but with the help of powerhouse books like this one, there may at least come greater understanding."
—Steve Donoghue,
The Christian Science Monitor

"In *Civil Wars* Armitage traces the evolution of an explosive concept, not to pin down a proper meaning but to show why it remains so slippery. . . . In an era of transnational populism and anti-globalist revolt, this [book] is resonant. The meaning of civil war, as Mr. Armitage shows, is as messy and multifaceted as the conflict it describes."
—*The Economist*

"Unusually timely. . . . Armitage is a historian of ideas and his discussion of the subsequent vicissitudes of the idea of civil war is at the core of his book. He moves fluently from Rome, through early modern Europe to the American Civil War."
—Mark Mazower,
Financial Times

DAVID ARMITAGE

CIVIL WARS

David Armitage is the Lloyd C. Blankfein Professor of History at Harvard University, where he teaches intellectual history and international history, and former chair of Harvard's History Department. His many publications include *The Ideological Origins of the British Empire* (2000) and *The Declaration of Independence: A Global History* (2007).

ALSO BY DAVID ARMITAGE

The Ideological Origins of the British Empire

Greater Britain, 1516–1776: Essays in Atlantic History

The Declaration of Independence: A Global History

Foundations of Modern International Thought

The History Manifesto

Civil Wars

CIVIL WARS

A History in Ideas

DAVID ARMITAGE

VINTAGE BOOKS
A Division of Penguin Random House LLC
New York

FIRST VINTAGE BOOKS EDITION, JANUARY 2018

Copyright © 2017 by David Armitage

All rights reserved. Published in the United States by
Vintage Books, a division of Penguin Random House LLC,
New York. Originally published in hardcover in the
United States by Alfred A. Knopf, a division of
Penguin Random House LLC, New York, in 2017.

The Library of Congress has cataloged the Knopf edition
as follows:
Names: Armitage, David, [1965–] author.
Title: Civil wars : a history in ideas / David Armitage.
Description: First edition. | New York : Alfred A. Knopf, 2017. |
Includes bibliographical references and index.
Identifiers: LCCN 2016023404 (print) | LCCN 201641142 (ebook)
Subjects: LCSH: Civil war—Philosophy. | Military history. |
BISAC: PHILOSOPHY / Political. | HISTORY / World.
Classification: LCC JC328.5 .A75 2017 (print) | LCC JC328.5 (ebook) |
DDC 355.02/1809—dc23
LC record available at https://lccn.loc.gov/2016023404

Vintage Books Trade Paperback ISBN: 978-0-307-45617-5
eBook ISBN: 978-0-385-35309-0

Author photograph © Lauren McLaughlin
Book design by Soonyoung Kwon

www.vintagebooks.com

Printed in the United States of America
10 9 8 7 6 5 4 3 2 1

In memoriam

Nicholas Henshall (1944–2015)
Christopher Bayly (1945–2015)

Civil war? What does this mean? Is there any foreign war? Is not every war between men, war between brothers?

—VICTOR HUGO, *Les Misérables* (1862)

Whatever brotherhood human beings may be capable of has grown out of fratricide, whatever political organization men may have achieved has its origin in crime.

—HANNAH ARENDT, *On Revolution* (1963)

Contents

Note on Conventions

Following the convention among classicists and others who study the ancient world, I have used B.C.E. (before the Common Era) and C.E. (Common Era) to describe dates otherwise written as B.C. and A.D.

In quotations from original sources, I have silently modernized some spellings for intelligibility, so that *i* becomes *j*, *u* becomes *v*, and vice versa. I have retained punctuation and italicization.

I cite Greek and Latin sources according to the conventional numbering of books, lines, and so on, found in the volumes of the Loeb Classical Library.

Translations are my own, unless otherwise specified.

Civil Wars

Confronting Civil War

Since 1945, Europe, North America, and countries of comparable wealth elsewhere, like Australia and Japan, have experienced what has been termed a "Long Peace." Coming in the wake of World War II, this period without war between states now stands as the most enduring in modern history. Previously the calmest moments, within Europe at least, ran from the end of the Napoleonic Wars to the Crimean War (1815–53) and then from the Franco-Prussian War in 1871 to the beginning of World War I in 1914, but the recent international peace in the Global North has already lasted two decades more, even if over-shadowed by the Cold War for much of its duration.[1] Current global trends are also encouraging. In 2016, the latest year for which we have data, there were only two inter-state conflicts, between India and Pakistan and Eritrea and Ethiopia, each over border disputes; the latter lasted for only two days.[2] Despite Russian intervention in Ukraine and the combustible disputes over islands in the South

China Sea, the Long Peace increasingly looks as if it might expand and become all encompassing around the globe.

And yet our own age is plainly no piping time of peace. The world is still a very violent place.³ In 2016, there were forty-nine armed conflicts in progress from Afghanistan to Yemen, not counting acts of terrorism, insurgency, or other forms of "asymmetrical" warfare, in which non-state forces attack states or their inhabitants. The activities first of al-Qaeda and now of Islamic State (Daesh) and its sympathizers have brought the weaponry of war onto the streets of the world's cities, from Manhattan to Mumbai and from Sydney to Brussels. While states may, in fact, be at peace with one another, their peoples can hardly feel at ease or secure amid the effects of conflict taking place afar, where so many still know war within their own borders. The Long Peace stands under a dark shadow—the shadow of civil war.

In the early 1990s, theorists of the "end of history" assured us that capitalism and democracy were poised to blanket the globe, uniting all humanity in the enjoyment of flourishing trade and secure rights. Subscribers to such thinking argued for the so-called democratic peace, the view that as democracy spreads, universal peace would follow in its wake because democracies (they allege) do not go to war with one another. They built on the arguments of the philosopher Immanuel Kant (1724–1804), who in turn drew on the European Enlightenment's long tradition of discourse on the possibility of securing lasting peace.⁴ Kant was no naïf; he wryly observed that a Dutch innkeeper had painted the very words "perpetual

peace" on his tavern sign alongside a picture of a graveyard, implying that the only true and lasting peace would
be the eternal sleep of death. Yet Kant believed that peace
among states was "no empty idea" but rather "a task that,
gradually solved, comes steadily closer to its goal."[5] Not
that perpetual peace would draw any nearer in his own
lifetime: the great general and empire builder Napoleon
was crowned emperor only ten months after Kant died in
February 1804 and would spend the next decade menacing the world. Even so, a little over two hundred years
later, many dare to believe that humanity might finally
have moved beyond armed conflict between states—that
following "the better angels of our nature," we may well
be able to fulfill Kant's dream and at last "win the war on
war."[6] Yet with death and destruction all around us, the
peace we have feels more like that of the graveyard. And
more than any other form of conflict, the one that has
lately filled the graveyard is not war between states, not
terrorism, but *civil* war.

Civil war has gradually become the most widespread,
the most destructive, and the most characteristic form of
organized human violence. The decades following the
Cold War saw a major spike in its incidence. Since 1989,
an average of twenty intrastate wars have been in progress at any moment—about ten times the annual average globally between 1816 and 1989. There have been
roughly twenty-five million "total battle deaths" in these
wars since 1945, or about half the military casualties of
World War II. Even that count does not include wounded,
displaced, and dead civilians, let alone all those afflicted

by disease and malnutrition. The material and economic costs have been no less staggering. Hard-nosed analysts of global development have focused on the impact of war on growth, factoring in the loss of life and, consequently, of productivity, as well as the value of wasted resources, military spending, the spread of crime and disease, and the disruption of neighboring economies. The result of their calculations? The annual price tag for civil war has been about $123 billion—roughly what the Global North budgets for economic aid to the Global South each year. Not without reason, then, has civil war been chillingly described as "development in reverse."[7]

Wars within states tend to last longer—some four times longer—than wars between them, and in the second half of the twentieth century they have generally lasted three times as long as in the first half. These conflicts are also much more prone to recur than any others, as "the most likely legacy of a civil war is further civil war"; indeed, almost every civil war in the last decade was the resumption of an earlier one.[8] Civil wars seem disproportionately to befall the world's poorest countries—especially those in Africa and in Asia—which the development economist Sir Paul Collier has called "the bottom billion."[9] If the developed world has enjoyed a long peace since 1945, large parts of the global population have undergone an equally long trauma. The Centre for the Study of Civil War in Oslo proclaims all these distinctions on its website, adding, "Yet civil war is less studied than interstate war."[10] It seems that civil war, like the poor, may always be with us. And so long as it is, it will generally afflict the world's poor.

But civil war shouldn't also remain an impoverished area of inquiry. As many have noted, civil war has remained undertheorized and resistant to generalization. There is no great work titled *On Civil War* to stand alongside Carl von Clausewitz's *On War* or Hannah Arendt's *On Revolution*; indeed, as we shall see, Clausewitz hardly discussed civil war at all, while Arendt herself dismissed it, along with war itself, as atavistic and antimodern. The postwar German poet and political commentator Hans Magnus Enzensberger (b. 1929) observed in 1993 that "there is no useful Theory of Civil War."[11] So, too, the Italian political theorist Giorgio Agamben (b. 1942) has noted more recently that "there exists, today, both a 'polemology,' a theory of war, and an 'irenology,' a theory of peace, but there is no 'stasiology,' no theory of civil war."[12] Such laments are long-lived, too. It is not my aim to provide an overarching theory of civil war. Nor can I supply that missing treatise. What I can do as a historian is to uncover the origins of our present discontents, to explain just why we remain so confused about civil war and why we refuse to look it in the face.

Our own time demands an unblinking encounter with civil war. The three hundred years between 1648 and 1945 constituted an era of war *between* states; the last sixty years appear to be an age of war *within* states.[13] Indeed, this is the most striking change in patterns of human conflict for centuries. According to one widely cited estimate, since 1945 there have been 259 conflicts around the world that have risen to the level of a war, and the vast majority of those were internal conflicts. Since 1989, barely 5 percent of the world's wars have taken place between states. One has only to think back to the Balkan wars of the 1990s, or to those in Rwanda, Burundi, Mozambique, Somalia, Nicaragua, and Sri Lanka, for instance, to realize how prominent and how deadly internal struggles have been in recent memory, to say nothing of the ongoing suffering of those who live in their wake. To make matters even worse, civil wars do not usually stay "civil" for long. In 2016, eighteen of the forty-seven internal conflicts, from Afghanistan to Yemen, were so-called internationalized civil wars, ones that drew in forces from neighboring countries or intervention by outside powers.[14] Civil war is no respecter of borders. Indeed, it often turns countries inside out, as conflict drives people from their homes in search of safety. The populations displaced by civil war— not least the almost five million refugees from Syria over the course of the conflict there since 2012—are the most conspicuous victims of its overspill. Their plight has fueled a refugee crisis that will reshape the Middle East, North Africa, and Europe for generations. The attendant challenges to security and stability make it appear that ours is not a world at peace. It is a world of civil war.

*

War is hell, the U.S. Civil War general William Tecumseh Sherman is supposed to have said, but surely the only thing worse is *civil* war.[15] On that fact, there has been general agreement across the centuries. Internal wars are felt to be more destructive than ones against external enemies.

Writing in the wake of Rome's civil wars, in the first century B.C.E., the poet Lucan concluded from the shattered cities, abandoned fields, and droves of the dispossessed, "No foreign sword has ever penetrated / so: it is wounds inflicted by the hand of fellow-citizen that have sunk deep." Civil wars are like a sickness of the body politic, destroying it from within. Likewise, the Renaissance essayist Michel de Montaigne would warn his readers during the French Wars of Religion, "In truth *a forraine warre is nothing so dangerous a disease as a civill*." Dangerous and morally degrading, too. Just before the Irish Civil War of 1922, an elderly priest lamented, "War with the foreigner brings to the fore all that is best and noblest in a nation— civil war all that is mean and base."[16] And even when the battles have ceased, they leave wounds that will not heal: "I question whether any serious civil war ever does end," T. S. Eliot observed in 1947.[17] On a visit to Spain in 1970, the former French president Charles de Gaulle agreed: "All wars are bad . . . But civil wars, in which there are brothers in both trenches, are unforgivable, because peace is not born when war concludes."[18]

Civil wars are doubtless inhumane but they have been so widespread and persistent that some have suspected them of being essential to our humanity. As Hans-Magnus Enzensberger argued, "Animals fight, but they don't wage war. Only man—unique among the primates—practises the large-scale, deliberate and enthusiastic destruction of his fellow creatures." And what could be more characteristically human, yet more shamefully different from the habits of other animals, than inflicting aggression on your immediate neighbors? Formal warfare, conducted by professional armies and constrained by the laws of war, was something modern and recent, but what lay behind the outward show was a more basic, more enduring, form of inhumanity: *civil war*. "Civil war is not merely an old custom," Enzensberger concluded, "but the primary form of all collective conflict."[19]

Enzensberger was writing in the shadow of ethnic conflict in Africa and the Balkans and not long after the Los Angeles riots of April–May 1992 that followed the acquittal of police officers for beating an African American motorist the previous year. This was just the moment when human-on-human violence seemed to be cresting around the world, across continents and within cities, as if to reassert the prevalence of what is worst in humankind and to confirm our destiny as civil warriors. Enzensberger could be forgiven for assuming that civil war had always been with us. So many of the world's primal myths—Krishna and Arjuna in the Mahabharata; the Hebrew Bible's Cain and Abel; Eteocles and Polynices in Greek mythology; Romulus and Remus for the Romans—concern internecine violence, specifically fratricidal violence, in a way that suggests it is foundational.[20] Such myths can help us grasp the emotional dimensions of conflict but their durability should not be mistaken for civil war's inevitability.

Long-lived too is the reputation of civil war as the most destructive and invasive of all kinds of human conflicts—and with good reason. At the height of Rome's civil wars in the first century B.C.E., perhaps a quarter of all its male citizens aged between seventeen and forty-six were in arms.[21] Seventeen hundred years later, a greater proportion of England's population likely died in the civil wars of the 1640s than would later perish in World War I.[22] And the death toll of the U.S. Civil War was vastly larger, relative to population size, than the American casualty rate in World War II: estimated at 750,000, from both North and South, it would be equivalent to roughly 7.5 million deaths among the present-day population of the United States.[23] Slaughter on such a scale scythes through families, shatters communities, shapes nations. It can scar also imaginations for centuries to come.

Yet we should be cautious about assuming civil war is an inevitable part of our makeup—a feature, not a bug, in the software that makes us human. For that would be to doom us to suffer civil war ad infinitum, never to reach Kant's promise of perpetual peace. To unsettle the notion that we are condemned to interminable civil war, rather than destined for perpetual peace, I here bring historical tools to confront the challenge of civil war. Over the course of this book, I show that civil war is neither eternal nor inexplicable. I argue that the phenomenon is coterminous with its historical conception, from its fraught origins in republican Rome to its contested present and its likely no less confusing or controversial future. It has a history with an identifiable beginning, if not yet a discernible end. A historical treatment reveals the contingency of the phenomenon, contradicting those who claim its permanence and durability. It is my aim to show that what humans have invented, they may yet dismantle; that what intellectual will has enshrined, an equal effort of imaginative determination can dethrone.

My goal is not just to excavate the history of civil war but to point up its significance in forming how we think about the world. I argue that despite its destructiveness civil war has been, throughout history, conceptually generative. Without the challenges it posed, our conceptions of democracy, politics, authority, revolution, international law, cosmopolitanism, humanitarianism, and globalization, to take just a few, would have been very different, even poorer.[24] The experience of civil war—the efforts to understand it, to ameliorate it, even to prevent it—has also shaped and continues to inform our ideas of community, authority, and sovereignty to this day. Civil wars spring from deep and deadly divisions but they expose identities and commonalities. To call a war "civil" is to acknowledge the familiarity of the enemies as members of the same community: not foreigners but fellow citizens. "Civil war has something atrocious about it," remarked the German legal thinker Carl Schmitt (1888–1985). "It is fraternal war, because it is conducted within a common political unit . . . and because both warring sides at the same time absolutely affirm and absolutely deny this common unit."[25] That is the source of our horror about civil wars; we should not underestimate the effect of civil wars in forcing a recognition of commonality amid confrontation, of making us see ourselves in the mirror of enmity.

Civil wars have been so paradoxically fertile because there has never been a time when their definition was settled to everyone's satisfaction or when it could be used without question or contention. This is in part because conceptions of civil war have been disputed and debated within so many different historical contexts. Naming, however, is always a form of framing. Understanding an object means first distinguishing it from similar things, and that often entails settling its identity by taming it in words. Once we can see what makes it peculiar, we can begin to recognize patterns, continuities, and differences, thereby developing our understanding.

This problem of naming becomes particularly acute when political ideas are at stake. We frame these terms to persuade our friends and to combat our enemies. And we have to invent new terms for new phenomena, both to make sense of them—what is this we are experiencing?— and to help others share our conception of them. When the framing term is one like "civil war," however, politics precedes even attempts at definition. What makes a war "civil" rather than, say, "foreign"? That difference will always raise hackles. And what makes violence identifiable as "war"? Again, wars have implications that serial skirmishes do not. Even to ask these questions demands fixing some points at least: an idea of what is "civil" (and what is not), as well as what counts as war (and what does not). It has never been easy to decide what is, or is not, a civil war, but that distinction was literally inconceivable before the category had been invented.

Civil war is not solely in the eye of the beholder, but the use of the term is itself often one source of strife among the combatants. Established governments will always view civil wars as rebellions or illegal uprisings against legitimate authority, particularly if they fail. The Earl of Clarendon (1609–74) titled his Royalist account of England's mid-seventeenth-century troubles *The History of the Rebellion and Civil Wars in England* (published in 1702–4) precisely to deprive the "rebels" of legitimacy.[26] For the same reason, the seventy-volume official history of the U.S. "Civil War" published between 1880 and 1901 was called *The War of the Rebellion*, a title clearly meant to deny standing to the defeated "rebels."[27] By contrast, the victors in a civil war will often commemorate their struggle as a revolution, as did those in the American and French "Revolutions," for example. It's easy to perform the conjugation: *I* am a revolutionary. *You* are a rebel. *They* are engaged in a civil war.

For those of us lucky enough to live under the reign of the Long Peace, civil war is more a matter of memory and metaphor than lived experience. Civil wars now take place as historical reenactments and science-fictional video games, and more seriously in the debates of assemblies and power struggles of political parties. For example, in 1988, the U.S. congressman Newt Gingrich described American politics as if it were a civil war: "The left at its core understands in a way Grant understood after Shiloh that this is a civil war, that only one side will prevail, and the other side will be relegated to history." He then sketched out the terms of the fight: "This war has to be fought with the scale and duration and savagery that is only true of civil wars. While we are lucky in this country that our civil wars are fought at the ballot box, not on the battlefields, nonetheless it is a civil war."[28] More recently, in the aftermath of the Daesh terrorist attack on Paris in November 2015, the French prime minister, Manuel Valls, charged that the right-wing National Front was stirring up civil war in France. "There are two options for our country," he said. "There is the option of the extreme right which, basically, foments division. That division can lead to civil war [*guerre civile*], and there is another vision, which is that of the Republic and its values, which means pulling together."[29] As I write, the instability of party politics has fomented charges of "civil war" among Republicans in the United States, within the British Labour Party, throughout Brazil's fractious political elite. Around the world, democratic politics now looks ever more like civil war by other means.

Civil wars are everywhere, in the headlines and on the ground, in hearts and minds, as well as in commemorations of civil wars past. Some countries have thought themselves free from civil war. Others can hardly imagine themselves except through the memory of it: the United States, for one. And the international community perceives still others—Iraq, for example—as the perpetual battleground of unending civil wars. The benefit of history, and perhaps the curse of remembering it, is the knowledge that civil war has never been quite as stable or transparent a category as its popular usage would imply.

Yet how do we tell civil wars apart from other kinds of wars, when so many internal conflicts spill over their countries' borders or draw in combatants from outside, as happened in Liberia and Rwanda in the 1990s as well as Iraq, Afghanistan, and Syria more recently? Can such wars even be considered "civil"—in the sense of taking place among fellow members of the same community—

when insurgent groups comprise transnational elements, like al-Qaeda, or deliberately set themselves against the existing world order of states by proclaiming their wish to form supranational communities like the caliphate pursued by IS/Daesh? Is every civil war really a specimen of the same species, when so many distinct dynamics—ethnic conflicts, wars of secession and national liberation, battles for succession, and so on—can be found across history and around the world and when local contexts may make it impossible to analyze specific incidents of violence as part of larger patterns of collective action?[30] Can we distinguish particular civil wars from any larger global phenomenon of "new" wars in the aggregate?[31] What, in short, *is* civil war?

Any complex idea like civil war has multiple pasts. Historians can show the paths not taken as well as the many and winding roads by which we came to our present understandings. One fashionable term of art for this procedure is "intellectual genealogy." This method does share some features with tracing family history: it digs back through the past; it searches for roots; it is always open to wandering along the byways of a tangled history. But there are also important differences.[32] Genealogical research fastens on continuities: who descended from whom, who begat whom. And if the overall aim of family genealogy is self-affirmation, intellectual genealogy encourages skepticism and humility. It traces breaks or discontinuities and shows how our own arrangements are accidental, not inevitable, the outcome of choices, not the product of design, contingent and therefore temporary and changeable. "When we trace the genealogy of a concept," one distinguished exponent of the approach has argued, "we uncover the different ways it may have been used in earlier times. We thereby equip ourselves with a means of reflecting critically on how it is currently understood."[33]

The originator of this form of conceptual genealogy was Friedrich Nietzsche (1844–1900). In his *On the Genealogy of Morality* (1887), he pointed out that "anything in existence, having somehow come about, is continually interpreted anew, requisitioned anew, transformed and redirected to a new purpose by a power superior to it." Nietzsche wanted to try to explain why an idea might have arisen, what purposes it once served, how power relations allowed it to endure, and what marks of its beginnings it still carried long after the original intent behind it had fallen away.[34] As an outstanding classicist, Nietzsche knew the importance of philology, that study of the strata of meanings laid down in complex words, and he applied its tools to the analysis of ideas and practices. His prescription was at once stringent and succinct: "All concepts in which an entire process is semiotically concentrated defy definition; *only something which has no history can be defined.*"[35] That is, the weight of history may be so densely compacted into a given concept that no effort of refinement can remove all its accreted complexities. And nothing that has a past, particularly one deep or controversial, can be specified so exactly that its meaning can be agreed once and for all.

Civil war was not one of Nietzsche's examples, but it easily could have been. (After all, his *Genealogy of Moral-*

ity bore the subtitle "Eine Streitschrift": a polemic or, literally, "conflict writing.") Only by ignoring the multiple histories of civil war would it be possible to define it. For history shows that civil war has had no stable identity or agreed definition. A fundamentally *political* concept, it has been reinterpreted and redeployed in multiple contexts for multiple purposes throughout the centuries. It may look descriptive, but it is firmly normative, expressing values and interpretations more than any stable identity.

Civil war is an example of what philosophers term an essentially contested concept, so called because their deployment "inevitably involves endless disputes about their proper uses on the part of their users." This occurs because there is so much to be gained—and so much can be lost—from the application of the concept to particular cases and because, as with other contested concepts—art, democracy, and justice, for instance—the use implies a value judgment. Is that object a work of art? Is this political system democratic? Is your procedure just? Anyone who uses these terms should have some inkling of being in for a potential fight over the prestige they carry.[36] At the same time, the user should also be advised that any use of such concepts "must be understood historically, as a phase in an inherited and unending intellectual task," and that "their conflicting interpretation" is "limited by the inheritance from the past" but "never preclude[s] the possibility, and indeed the necessity, of future debate."[37]

In this light, the most useful critical reflection on conceptions of civil war would trace their history over a long stretch of time, centuries beyond the horizon of 1989 or 1945. Yet this approach runs counter to most current research on civil wars, dominated as it has been by disciplines that typically impose a much narrower chronological focus. After the end of the Cold War, there was a "boom in the study of civil war" among professional social scientists.[38] Economists who study underdevelopment, especially in Africa, isolated civil war as one of its main causes. The phenomenon has also drawn students of international relations who have seen their traditional subject of wars between states disappearing before after very eyes. And the rise of apparently ethnic conflict after 1989 excited interest in the various causes of civil strife in regions across the world from the Balkans to the Horn of Africa.[39] Social scientists often study only those conflicts that have taken place since World War II, when one of their standard databases, the Conflict Data Program at Sweden's Uppsala University, begins.[40] Some extend their horizons further with the help of the vast databases forming the Correlates of War Project (founded at the University of Michigan and now at Pennsylvania State University), which goes back to 1816.[41] But few have examined civil wars in comparative, long-range perspective over more than the past two centuries.[42]

As for historians, they have not helped. They—I should say, *we*—have tended to study particular conflicts: the English Civil Wars, the American Civil War, the Spanish Civil War. We have rarely treated civil war as a serial phenomenon, across time and around the world. Instead, we have preferred the rich reconstruction of historical particularity over what clarity might be produced by revealing underlying patterns or models.[43] By no coincidence, most professional historians were content, until recently, to undertake quite sharply focused studies on time frames approximating a natural life span: rarely more than a century, often a few decades or even years. Lately, however, many have been returning to the historical big picture, the long-range view that had been out of fashion, not infrequently aiming to uncover the origins of some of the most pressing problems of our time—climate change, inequality, the crisis of global governance—which lie decades or centuries in the past.[44] A longer perspective, history's traditional perspective, is essential if we are to see just what has been at stake, and what still remains at issue, in civil wars over the past two thousand years.

I have called this book a "history *in* ideas" to distinguish it from a long-established strain of intellectual history known as the "history *of* ideas."[45] The latter reconstructed the biographies of big concepts—nature; Romanticism; the great chain of being—across the ages, as if the ideas themselves were somehow alive and had an existence independent of those who deployed them. But in time, the sense that ideas inhabited some Platonic sphere, far above and beyond the mundane world of human life, came to discredit the history of ideas among more rigorous intellectual historians, to the impoverishment of historical understanding of important concepts. Only recently have they—again, I should say "we"—regained the courage to construct more subtle and more complex histories *in* ideas over broader periods, with notions like happiness and genius, toleration and common sense, sovereignty and democracy, among others, now emerging again as central topics of study.[46] This book joins these new histories by investigating a key idea in Western, and global, argument in its multiple historical contexts. The point of origin it proposes is quite particularly Rome, not any earlier setting, such as Greece. Not all roads lead from Rome in the formation of modern political vocabulary, but a great many do. Among them are some of the most enduring ideas in the contemporary lexicon, including liberty, empire, property, rights—and civil war.[47]

The "ideas" that lend this kind of history its structure are not disembodied entities, making intermittent entries into the terrestrial world from idealism's heavenly realm, but rather focal points of arguments shaped and debated episodically across time, each instance being consciously—or at least provably—connected with both earlier and later ones. Even amid changing assumptions, such "ideas" are linked through time by a common name. They also remain connected by the freight of meanings accumulated from their dialogue with the past and, occasionally, with the future. Civil war is a prime candidate for such a history in ideas.

*

My history of arguments about civil war over the past two thousand years is purposefully more symptomatic than systematic. It is not meant as a complete history, or even a comprehensive *intellectual* history, of civil wars across time and space. A truly all-encompassing work, in multiple volumes written by many historians, collecting accounts of every conflict in world history that contemporaries or later observers thought was a civil war, is certainly imaginable. What is less conceivable is that anyone would want to read such an encyclopedic work.[48] To hold the reader's attention, my focus is more precisely trained. I treat three major moments, successively Mediterranean, European, and global, over the *longue durée* of civil war to illustrate its genesis, its transformations, and its contemporary applications: the first in ancient Rome, the second in early modern Europe, and the third since the middle of the nineteenth century. Other histories of civil war can and should be written. This one nonetheless represents the first attempt to portray its metamorphoses over two millennia.

Treating such a vast expanse of time constrains my coverage of space. In all of the world's major cultures, there are, of course, histories of violence within particular communities, at least four such traditions of which I am aware, and no doubt others of which I am not. The first is the Greek tradition of *stasis*—meaning literally "standing" or "taking a stand," with its associations of "faction," discord, and internal dissension.[49] I touch upon it in the first chapter, if only to explain why I give a second tradition, the Roman formulation "civil war" (*bellum civile*), greater prominence. In English, French, Italian, Spanish, German, Irish, Russian, and many other languages, the words for my subject are direct calques of the Roman one, or nearly so: "civil war," *guerre civile*, *guerra civile*, *guerra civil*, *Bürgerkrieg*, *Cogadh Cathartha*, гражданская война (*grazhdanskaya voyna*). The Russian phrase comes from the German; the German phrase translates literally a term found in the Romance languages and in English. We need not assume that they all represent exactly the same concept to see that they all have two elements in common. The root of each is the word for citizen: a "civil" war is literally a "citizens' war" or war among fellow citizens. And the original term for citizen lying behind them all is the Latin noun *civis*, from which the adjective "civil"—in Latin, *civilis*—derives, along with such weighty words as "civility" and "civilization."

The third tradition is the Arabic, in which the term *fitna*—meaning, variously, anarchy, discord, division, and schism, particularly the fundamental doctrinal schism within Islam between Sunnis and Shi'as—carries some of the same connotations as its equivalent in the Roman tradition.[50] And, lastly, there are Chinese conceptions of "internal war," or *nei zhan* (內戰), which can also be found in Japanese (*naisen*, 内戦).[51] To my knowledge, no attempt has been made to reconstruct these traditions over the long term; any comparison with them would therefore be impossible for the time being. It will, however, be part of my argument that Western conceptions of civil war are the ones that have shaped global debates through adoption by international organizations like the United Nations and by global communities of lawyers, scholars, and activists in the twentieth and twenty-first centuries.

Tracing the legacies of Roman conceptions of civil war across the following centuries, my argument identifies three important turning points in the meaning of the term. The first, in the late eighteenth century, came at the moment when contemporaries needed to distinguish civil war from another category of violent and transformative political upheaval: revolution. The second, in the mid-nineteenth century, occurred when the first attempts were made to pin down a legal meaning of civil war, an effort made, not coincidentally, during the conflict widely known, at least in the United States, as the American Civil War of 1861–65. And the third came during the late phases of the Cold War, when social scientists decided to define the term to help them analyze conflicts all around the world during an era of proxy wars and decolonization. Our confusion about the meaning and application of civil war to contemporary conflicts is the product of this long and layered history. But only with the help of history, I argue, can we understand just why its meaning remains so controversial today.

At least until the nineteenth century, and the great historical watershed marked by the U.S. Civil War, civil wars were understood as cumulative phenomena whose succession gave a shape—though hardly a comforting one—to the past and whose avoidance might yet be an achievement of the future. The experience was typically refracted by history and memory, through the record of past civil wars, in distant times and far-flung places, and through fears that the civil wars in one's own country's history might repeat themselves. We have no other way to approach such fears except through history if we want to understand what the victims of civil war anticipate returning. And the best means of tackling this history is through language. As we will see, civil war is such a contested phenomenon because it carries such a weight from the past and can only be discussed in words that are endlessly arguable. Conflict over its meaning, as much as the meaning of the conflict, are prime subjects for long-range historical treatment.

To tell this story, I have broken the book into three parts, each with two chapters.

The first part, "Roads from Rome," traces changing conceptions of civil war chronologically over six hundred years from the first century B.C.E. to the fifth century C.E. During this period, I argue, Roman debates decisively shaped conceptions about civil war: about its genesis, about its normative definition, about how to recognize its outward signs, and about the likelihood of its recurrence. Thereafter, all roads would lead from Rome and not, I argue, further back from Athens and the world of Thucydides, where conflict within the community was understood very differently. The Roman heritage itself contained many different explanations of civil war and transmitted various competing narratives of its place in Roman history.

As I show in the second part, "Early Modern Crossroads," in Europe between the sixteenth and the eighteenth centuries, those explanations and narratives derived from Rome provided the repertoire from which European thinkers drew their own conceptions of civil war. Since the Enlightenment, however, two conceptual clusters, regarding civil war and revolution, would drift apart from each other and even be set in deliberate opposition, with quite distinct moral and political implications: the first deemed backward looking, destructive, and regressive; the second, future oriented, fertile, and progressive. Successful civil wars would thus be "rebranded" as revolutions, while revolutionaries would deny they had been engaged in civil wars.[52] But matters are never so simple; as we shall see, the two categories would continue to overlap and interpenetrate well into the twentieth century.

The book's third part, "Paths to the Present," traces the conceptual heritage of civil war from the era of the U.S. Civil War to our own time. The nineteenth century's great contribution to this history was the attempt to ameliorate the severity of civil war by bringing it under the domain of law. Civilizing civil war remains an objective for the international legal community right down to our own time; the roots of its concern, and the tensions civil war presented within what we now call international humanitarian law, are the subject of the final chapter of this book, which traces developments as civil war goes global over the course of the twentieth century. At this time, the frontiers of the community beset with "civil" wars expand beyond the physical boundaries of state and empire to encompass the whole world. That expansion may be traced to various strains of cosmopolitan thought, which had long suggested that all wars, being among humans, were civil wars.[53] Yet the impulse is at odds with another twentieth-century effort, by social scientists beginning in the Cold War, to bring conceptual clarity to the study of civil war—a doomed enterprise, as we shall see.

As I argue in the conclusion, "Civil Wars of Words,"

past definitions and conceptions of civil war persist to this day in the intellectual DNA of international organizations, journalistic organs, and scholarly discussions. Hence much of our own confusion about what is, and what is not, a civil war. The sedimentary conceptual history going back to the Roman republic has only grown more complex and more perplexing since the modern languages of law and social sciences have added layers of their own. I suggest in conclusion that the contested pasts of civil war will continue to generate multiple futures. How the knowledge of history equips us to face those futures may have consequences for tens of thousands, even millions, of people— often the most vulnerable and unfortunate—across the globe. To see why, we must first head back more than two millennia into the past, to observe the invention of civil war in republican Rome.

PART I

Roads from Rome

Inventing Civil War

The Roman Tradition

Civil war was not a fact of nature, waiting to be discovered. It was an artifact of human culture that had to be invented. That invention, a little over two thousand years old, can be dated quite closely to the first century B.C.E. The Romans were not the first to suffer internal conflict but they were the first to experience it as civil war. Perhaps having been first to define what was "civil"—meaning, among fellow citizens—they inevitably understood their most wrenching conflicts in definitively political terms, as clashes among citizens that rose to the level of war. Those elements would remain at the heart of concepts of civil war for much of its history.

Thus, having conceived the "civil" and then joined it—reluctantly, paradoxically, but irreversibly—to the idea of war, the Romans created the unstable, fissile compound that remains disturbingly with us today: "civil war." The inventor is unknown. He—and it must have been a man, because he was surely a Roman citizen—joined together two distinct ideas to make an explosive new amalgam. No one before that obscure Roman had yoked these two elements together.

The Greeks had a clear understanding of war, or what they called *polemos*—from which many modern languages derive the fighting word "polemical." But they imagined the "wars" within their own communities as "something completely different" from what the Romans had.[1] This is not to say that there was an unbridgeable chasm between Roman and Greek ideas of internal strife. Roman writers sometimes attributed the origins of their own political divisions to the importation of dangerous Greek notions like "democracy."[2] The primal Greek historian Thucydides influenced his successors among Roman writers, most notably Sallust, "the rival of Thucydides" (as another Roman chronicler called him).[3] And in the first century c.e., Roman historians writing in Greek naturally used Greek terms to describe Rome's civil wars.[4] And yet, despite these continuities, the Romans were sure they were experiencing something new, for which they needed a new name: civil war, or, in Latin, *bellum civile*.

For the Romans, war had traditionally implied something quite specific. It was an armed conflict, in a just cause and fought against an external enemy. Mere aggression did not count, for that could hardly be just. Nor did individual violence rise to the level of war, because that could not be constrained by the laws of war, which the Romans had. And the enemy (*hostis*) was by definition unfamiliar, either from outside Rome or at least beyond the community of free Roman citizens: Romans fought wars against slaves, like the great leader of the slave revolt Spartacus, and they battled against pirates in the Mediterranean; they also warred against enemies on their frontiers, such as Parthians and Carthaginians. What made "civil" war so different was that the enemies were all too familiar and could even be thought of as familial: it was one's fellow citizens—or *cives*—who were on the other side. Such a war, then, challenged the standard Roman criteria, their very definition of war, to the breaking point. The enemies were not others; they were, in effect, the same. And it was hard to see a struggle against them as just when it so obviously affronted their conception of just war, which implied a legitimate enemy as well as a proper cause for self-defense.

The resulting idea of civil war was deliberately paradoxical: a war that could not be a war, fought against enemies who were not really enemies. In the propaganda battles during Rome's civil wars, the competing sides trumpeted the rightness of their cause to win support and also to assimilate their conflicts to the conventional understanding of war as fought for a just cause.[5] To call this kind of war "civil" followed the Romans' practice of naming their wars after the opponents they were fighting.[6] This tradition lasted into the nineteenth century, with the "Napoleonic Wars" in Europe and Britain's "Zulu War," "Boer Wars," and "Māori Wars," for example.[7] It has not persisted into our own time; even in the United States, there are few who would now call the U.S. Civil War "Mr. Lincoln's War," and no one there, or anywhere else for that matter, called the Gulf Wars "Saddamic" wars. In the West, we generally give wars the names of the places where they are fought, and so we have the Korean and Vietnam Wars, the first and second Gulf Wars, and even the "world" wars of the twentieth century.

This is not to say that the Romans never thought of their wars in terms of geography, only that they more typically named them for the opposing ruler or people. In this way, they called the three wars they fought against Carthage in the third and second centuries B.C.E. the "Punic" Wars, the Carthaginians being descendants of the Phoenicians, or *Poeni;* a later war against the North African king Jugurtha in 112–105 B.C.E. would be named the "Jugurthine" War. In the years 91–89 B.C.E., Rome also struggled with its various allies, or *socii,* in Italy over the question of extending the full rights of citizenship throughout the peninsula; collectively, those contentions became known as the Social War. Likewise, the military efforts to crush slave revolts, most notably that of Spartacus in Sicily in 71 B.C.E., were known as the Servile Wars, or the wars against slaves (*servi*).[8] Each of these terms would have an intermittent afterlife, as, for instance, when writers during the American Revolution compared the revolt of the British American colonists to the Social War or slaveholders spoke of the threat of "servile war" in the early nineteenth-century U.S. South. Neither, however, would take root as firmly or enduringly as "civil war."

The Romans adopted the idea of civil war reluctantly at first. For a long time, they used it only with trepidation. They faced it as something novel and unsettling, and it still takes a feat of the imagination to recall just why civil war was originally so disturbing and invoked only with fear. "'Civil war' in English has lost the paradoxical sense it held in Rome," one scholar of the Roman tradition has noted. There "the distinction between *ciues* and non-*ciues* was a crucial determinant of status, obligations, and rights" in a way that was not clear before the Roman invention. It left only ghostly etymological traces that can now barely be discerned.[9]

For the Romans, civil war was the subversion of city-dwelling civilization. Yet there was also an enduring and disturbing strain of Roman history that suggested there was a tight relationship between civil war and civilization itself. These conflicts came back so often across the history of the republic and into the early empire that they appeared to be woven into the fabric of Roman public life. For this reason, the Romans were at pains to explain the causes of their civil wars. They soon saw links between occurrences and likened them to natural phenomena, like the activity of a volcano, which could fall dormant after an eruption but with no certainty that it would not explode again. Seen in this light, Rome's history appeared to be nothing less than a series of civil wars and the brief moments of calm between them. This created a narrative—in fact, a set of narratives—of civilization as prone to civil war, even cursed by it—that would last for centuries and inform later understandings of civil war across early modern and modern Europe and beyond.

At this point, we should ask just what conception of internal conflict there was before the Romans invented their ideas of civil war. The Romans themselves had two

places to look for answers to that question: in the history
of the city-states of ancient Greece and in their own early
history, all the way back to the founding of the city of
Rome. In the Greek past, especially Athenian history, they
would have found something that looked like civil war,
but they did not recognize it as being the same as their
own turmoils. Nor could they find the thing itself in the
early Roman past, though they could uncover some of its
roots—that is, the moral and often immoral causes that
had ultimately led Rome to perhaps its most destructive
innovations. Out of their analyses of the long-term causes
of civil war emerged a set of historical narratives to explain
the present and predict the future. All of these stories were
highly political, and therefore all highly contested. To see
why, let us look first at the Greek and Roman histories of
internal conflict in turn.

*

Conceptions of civil war have changed with understandings of civilization and of war itself. For much of its history, civil war has been closely associated with ideas of the
city. This should not be at all surprising if we recall that
the very foundations of Western ideas of both civilization
and politics derive directly from the experience of organiz-
ing human beings into the complex, highly ordered, and
often tightly bounded communities we call cities. For the
Greeks, the city was the *polis*, the self-sustaining paradig-
matic community described by Aristotle and others, from
whose name we still derive the word "politics." For their

Roman heirs, the city was the *civitas*, inhabited by citizens or *cives*, whom we distantly commemorate every time we use words like "civil," "civility," and "civilization."[10] By no coincidence, for the last two thousand years, the city has frequently been the stage for civil war, that contention between citizens who are also (as the name suggests) city dwellers.[11] Civil wars were struggles between citizens, then, but they were also often fought within cities, actual as well as imagined.

For classical thinkers, the city was a metaphysical space as much as it was a physical place—Athens or Rome within its civic boundaries, for example. It was a zone of cooperation and peace, where humans could cultivate their humanity under the rule of law. It was increasingly distant from the perils and incivility of wild nature, literal and figurative, because the city was constructed and maintained to keep the threats of irrationality, savagery, and animality at bay, outside its bounds.[12] When such evils returned, it was in the form of violence that broke into the pale of civilization itself. That is the reason why so much of the imagery of civil wars, from classical times to the present, has reflected barbarism, bestiality, and inhumanity, the very picture of nature red in tooth and claw.

Greek thinking about politics prized harmony above all other values, at least to judge by the broadly aristocratic defenses of city life we have from Plato and Aristotle. "Do we know of any greater evil for a *polis* than the thing that distracts it and makes it many instead of one," asks Socrates in Plato's dialogue *The Republic*, "or a greater good than that which binds it together and makes it one?"[13] This would be at the heart of Plato's vision of the ideal city, in which the balance of an individual soul mirrored the ideal balance of elements within the *polis* itself. And if harmony was the greatest good, then division would be the greatest evil.

The Greek name for the evil that divided the polis was *stasis*. Like the Roman conception of civil war, *stasis* was founded on a paradox. The word is the root of "static," and one of its literal meanings was the absence of movement; however, another meaning was "position" or "standing," and hence by implication "taking a stand" in a political dispute.[14] (It can even mean a literal place to stand patiently; *stasis* is still the term for bus stop in Modern Greek.) But the meaning that concerns us here is the one connected with the idea of the *polis*, as a condition in that most fundamental and natural community. As a hostile and divisive political stance, one defying the *polis*'s unity and common purpose, *stasis* also became synonymous with faction, partisanship, and something close to what would later be called civil war: close, but not in fact the same thing. For the Athenians, politics—as an art of rule, the mechanism for distributing honor and office among citizens, and as the means to manage conflicting interests for the public good and without bloodshed—was in effect the cure for *stasis* and its replacement.

Stasis for the Greeks remained a state of mind rather than an act of physical resistance. It might lead to war, or even arise from war, but it did not in itself entail actual warfare; in this sense, it could mean what we might call a standoff or impasse without actual aggression or combat.[15]

And the Greeks never qualified *stasis* with any adjective implying a political or legal definition of those who stood on each side of the internal division. In short, it was not "civil," nor did it necessarily entail the presence of "war."

The Greeks did however distinguish between two particular kinds of struggles: division within the *polis*, and war between political communities. They did not treat the distinction systematically, but it was a meaningful one for them. For example, in Plato's *Republic*, Socrates tells Glaucon, his partner in the fictional dialogue, that those who would defend the ideal city he envisages should respect the distinction between Greeks, who are friendly and civilized, and barbarians, who are hostile and alien; if Greeks fight against fellow Greeks, they should not destroy their lands or burn their houses as they might when battling barbarians. The boundary between Greeks and barbarians was, thus, also the border between the two kinds of conflicts—one among Greeks, the other with outsiders. According to Plato, conflict among "the friendly and the kindred" was called faction or, in Greek, *stasis;* conflict with "the alien and the foreign" was instead war, or *polemos.*[16]

Similarly, in Plato's very last work, the *Laws*, the Athenian—a character who seems to voice Plato's own views—questions whether anyone setting up a *polis* would want to organize it to face the threat of warfare from without: "Would he not much rather pay regard to the internal warfare which arises, from time to time, within the city, and is called, as you know, *stasis*—a kind of war any man would desire never to see in his own city?" The Athenian goes on to draw a contrast between *stasis,* "the most dangerous kind of war . . . [and] the other, and much milder form . . . [which] is that waged when we are at variance with external aliens."[17]

The ancient Greeks also spoke of *stasis emphylos*, a faction or division within the community bound by blood and kinship, *phylos* being the word for family or clan. But they used the word "war" (*polemos*) for their most dangerous discords, even intra-communal, though they did so in a way that was different from later Roman conceptions. When conflict took place within the community, they called it a war within the extended clan, or *emphylios polemos*. In much later centuries, Byzantine historians would use this term to describe armed conflicts within the empire, though they rarely deployed it referring to contentions with fellow Christians, and by the thirteenth and fourteenth centuries it had lost its strictly cultural or ethnic connotations.[18] The expression also persists in Modern Greek usage, for example to describe the divisive conflicts in Greece between 1944 and 1949.[19]

The idea of community shifted somewhat, depending on context. Plato, as we have heard, distinguished firmly between contentions among Greeks, on the one hand, and wars against barbarians, on the other. Wars between Greek communities—like that between the Athenians and the Spartans and their respective allies chronicled by the historian Thucydides—were in the nature of conflicts within a single extended family.[20] This blurs the later distinction between what the Romans would call civil wars—those taking place within a single *political* community—and wars between states or cities. For the time being, as Plato's

Socrates observes in the *Republic*, they will "regard any difference with Greeks who are their own people as a form of *stasis* and refuse even to speak of it as war."[21]

The classic Greek account of *stasis* appears in the third book of Thucydides's *History of the Peloponnesian War*. This is the episode of the seditions in Corcyra (the Ionian island known as Corfu) in 427 B.C.E. invoked by countless modern commentators as the primal image of civil war itself. As Thucydides relates, in the course of the war between Sparta and Athens, Corcyra had changed sides to support the Athenians; four years into the struggle, a group of Corcyrean captives were sent back to their home city to stir up revolt and to persuade the city to restore its earlier alliance with Corinth. The diplomatic division between Sparta and Athens followed the political split within Corcyra between the pro-Athenian democrats, who supported the rule of the common people, and the oligarchs, who supported the alliance with Corinth.

The fifth column of released Corcyrean prisoners tried to overturn the alliance with Athens by peaceful means but failed to persuade the assembly of Corcyra. They then tried to have the leader of the democrats, Peithias, prosecuted for enslaving Corcyra to Athens. That move also failed. When Peithias struck back against his accusers, they killed him with sixty of his allies. The oligarchs temporarily won out over the democrats, but after the arrival of a Corinthian galley an uneasy truce broke out into open factional fighting.

Thus war between foreign cities stirred the internal seditions between the two groups who skirmished from

the different parts of Corcyra they had respectively occupied. Each tried to secure the support of the city's slaves
with promises of emancipation. The slaves chose the democratic faction, who, aided by the Athenians, gained the
upper hand. The arrival of fleets from both Corinth and
Athens further increased tensions, before a détente was
reached, only to explode after an even larger fleet came
from Athens. With that, the democrats launched a reign of
terror that would become a historical byword for political
subversion and the upending of established order. As the
seventeenth-century English philosopher Thomas Hobbes
put it in his classic translation of Thucydides in 1629, "All
formes of death were then seene . . . For the Father slew
his Sonne; men were dragged out of the Temples, and then
slaine hard by; and some immured in the *Temple* of *Bacchus*,
dyed within it. So cruell was this Sedition."[22] It is notable
that Hobbes nowhere uses the translation "civil war" in
his version of the *Eight Bookes of the Peloponnesian Warre*;
indeed, not until the nineteenth century would the words
become the commonplace equivalent of Thucydides's own
terms in later versions.[23]

Thucydides had portrayed *stasis* as a disease that
spread through the cities of Greece.[24] In time of war, these
divided communities became more vulnerable to the infection than they would have been in peacetime: "War taking
away the affluence of daily necessaries, is a most violent
Master, and conformeth most mens passions to the present occasion." The symptoms of the disease were mani-
fold. Evil deeds were commended, not decried. Laws were
ignored, lawlessness reigning in their place. Oaths were

broken. Fraud, dishonesty, and revenge prevailed, and all manner of crimes became causes for pride, not shame. "The received value of names imposed for signification of things, was changed to arbitrary": foolhardiness became courage; modesty, cowardice; and wisdom, laziness. Truly, this was a world turned upside down. "Thus was wickednesse on foot in every kind, throughout all *Greece*, by the occasion of their sedition," as Hobbes's translation has it.[25]

In his treatment of *stasis*, Thucydides consistently distinguishes the war between Sparta and Athens from the strife within Corcyra. His account would be so influential on later theorists of civil war in part because he demonstrated how the strains of external warfare could encourage internal division, but his survey of the causes that connected them never identified the two forms of violence with each other. War, or *polemos*, was the activity of cities and their rulers, leading armies or navies against their enemies. Faction, or *stasis*, took place within the *polis* between sharply divided groups without such formal military arrays and often wielding little more than what came to hand, such as the roof tiles hurled by women against the oligarchs early in the seditions of Corcyra.[26] The parties were wrestling for control of the city, as they would later in Rome, but in the Greek cases questions of legitimacy did not arise.

In Thucydides's account, what matters is the larger moral breakdown of the *polis* itself. There could be no question of arguing a just cause when all justice is shattered and stable moral criteria no longer applied. Nor is the scale of violence remotely that of the armies later assembled in the Roman civil wars, in which whole legions were deployed, with control of not just a city but whole provinces at stake. The sheer scale of Rome's conflicts and the areas over which they were fought would have been unimaginably vast to the Greeks. It was, in fact, only when conflict overflowed the bounds of the city that it became civil war—a war among citizens that engulfed the city but could not be contained by it. Nothing on that level, or of that kind, afflicted the Greeks in the times chronicled by Thucydides.[27]

Moreover, in the Greek setting, the parties did not consider each other formal enemies. But nor did they see each other within the categories of citizenship that defined Roman conceptions of civil violence. "Many writers call the Peloponnesian war . . . the great civil war of Greece," noted the English essayist Thomas De Quincey in 1844. " 'Civil'!—it might have been such, had the Grecian states had a central organ which claimed a common obedience."[28] Without that political unity, then, there could be no common citizenship, either legal or political. And without such a conception of citizenship, there could be no "war" between citizens—no *civil* war. As Thucydides's most recent and most authoritative English translator wisely remarks, "The usual translation of *stasis* as 'civil war' seems anachronistic and inappropriate to the scale of these conflicts."[29] For all these reasons, and despite any imputed resemblance, *stasis* for the Greeks was simply not equivalent to the Romans' *bellum civile*.

Every conception of civil war is paradoxical in its own

way. The Greek paradox was different from the one the Romans would face. Assuming the ethnic or even genetic unity of the people divided, Thucydides paints *stasis* as an affliction common to all Greeks and destined to sunder all their communities in ways that "shall be ever as long as humane nature is the same."[30] To conceive of faction this way has at least the redeeming feature of implying a community sufficiently well integrated to confront the challenge. It was understood to be unified fundamentally, before politics, and beyond law, because all its members were descended from the same ancestors. Belonging to the city was thus a hereditary matter, not an acquired status, and so divisions did not need to be defined legally and politically, as they would be at Rome.[31] In this way, the Greeks could conceive of a war within the household, or the *polis*, if understood as an agglomeration of households; this was what they called a domestic war (*oikeois polemos*).[32] What they could not conceive of was a war within the *polis* understood metaphysically; that would have been like being at war with oneself.

The Romans were well aware that their own internal dissensions were different—horrifyingly so—from those suffered by the Greeks. The Greeks never spoke of a political war, a *politikos polemos*; it was almost literally inconceivable in Greek. The Romans alone would bear the guilt of inventing civil war and of learning how to tell its stories and determining what its history meant.

*

Instead of looking back to the strife of Greece for answers to their questions about internal conflict, Romans could also turn to the early history of their own commonwealth. Every kind of political violence studded that history: murders and assassinations, tumults and seditions, conspiracies and uprisings—every kind, that is, except for civil war.[33] Most of these earlier disturbances took place within the citizen body, but none of them had risen to the level of outright war.[34] This absence reinforced the argument that civil war was not only something peculiar to Rome but something altogether new in history.

Roman mythology told how Rome itself had been born from an act of murder. In fact, fratricide would become the central metaphor of the unnatural dissension at the heart of civil war. The legend told how Rome's founders, the brothers Romulus and Remus, had quarreled over where to settle their new city and then about how to create a new line of kings to rule over it. Because they were twins, neither could yield regal precedence to the other. In the most common version, as relayed by Livy, the historian of early Rome, Romulus killed Remus for mocking his brother's claims and "thus became sole sovereign and gave his name to the city so founded": Rome, from Romulus.[35] "Rome's first walls were drenched with a brother's blood," the poet Lucan noted in his epic poem of the wars between Caesar and Pompey, *The Civil War* (*De bello civili*).[36] The truth of the story is typical of myth, but its appearance in later Roman narratives of civil war is "hugely revealing of big Roman concerns" about the problem and the primordial terms in which its horror was considered.[37]

Among Roman historians and poets, the expulsion of Rome's last king, Tarquinius Superbus, at the turn of the fifth century B.C.E., had seemingly provided some atonement for the shame of its very founding. That overthrow, achieved without violence, allowed the bloodstained city to be founded anew as a republic (*res publica*), literally the people's business or the common wealth shared in by all its citizens.[38] Rome now had the chance to become what Livy called "a free nation in peace and war," a political community that showed "greater obedience to the commands of law than those of men." Citizens were only truly free when they lived in a free commonwealth: their liberty depended on that of the *res publica* itself.[39]

Free and law-bound the Roman republic might have been in theory, but the reality was far from peaceful or untroubled. From the fifth through the third century B.C.E., for instance, those of humble birth, plebeians, had battled for political recognition with those of more ancient lineage, the patricians, in a series of struggles later known as the Conflict of the Orders.[40] It is from this period that the modern world has inherited some of its key designations of social and class conflict: the word "class" (*classis*) itself; "patrician"; "plebeian"; and "proletariat," that is, those who contribute to the commonwealth by bearing children, or *proles*. All these were terms of art in Roman life long before they entered other languages, not least through the writings of Karl Marx (1818–83), that keen nineteenth-century connoisseur of civil conflict, who was a student of classical history in general and of Roman political turmoil in particular.[41]

Roman aristocrats controlled street gangs and could conjure private militias from among their dependents and clients. Gruesome killings punctuated the last century of the republic, beginning with the death of Tiberius Gracchus, a populist tribune of the people. In 133 B.C.E., a politically inflamed mob killed three hundred of Gracchus's supporters and threw his body ignominiously into the river Tiber: "This is said to have been the first time since the revolution against the monarchy that civil strife in Rome ended in bloodshed and the loss of citizens' lives," the historian Plutarch lamented in the early second century C.E. It might have been the first time, but it would hardly be the last. In 121 B.C.E., Tiberius's younger brother, the tribune Gaius Gracchus, was killed, decapitated, and his skull filled with molten lead before his headless corpse was also pitched into the river.[42]

All these murders were "civil" acts because they took place within the citizen body, but none of them could be designated as "war." Only in hindsight did Rome's historians regard such incidents as the symptoms of full-blown civil wars and harbingers of such notorious acts of bloodletting as the assassination of Julius Caesar a century later, in 44 B.C.E., and the execution of Cicero a year after that. Here is the Greek-speaking historian Appian (ca. 95–ca. 165) looking back over more than five centuries of Roman history from the second century C.E.

> At Rome, the common people and senate were frequently at odds with each other over the passing of laws and the cancellation of debts or the

distribution of land, or during elections, but there was never any outbreak of civil violence ... No sword was ever brought into the assembly, and no Roman was ever killed by a Roman, until Tiberius Gracchus, while holding the office of tribune and in the act of proposing legislation, became the first man to die in civil unrest.

This was civil unrest—in Appian's Greek, the word was, of course, *stasis*, but, again, it was not yet civil *war*.[43]

Looking back with the critical distance afforded by both the passage of time and his writing in Greek, Appian could see just what distinguished Rome's contentions in the first century B.C.E. from the dissensions of the Greeks, on the one hand, and the primal violence in Rome's early centuries, on the other. To begin with, swords had been drawn in public; that marked the crossing of one threshold, a breach of the peace among citizens. But this was still an interpersonal threat, individual menacing individual. It did not involve collective action, nor did it upset the delicate balance that Roman law had achieved between the spheres of civil life and military discipline. Appian argued that civil war would be the result of ambition and injustice sapping the republic until still greater conflict divided Rome: "Open revolts took place against the republic and large armies were led with violence against their native land ... If one side took possession of Rome first, the other nominally made war against their adversaries but in fact against their homeland: they attacked it as if it were an enemy city." This was not a recurrence of some timeless enmity. It was something frighteningly new and unprecedentedly disturbing: a war by the people against the people, and hence (finally) a civil war.[44]

By definition, anything that took place within the bounds of the commonwealth was "civil" because it took place among citizens. The Latin word *civilis* seems to have first appeared in the second century B.C.E., becoming a highly charged term of art in Roman legal and political vocabulary. The term *bellum civile* might even have been patterned after the term *ius civile*, or "civil law," which governed relations between members of the same political community or commonwealth, a set of norms different from the "law of peoples" (*ius gentium*) governing relations among foreigners or between Romans and outsiders. Romans had pursued their wars only against these literally hostile enemies—*hostes*—who populated the world beyond the Roman republic.[45] The forms of authority held by a magistrate inside Rome and by a general outside it were likewise supposed to be entirely distinct; to breach the separation between them by bringing military command within the city and treating its citizens as if they were enemies was to commit the ultimate form of treason and sacrilege against the republic. The enormity of that crime helps to explain why Romans were so hesitant about giving civil war a name and why they remained so reluctant to use it long after its invention.[46]

A civil war was a struggle against intimate enemies: indeed, against those who should never have been thought of as enemies at all. Citizens enjoyed the protection of the civil law and were the only people eligible for the offices and honors afforded by the republic, even if not all citizens could grasp all those prizes, as the Conflict of the Orders had shown. They were also responsible for defending the commonwealth militarily by serving in its legions.[47] Civil rights, or the rights of citizens, were legally and politically defined, and their corresponding duty was to defend Rome against its enemies. Civil war overturned all these certainties. It was nothing less than the transformation of the republic from a zone of amity to an arena of enmity, an incursion of hostility within the very pale of civility itself. What caused this disturbing new idea of civil war to enter the Roman political lexicon? The answer, in short, was a set of new threats to Rome itself.

*

By general agreement, Rome's sequence of civil wars began when the consul Lucius Cornelius Sulla marched on the city at the head of an army in 88 B.C.E. Sulla thereby violated the ultimate taboo for any Roman magistrate or military commander. His consulship—the highest political office in Rome—had been in part a reward for his victory against Rome's allies in the Social War. The members of the Italian confederation headed by Rome had demanded equality, especially the rights of Roman citizens. Rome had refused. In 90 B.C.E., the frustrated allies rebelled to secure their independence, eventually to be repressed by a two-year campaign. By that time, however, citizenship had been granted grudgingly to most of the allies, but in such a way that their votes would count for little in the Roman assemblies. When the tribune Publius Sulpicius Rufus introduced a bill into the Senate extending the franchise in 88 B.C.E., the new consul, Sulla, having returned from mopping-up operations against the allies, declared the legislation illegal. Enraged, Sulpicius turned to another Roman commander in the field, Gaius Marius, who was a rival of Sulla's. This set in train the explosive events that would lead to Sulla's march on Rome. In return for Marius's support, Sulpicius promised him a rich plum, the command of Rome's armies against the Persian king Mithridates, a post that offered ample opportunity for plunder as well as for glory and a triumph. Because the command had already been promised to Sulla, a collision between two of Rome's greatest generals became inevitable.[48]

Sulla, that pioneer in the history of civil war, was reluctant and hesitated to turn his troops upon Rome itself. When he and his fellow consul attempted to block Sulpicius's bill, violence flared in the city streets; Sulpicius was rumored to have three thousand swordsmen at his command. After a confrontation that turned violent, Sulla escaped, finding himself briefly in Marius's house, where he might have negotiated with his rival before withdrawing from Rome for his own safety. In his absence, Sulpicius passed his laws without opposition and revealed his previously secret plan to transfer command of the forces against Mithridates to Marius.

Facing political as well as personal ruin if he accepted these moves, Sulla turned to his troops for support, describing the wrongs that had been done to him. He seems to have had no plan to march against Sulpicius or Marius, but his loyal soldiers urged him on. His officers, meanwhile, were horrified and would desert him. The entrails examined by his soothsayer boded well. Then a goddess appeared to Sulla in a dream, handing him a thunderbolt, and told him to strike his enemies. Emboldened by these auspicious omens, and his regulars' goodwill, Sulla set off leading the first army to march on Rome in its history. It would be the first of many.

The Senate met Sulla's approach with embassies; indeed, they could do little else, having no organized force to confront his. When three sets of senatorial envoys questioned his intent, Sulla answered that he had come to free the fatherland from tyrants, implying that he was engaged in a defensive operation and hence one that could be construed as just. Julius Caesar would make much the same claim, forty years later, when he turned his army against Rome upon crossing the river Rubicon.[49]

When Sulla's army came within five miles of Rome, the Senate made one last effort to halt his progress. Sulla promised to relent but sent a contingent ahead nonetheless. When his men entered the city, they met fierce civilian resistance, amid a hail of stones and roof tiles, until Sulla arrived to take charge. Sulpicius and Marius tried to array their followers against him, but Sulla marched through the Forum and took the Capitol. When asked the next day to explain himself, he replied again that he was using his authority as consul to defend the commonwealth against its enemies. He soon formally declared Sulpicius, Marius (who had already fled to Africa), and ten of their closest supporters to be public enemies (*hostes publici*) and hence outlaws. Only Sulpicius was captured and executed. Otherwise, Sulla's reverse coup was bloodless, because both sides strove to prevent collisions between soldiers and citizens within the city.

Tidy though Sulla's action might have been, it clearly marked a turning point in Rome's fortunes. The immediate effects were hardly calamitous. Only Sulla's later actions as dictator—an office invested with emergency powers for a limited time, which he extended—would make clear that his initial moves had marked the beginning of a cycle of civil violence, one that would not end until the creation of the empire with the elevation of Augustus as emperor in 27 B.C.E.

Sulla had not intended anything remotely resembling a military takeover of the republic. To be sure, he had brought an army into the city and formally treated Roman rivals like external enemies, both for the very first time in Roman history. And the army did remain in the city, quiescent but no doubt intimidating, while he rolled back Sulpicius's legislative program. But as soon as he had done so, he sent his troops away, leaving Rome to its two newly elected consuls, Gnaeus Octavius and Lucius Cornelius Cinna. Soon, however, the consuls clashed over the matter of how to treat the recently enfranchised Italians. Their respective supporters came to blows, and then violence rapidly escalated when Octavius had some of the new citizens killed and Cinna left Rome to drum up support for a military solution to his political problems.

It was the second time a citizen was branded as an

enemy of Rome when the Senate declared Cinna a *hostis*.
Maneuvering himself into an alliance with Marius, he
returned with an army and surrounded Rome. As on the
first occasion when the city had come under direct military threat, envoys were sent; and again a consul and commander returned to power with an army at his back. This
time, however, Sulla would be declared a public enemy
and pitted against Marius, who would join Cinna as consul
the following year.

And so the stage was set for the next great
confrontation—what would be seen as the second of
Rome's civil wars—between the two bitter rivals. In late
85 B.C.E., Sulla wrote to the Senate from Greece recalling
his victories on behalf of Rome and vowing revenge on
his enemies. This was no empty threat. He had refused to
recognize the earlier declaration of him as a public enemy,
and believing himself to be rightfully in command of the
army he had been leading against King Mithridates, he
was, as his opponents knew, planning to lead his forces
back against Rome.

After abortive negotiations with the Senate, in the
spring of 83 B.C.E. Sulla made his advance and was soon
joined by Crassus and by Pompey, who would in due course
earn his first precocious triumph at the age of twenty-four
for his campaigns in Africa during the civil war. Over the
course of the following year, Sulla and his men gradually
made their way toward Rome, and by the time he reached
the city, all his enemies had left. He followed his occupation with a series of proscriptions that led to the execution

and dispossession of prominent opponents and debarment from office of their descendants. As for Sulla, he returned to the position of dictator.

Ever after, in Rome and among Rome's heirs, Sulla would be the very embodiment of the bold military leader who claims emergency powers to pursue his own agenda, an image that would attach to later leaders in arms from Julius Caesar to Oliver Cromwell eighteen centuries later. But he should also be credited with giving human form to civil war and defining its features for generations of Romans. As Appian forcefully notes, when Marius and Sulpicius had confronted Sulla on his way to the Forum, "there took place a struggle between political enemies which was the first conducted in Rome not under the guise of civil dissension, but nakedly as a war, complete with trumpets and military standards . . . In this way the episodes of civil strife escalated from rivalry and contentiousness to murder, and from murder to full-scale war; and this was the first army composed of Roman citizens to attack their own country as if it were a hostile power."⁵⁰ That moment marked the arrival of civil war as an event, not just as an idea.

Appian's considered view of what made Sulla's move so momentous would shape later understandings of just what was warlike about civil war. He begins his account with a typically Greek analysis of a commonwealth bitterly divided between plebeians and patricians over such matters as laws, debts, the distribution of land, and the conduct of elections. Despite this acrimony, however, the two sides, as Appian explains, never came to blows, and even their most violent clashes could not be compared with the moment when the renegade general Coriolanus had allied with Rome's enemies and turned against the city in 491 B.C.E., for example.

For Appian, as for most other Roman commentators, it is the possession of arms and the adoption of the rules of war that distinguishes civil war from other internal disturbances. Only when "the faction leaders struggled against each other with great armies in military fashion for the prize of their native land" under Sulla and Marius could civil war be said to have begun in earnest.[51] Trumpets and standards were the visible signs, conventional warfare the means, and political control of the commonwealth was the end. All told, these were the peculiar marks of civil war as opposed to mere tumult, dissension, or sedition.

The Romans introduced two elements of civil war that would create a family resemblance among later conceptions. The first was the idea that the war takes place within the boundaries of a single political community. In the Roman case, this community was ever expanding, from the city of Rome itself, to the Italian peninsula, and then outward into the Mediterranean basin as Roman citizenship itself encompassed more and more peoples. That expansion of the limits of the community as defined by civil war would recur in later centuries, reaching its greatest extent in our own generation with the notion of a "global civil war," as we will discover later. The Romans also knew that there should be at least two contending parties in a civil war, one with a legitimate claim of authority over that community. These elements would be transmitted through the very language of civil war as well as in the several civil war narratives that the Roman historians, whether in Latin or in Greek, spun to explain and understand their commonwealth's serial calamities.

Civil war came to define the history of Roman civilization, whether as a curse the commonwealth could not shake off or as a purgative for the republic's popular ills, allowing the restoration of monarchy. Rome's heirs in the Latin West would then perceive their own internal troubles with the help of the repertoire of examples and images drawn from the Roman corpus of writing on the subject. Columns and capitols, amphitheaters and aqueducts, laws and Latin, would not be the only legacies of Rome to the world; among the most enduring, and the most unsettling, was the category of civil war itself. Indeed, for more than a millennium and a half, civil war was viewed through Rome-tinted spectacles.

Remembering Civil War

Roman Visions

"Forgetting is the best defense against civil war." So thought the Roman orator and historian Titus Labienus.[1] We might now call this, in the language of popular psychology, repression: an attempt to suppress painful memories through an effort of willful amnesia. But because repression is often linked to trauma, it can take much energy to push such memories deep into the unconscious, and it cannot be done indefinitely. Even those Romans who tried hardest not to speak of civil war found themselves reliving it in their writings and speeches. And their contemporaries and successors could hardly avoid addressing it in terms derived from Roman experience itself.

For many Romans, civil war remained the war that dared not speak its name. The words *bellum civile* had to be weighed carefully and spoken sparingly, if ever at all, because of the harsh memories of major conflicts. The clearest example of such reluctance may be that of the civil warrior and historian Julius Caesar. Caesar narrated his power struggle with Pompey in a work now known simply as *The Civil War*. Part campaign history, part autobiography, and part self-justification, the work carried on directly from his seven books of similar purpose respecting the conquest of Gaul, usually known as *The Gallic War*. The opening of the succeeding unfinished, indeed abandoned, history is lost, but one thing seems certain: Caesar himself did not call it "the Civil War." This title, which appeared only in later manuscripts, would have been for the author an unusual, even unthinkable, choice. In fact, Caesar did all he could to avoid using the phrase in his text. In its three surviving books, *bellum civile* appears only twice: once in an otherwise corrupt passage where Caesar places it in the mouths of some nervous and possibly deluded soldiers in his army describing their greatest fear; and once when he himself uses it, casually and only in retrospect, to describe his struggle with Pompey.[2]

Caesar and Pompey had made an expedient alliance in 60 b.c.e. against their common enemies in the Senate, an alliance strengthened in 59 b.c.e., when Pompey married Caesar's daughter, Julia. Their political arrangement also included a third man, Marcus Crassus, and for that reason became known as the first triumvirate (that is, the rule of three men, or *viri*). The same year that Caesar and Pompey were united by marriage, Caesar assumed the republic's highest political positions as one of the two annual consuls who directed the commonwealth and headed its armies. While in office, he engineered a five-year military command in Cisalpine Gaul, close to Rome, in part to ensure immunity from prosecution by the Senate for acts that he had undertaken as consul. In 56 B.C.E., Pompey and Crassus also secured similar five-year commands and then passed legislation extending Caesar's position until 50 B.C.E.

By the time that moment arrived, both Julia and Crassus were dead, and the supporters of Caesar were maneuvering on his behalf at Rome, while those of Pompey were doing likewise. The crisis came to a head when the Senate voted that both Caesar and Pompey should give up their commands. Neither did. After the reigning consul, Lentulus, overruled the tribunes of the people, Antony and Cassius, who had the power to maintain Caesar in his post, the Senate declared a state of emergency to "see to it the Republic suffers no harm." That prompted Caesar to march on Rome. He made every effort to deny that his actions and those of his army constituted an offensive move against his fellow Romans. Like any Roman commander, he insisted on the justice of his cause and explained it as a purely defensive maneuver. The true offenders, he insisted, were a powerful minority in the Senate who had plotted to deprive him of consulship in violation of the Roman constitution:

> I did not leave my province with harmful intent but to defend myself from the insults of my enemies, to restore the tribunes—who have been expelled from Rome in connection with this business—to their proper dignity, and to liberate myself and the Roman people from oppression by a small faction.[3]

The step Caesar referred to here—"leav[ing] my province"—was the act that would become one of Rome's greatest bequests to the later repertoire of civil war. This was the moment in January 49 B.C.E. when Caesar took his army across the river that marked the frontier between the province of Gaul, where he held authority as a military commander, and Rome itself, from which such military power was firmly debarred. The name of the narrow river went down in history: the Rubicon. "Crossing the Rubicon" thus came to speak of any political decision that was fraught, swift, and irreversible.[4]

Breaching the strict separation between military and civilian command, the act brought the zone of war, so carefully controlled outside the boundaries of Rome, within the peaceful sphere of the commonwealth. The keepers of Rome's memory, its historians and poets, would tell various versions of the event. Plutarch and Appian report that Caesar sent a small force ahead into Ariminum, the present-day resort of Rimini, ten miles south of the Rubicon, to infiltrate the town. He then excused himself from dinner before inconspicuously taking a carriage there along with a small group of attendants. Deep in thought, Caesar at nightfall hesitated at the river before airing his doubts to his companions. "If I refrain from this crossing, my friends, it will be the beginning of misfortune for me," Appian portrays Caesar as saying, "but if I cross, it will be the beginning for all mankind." In a burst of emotion, he quickly crossed the river, speaking the proverbial words of a bold and calculating gambler: "Let the die be cast!"[5]

The historian Suetonius adds to the scene an enthralling and mysterious pipe-playing woman who snatches a trumpet from one of Caesar's men and, leaping across the river, summons the army from the other bank. Lucan also places a woman at the scene, a grief-stricken, disheveled embodiment of Rome herself, who terrifies the general with her warning: "If lawfully you come, / If as citizens, this far only is allowed." But in Lucan, Caesar takes the plunge with full knowledge of the enormity of his action: "Here I abandon peace and desecrated law; / Fortune, it is you I follow. Farewell to treaties from now on; / I have relied on them for long enough; now war must be our referee."[6] Later artists would have to choose whether or not to add the curious piper or the distraught figure of Rome to their depictions of the scene.[7] Caesar himself has none of it.

In Caesar's third-person version of events, the general and his legion simply materialize in Ariminum, as if by magic. There is no mention of the crossing or any indication of anguished discussion, nothing to suggest that Caesar viewed the transit as pivotal for Rome or his own fortunes. There are no ominous attendants, indeed no other characters in the drama apart from Caesar himself. All he writes of the incident is this: "Apprised of the soldiers' goodwill he set out with the thirteenth legion for Ariminum, where he met the tribunes who had taken refuge with him."[8] In the eyes of the Senate, and in the judgment of most of posterity, Caesar had "declared civil war and defied the anathemas pronounced against generals who crossed the Rubicon in arms: they were damned to the infernal gods." So thought his great admirer Napoleon

Bonaparte as he dictated notes on Caesar's histories during his exile on the island of St. Helena in 1819.[9]

When it came to the matter of civil war, Caesar was the original master of denial. His great opponent, the lawyer, statesman, and philosopher Marcus Tullius Cicero, was not quite as repressed about it. Cicero has three claims to fame for the purposes of our history. First, he was the earliest writer known to have used the term, although for a long time he uttered it almost as rarely as Caesar himself: between 66 and 49 B.C.E., only twice in his voluminous writings and speeches.[10] Second, he showed how fluid the boundaries were between Roman conceptions of civil war and the understanding of other forms of organized armed threat. And third, he provides evidence that the Romans saw their own internal struggles as quite distinct from those of the Greeks they so admired.

Cicero first uttered the words "civil war" in a speech delivered in 66 B.C.E. He gave it on just the spot in the Forum where, twenty-three years later, his head and hands would be displayed on the Rostra after his execution. In the speech, he defends a proposal to offer the command of the war against Rome's most dangerous enemy in Asia Minor, Mithridates, king of Pontus, to the general Gnaeus Pompeius, or Pompey the Younger, better known to later generations simply as Pompey, Caesar's major adversary. After pointing out how nothing less than Rome's glory and honor and the future of its empire are at stake in this just war, Cicero asks his listeners to imagine the kind of great commander needed to lead Rome to victory, a man with military experience, ability, authority, and luck. Who better, who more possessed of these qualities than Pompey, the precocious young general who had taken his first major command at the age of eighteen? He had fought every new enemy, in every conceivable theater of war, the Romans had faced over the next two decades:

> What type of war can there be in which the fortune of the state has not made use of him? *Civil*, African, Transalpine, Spanish (a war involving both citizens and exceptionally warlike tribes), slave, and naval wars, wars and enemies different in character and locality, wars not only undertaken by this one man but also completed by him—all these demonstrate that there is no aspect of military experience which can escape the knowledge of this man.[11]

For vanquishing rebels in North Africa, Spain, and Gaul, as well as two other military triumphs, one while still in his twenties, Pompey had earned the nickname Magnus, "the Great," after his hero, Alexander the Great. He also easily crushed the remnants of Spartacus's slave rebellion in Sicily, swept pirates from the Mediterranean in a stunning three-month campaign, and had successfully battled the forces of Gnaeus Papirius Carbo in Sicily in 82 B.C.E. and Marcus Aemilius Lepidus in Etruria in 77 B.C.E.[12] Except for the wars against slaves and pirates, all of these exploits were conducted in whole or in part against fellow citizens. "Civil" wars were part of Rome's recent history, and they were already difficult to distinguish from wars against other external enemies.

Cicero's mention of "civil" war in his defense of Pompey shows that the term was already in general currency. He was, then, clearly not the first to deploy it, even if his use is still the earliest recorded. His listing of Pompey's wars also implies a hierarchy of enemies and challenges; most opprobrious of all were the pirates and slaves, but the hardest to defeat were Roman citizens. Thus, Cicero would have left his audience in no doubt that victory in the "civil" wars of the 80s B.C.E. stood first among Pompey's achievements, even if those wars became immediately unmentionable. Cicero was speaking, after all, as a partisan of Pompey's; that is the sense in which his audience would surely have taken his tendentious mention of civil war as something on a par with the defeat of Rome's external enemies and internal threats. And so, no sooner had civil war been invented than it was reinvented: first, as an almost inconceivable horror, but soon as a more slippery concept, capable of being turned into something, if not valuable or honorable per se, then at least an occasion when valor and military prowess might be shown.

This was tricky; civil wars were "wars which would bring no triumphs," as Lucan put it and as most Roman commentators agreed.[13] Roman ritual triumphs were the reward for victory in a just war against a foreign enemy—or so the convention ran. A victorious army proclaimed its general an *imperator*; he then requested the Senate's permission for various rituals of thanksgiving; in due course, a formal triumph was often granted. "No man," wrote the historian Valerius Maximus in the first century C.E., "though he might have accomplished great things eminently useful to the commonwealth in a civil war, was given the title of *imperator* on that account, nor were any thanksgivings decreed, nor did such a one triumph either in ovation or with chariot, for such victories have ever been accounted grievous, though necessary, as won by domestic not foreign blood."[14] Pompey, however, did receive triumphs for victories in Africa and Spain "that were in reality civil wars," and Caesar later celebrated a string of triumphs over his enemies—citizens and foreigners alike—in Gaul, Egypt, Pontus, and Africa, and then over Pompey's sons, in clear violation of the taboo against triumphs in civil wars.[15] When, finally, Octavian came to power as the emperor Augustus following his defeat of Mark Antony and Cleopatra at the Battle of Actium in 31 B.C.E., he too celebrated a triumph—but only after representing his victory as having been won over both foreign and citizen enemies. The boundaries between different types of wars remained porous and debatable; the logic of victor's justice could determine the definition, but only by suppressing the "civil" element in many of the wars of the late republic.[16]

The Romans believed their experience of civil war was anomalous when set against Greek history and their own city's beginnings. It took a peculiar kind of inverted pride to see the internal violence of the republic as an innovation over the less structured, less visibly warlike commotions of the Greeks. Cicero certainly acknowledged this. Shortly before Caesar's assassination in 44 B.C.E., the senator composed a work of advice for his only son, Marcus, then leaving Rome for further education in Athens. This work, known better as *On Duties* (43 B.C.E.), was in part a veiled argument for tyrannicide; in it, Cicero points out the difference between Greek and Roman conceptions of internal division. He quotes Socrates in Plato's *Republic* on the need to follow the common good and warns Marcus against the division of the Roman republic into factions of democrats and aristocrats. Cicero then notes that while the Greeks had indeed known great discords, the divisions in Rome were nonetheless different in scale, in form, and in name. The Romans had suffered not just seditions— the kinds of turmoil the Greeks would have called *stasis*— but something much worse and quite new: "accursed civil wars" (*pestifera bella civilia*). Any serious and courageous citizen would avoid and condemn civil war.[17] Nonetheless, Rome might be seen to have invented it.

*

Rome's orators, poets, and historians struggled to make sense of their commonwealth's descent into formal armed contention. They chewed over the question of blame for the civil wars, looking for signs of decay in Rome's moral health. They were particularly transfixed by the idea that civil war should repeat itself after periods of apparent calm. Finally, what they bequeathed to later readers was a vision of history structured around an ethically challenging, appallingly recurrent phenomenon that was, nonetheless, the paradoxical mark of civility, even (to take a much later term for it) of civilization itself. In all these ways, Romans became memory keepers of civil war, for their own people and for the ages to come.

Remembering civil war was always a risky business, as Titus Labienus implied when he counseled *oblivio* (forgetting). With remembrance came the danger of inflaming passions and reigniting civil war. We can see this most poignantly in one of the first Roman attempts at a history of civil war. This was by a companion of Caesar's, Gaius Asinius Pollio. In the estimation of the orator Quintilian, Pollio was the original "man for all seasons"; a writer, a politician, and a patron of poets (among them Horace and Virgil), he also founded Rome's first public library. His authority for writing about civil war came from his having fought with Caesar in 49 B.C.E. Indeed, he had been at Caesar's side as the general stood agonizing on the banks of the Rubicon and then took the plunge with him. Following Caesar's assassination in 44 B.C.E., Pollio had been crowned with the consulship, and he won a military triumph in 39 or 38 B.C.E. Soon after, when he retired from public life, Pollio, like many other Roman politicians in retreat, turned to literature as a form of politics by other means. We learn the subject of his major work from the ode his client Horace addressed to him on the subject:

The civil disturbance which began in the
   consulship of Metellus
and the causes of the war, its evils and the ways of it,
      the play of Fortune, the fatal friendships
     of the great, and armour

smeared with still unexpiated blood—
themes fraught with the hazard of the dice—
     all these you treat, and tread on fire
smouldering under ashes.[18]

As a supporter of Caesar's, working in the shadow of
his murder, Pollio would no doubt have thought his general's death still unavenged (hence Horace's "armour /
smeared with unexpiated blood"). His history would therefore have been somewhat an exercise in rehabilitation. As
Caesar had known, however, when crossing the Rubicon,
everything depends upon a gambler's throw; or, in those
words widely attributed to him, "the die is cast" (*iacta alea
est*). By recalling Caesar's aphorism, Horace artfully con-
flates Caesar's decision with Pollio's perilous undertaking
("themes fraught with the hazard of the dice"). For the
greatest danger lay in keeping the flame of memory alive.
Even if intended as simply a memorial pyre, it might grow
into something much more destructive because of the
smoking volcano always liable to erupt. The potential for
a new explosion of civil conflict was ever present. To treat
the history of civil war was always to tread on fire.

Civil war erupted repeatedly over more than a century of Roman history from the 80s B.C.E. to the 60s C.E.

and beyond. Sulla's first civil war against Marius in 88–87 B.C.E. led to a second series of contentions between them in 82–81 B.C.E. Two decades later, impoverished veterans of Sulla's wars supported the senator Catiline's conspiracy to take control of the city in 63 B.C.E. Cicero was one of the intended victims of that putsch, but he was alerted to the danger and led the political and oratorical charge to defeat this enemy of the republic. Almost twenty years later still, Caesar started a civil war that inaugurated a cycle of intermittent armed violence that engulfed first Rome, then the Italian peninsula, and ultimately much of the Mediterranean world as far as Egypt. In this cycle, the followers and descendants of Caesar and Pompey continued to fight out their differences in a series of wars that would culminate with the victory of Octavian over Mark Antony and Cleopatra at the Battle of Actium in 31 B.C.E. With Octavian's elevation to the emperorship as Augustus in 27 B.C.E., one sequence of civil wars had ended. The seeds for another were laid in the dynamics of succession to imperial authority.

The elevation of Octavian brought the temporary respite from conflict hymned as the "Augustan" age of peace and stability. But the decades after his death in 14 C.E. witnessed a boom in writing about civil war and, in turn, a recurrence of civil war itself. Those who opposed the imperial monarchy looked back nostalgically to the republic as an era when the common good (the *res publica*) had been maintained before corruption had set in. For others, however, the years before Julius Caesar and the emperor Augustus were fading by the day. "Even among the old men most had been born in the time of the civil wars: who was left who had seen a republic?" lamented the historian Tacitus in his *Annals*, writing of those alive at the end of Augustus's reign; by this account, tyranny was a continuation of civil war by other means.[19] The following decades, during the reign of the emperor Tiberius, witnessed more accounts of civil war than at any other moment in Roman history. Tacitus's is one of the few to survive; most went the way of Pollio's, including works by Seneca the Elder and those by the historian Aulus Cremutius Cordus, who had been charged with treason in 25 C.E. for allegedly inciting civil war just by writing about the earlier conflicts.[20]

There was another flare of remembrance during the reign of Nero, when Lucan wrote his epic poem, *The Civil War* (60–65 C.E.), on the struggles between Caesar and Pompey. It was an ambivalent poem, written under the emperor's patronage yet palpably nostalgic for the world before emperors, when the Roman republic had been vibrant, if battered by civil contention. Lucan looked back to civil conflicts a century earlier, envisaging a cosmos attuned to the political and military discords of the human world, with the heavens trembling in sympathy with the earth's calamity.[21]

Lucan's imagistic powers, republican leanings, and vivid re-creations of intimate violence ensured that he would be among the most widely read and admired of all Roman poets for almost fifteen hundred years, from the fourth to the early nineteenth century.[22] A translation of *The Civil War* was made in Middle Irish in the twelfth century.[23] By the thirteenth, a manuscript of it had reached

Iceland, where, combined with extracts from Sallust's *Jugurtha* and his *Catiline*, a prose synopsis formed the *Rómverja Saga*, an Icelandic history of Rome told through its tumults, conspiracies, and civil wars.[24] Dante in the early fourteenth century regarded him as "that great poet Lucan"; to Geoffrey Chaucer, later in the fourteenth, he was "the grete poete, daun Lucan."[25] And to Hugo Grotius (1583–1645), the Dutch scholar, theorist of rights, and scholarly editor of *The Civil War*, Lucan was nothing less than the "freedom-loving poet."[26] His popularity rose and fell with the incidence of civil warfare in Europe. In the sixteenth and seventeenth centuries, as we will see, he proved a crucial resource for understanding conflicts, both historical and contemporaneous, and while his fame declined in the nineteenth century, he would find new readers in the late twentieth.

Among Lucan's fellow writers under the emperor Nero was the politician, poet, and bon vivant Titus Petronius Arbiter (ca. 27–66 C.E.), author of *The Satyricon*. This notorious poem portrays a fictional dinner party at which the equally fictional poet Eumolpus recites a poem on the civil war between Caesar and Pompey. Eumolpus calls civil war a truly "great theme," perhaps as momentous as the *Aeneid*, which Virgil had called his own "greater work."[27]

Both Lucan and Petronius committed suicide under Nero. When the emperor himself was dead, too, in 69 C.E., the fires of civil war stirred back to life in the "Year of the Four Emperors" (Galba, Otho, Vitellius, and Vespasian). These wars over imperial succession would not be the last Roman civil wars—which, by some accounts, lasted into the fourth century C.E.—but they would bring to a climax the historical narratives of Rome as a commonwealth peculiarly prone to that kind of discord. That pattern became clear in retrospect. "Should I not have deduced the decline of the [Roman] Empire from the civil Wars, that ensued after the fall of Nero or even from the tyranny which succeeded the reign of Augustus?" the historian Edward Gibbon (1737–94) asked himself in the 1780s, after completing his famous account of Rome's decline and fall. "Alas! I should."[28]

Far from consigning civil war to oblivion, the Romans and their successors had repeatedly recalled it. It thus became as inescapable as it was unspeakable until, it seemed, they could talk of almost nothing else for centuries because civil war would never disappear. "These sufferings await, again to be endured," laments a character in Lucan's *Civil War:* "This will be the sequence / of the warfare, this will be the outcome fixed for civil strife."[29] There would be no end of making books about the Roman civil wars. Lucan's poem was followed four decades later by Tacitus's account of the Year of the Four Emperors in his *Histories* (ca. 109 C.E.). The Greek-speaking historian Plutarch composed a series of parallel lives of Greek and Roman figures, and among his Roman exemplars were the Gracchi and the successive civil warriors Marius, Sulla, Caesar, Pompey, and Antony (ca. 100–25 C.E.). Also in these years, another historian writing in Greek, Appian, composed the surviving books of his *Roman History*, titled *The Civil Wars* (ca. 145–65 C.E.). These attempted a comprehensive history, aiming to encompass all Rome's civil wars from Sulla to Octavian.

Less detailed than all of these, but even more wide-ranging, was Florus's popular *Epitome of Roman History* (ca. 117–38 C.E. or ca. 161–69 C.E.), which painted the seven centuries after Romulus as an unending run of different kinds of wars: foreign, servile, social, and civil. Though considering only the foreign ones were just, Florus deliberately blurs the boundaries between the other kinds of wars, noting, for example, that the Social War was in fact a civil war, because the allies who had been united with the Romans "in raising a rebellion within the bounds of Italy, committed as great a crime as citizens who rebel within a city." Moreover, after describing the Servile Wars as the most disgraceful of all, he ties the wars of Sulla and Marius to them in turpitude, as representing Rome's ultimate misfortunes, when citizens fought against citizens in the Forum as if they were gladiators—"men of the worst class"—in the arena. And to crown this confusion of categories, Florus traces the spread of the struggle between Caesar and Pompey outward from Rome, to Italy, and then the empire.[30]

Over the course of the almost five centuries to follow, roughly from Caesar to Augustine, Roman historians intrepidly struggled to understand their civilization's greatest curse.[31] They wrestled with the question of causes. What had sparked each of Rome's civil wars? Was there some fundamental flaw in the Roman republic that gave rise to them? They worried about the reasons for so many civil wars. Was there some deeper logic at work? And they tried to draw meaning from their tribulations. Was there an ideal form of the commonwealth that was immune to civil war? Or did some underlying structure of Roman civilization itself ensure that the scourge would always return? These questions would decisively shape *The City of God* (413–26 C.E.) by Augustine, the North African historian and bishop of Hippo; he remains among the greatest of the Roman histories of civil war. But first let us return to some of his predecessors.

Contemporary Romans' answers to those great questions generated some vivid and unsettling lessons that would be repeated and learned for centuries afterward. Civil wars came not singly but in battalions. They left wounds that would not heal, heirs who demanded vengeance, divisions that would split first the city of Rome and then the entire Roman Empire of the Mediterranean and beyond. As Tacitus puts it at the start of his account of the bitter disputes of the first century C.E., "The history on which I am entering is full of disasters, terrible with battles, torn by seditions, savage even in peace. Four emperors fell by the sword; there were three civil wars, more foreign wars, and often both at the same time."[32] Thus while civil wars were fought for control of the city itself, they could not easily be distinguished from foreign wars, their spillover reaching throughout the Roman world and later drawing in actors from across the empire.

The wider the grant of Roman citizenship, the broader the scope of civil war. As Florus argues, "The rage of Caesar and Pompey, like a flood or a fire, overran the city, Italy, tribes, nations and finally the whole empire, so much so that it cannot rightly be called a civil war, nor even a social or an external war, but it was a war with something of all of these—and yet worse than war."[33] Florus here echoes the opening lines of Lucan's *Civil War*, the classic summary of Roman anxieties about the subject:

> Of wars across Emathian plains, worse than
>   civil wars,
> and of legality conferred on crime we sing, and of
>   a mighty people
> attacking its own guts with victorious
>   sword-hand,
> of kin facing kin, and, once the pact of tyranny
>   was broken,
> of conflict waged with all the forces of the
>   shaken world
> for universal guilt, and of standards ranged in
>   enmity against
> standards, of eagles matched and javelins
>   threatening javelins.
>
> What madness was this, O citizens?[34]

If these wars between Caesar and Pompey are "worse than civil," it is because they were fought between two men who had been bound by marriage pact; in that sense, they were familial wars ("kin facing kin"), not merely between citizens.[35] The result is a phrase that would echo in later

history: a "warr without an Enemie," as the English parliamentary general Sir William Waller called the turbulence
of his own commonwealth in 1643. As a conflict among
kin and compatriots, such a war was agonizingly fraught
because it was being fought for political authority, and
with it the right to define the membership of the commonwealth itself.[36] But understood this way, as a test of
values, civil war was a necessary and natural struggle, as
unavoidable as it was terrible.

Civil wars were indeed wars, with the full panoply of
insignia and weapons, just like the first war identified as
civil—Sulla's war—with its conspicuous drums and trumpets, and now they engulfed the whole of the Roman Mediterranean: the "Emathian plains" lie in northern Greece
and were the location of the decisive Battle of Pharsalus in
48 B.C.E., from which Lucan's poem derives its alternative
name, the *Pharsalia*. If the physical frontiers lacked fixity,
the conceptual ones were even more fluid. The bounds
of the various kinds of wars that Cicero and others had
attempted to discriminate became blurred, as if by virtue
of the very effort, making it only more difficult to cor-
don off civil wars from other forms of conflict. Like some
implacable natural force, civil war no longer respected the
boundaries of the commonwealth, growing much more
destructive as it revealed its potential to be universal in
scope. And so it was precisely this nature, which made it
so imperative to understand civil war, that also made it so
hard to describe and to define.

*

The most fundamental problem all Rome's historians of civil war faced was exactly where to begin their narrative. Even Caesar did not begin his history with the crossing of the Rubicon; other poets and historians reached further back in search of the origins of their commonwealth's internal troubles. Horace's poem to Pollio neatly illustrates the difficulty of explaining the fact of recurrence; it refers to "the consulship of Metellus," even though *eleven* men named Metellus had been consul between roughly 140 and 60 B.C.E. Horace could have been referring to the one who held office in 60 B.C.E., when the alliance of Caesar, Pompey, and Crassus first formed, according to most Roman historians. Yet he might have meant another Metellus who held office in 123 B.C.E., the year Gaius Gracchus was tribune of the people, two years before his murder and decapitation by an angry mob. Now, if Horace meant the first Metellus, then he implies that Pollio's history began only two decades before Caesar crossed the Rubicon. If he meant the second, however, then Pollio had taken a much longer perspective on the troubles that split Rome and set its citizens at each other's throats.[37] The entire ethical history of Rome could hang on such choices.

A short-term explanation implied that civil war was accidental and unlikely to recur. The longer view would weave conflict into the very fabric of Roman history and imply deep-seated causes, perhaps even moral culpability for the descent into destructive violence. For some the problem was present at the very foundation of the city, with Romulus's murder of his brother, when, as Augustine would argue, "the city as a whole committed the crime which as a whole it overlooked."[38] Writing probably in the late 30s B.C.E., in the brief but uneasy period of peace brokered by the triumvirate in 39 B.C.E., Horace had asked his fellow Romans why they were thinking of drawing swords that had only just been sheathed, and why they should be so insane as to shed blood without conquering other peoples, like the Carthaginians or the Britons, choosing rather to perish by their own hands? There could be only one explanation—the primal sin of fratricide that had cursed the city ever after:

> Why this mad rush to join a wicked war? Your
>   swords
>   were sheathed. Why do you draw them now?
>
>   . . . It is harsh Fate that drives
>   the Romans, and the crime of fratricide
>   since Remus's blameless lifeblood poured upon
>   the ground—
>   a curse to generations yet unborn.[39]

By the time Horace wrote this poem, after two generations of civil war, Romulus's murder of his brother had become an established allegory of the political and social division between *plebs* and patricians, "with the permanent possibility of conflict between them."[40] It read back into Rome's origins its internal struggles—the Conflict of the Orders, the divisions under the Gracchi, and the civil wars. This bloody genealogy also cast a shadow over the future, as Horace himself would confirm a little over a year later with another poetic lament at the breakdown of relations between the triumvirate and Pompey's son Sextus Pompey: "A second generation is ground down by civil wars, / and Rome is falling, ruined by the might of Rome." It seemed once again as if "this city we, this doomed and godless generation, shall destroy."[41] The only way to escape Rome's original curse, Horace went on, would be to avoid Rome itself. Fleeing, not forgetting, might in fact be the only remedy for the curse of civil war.

But what if the roots of Rome's dissensions were not buried quite so deep in the city's early history? In his account of Catiline's conspiracy of 63–62 B.C.E., Sallust also attributes the great turn in the city's fortunes to a moral failing but one that is the unintended consequence of Roman success. The defeat of Rome's enemy Carthage in 146 B.C.E. had ushered in corruption on the coattails of victory. Before that time, Sallust thought, "citizens fought with citizens," but they had contended only for the honor that came with virtue. After the triumphs of the Punic War, however, "Fortune began to be cruel and confounded everything" by nurturing greed and ambition. Sulla had been able to conquer Rome by buying the loyalty of his army with the luxurious spoils of campaigns in Asia. By this understanding, civil war and corruption went hand in hand, sapping Rome's moral strength until Catiline tried to follow in Sulla's footsteps by aiming to overthrow the republic with the help of debased soldiers who "longed for civil war."[42] Elsewhere in his histories,

Sallust reaffirmed this narrative; Rome's earliest dissension arose from flawed human nature and its desires for freedom, glory, and power, but it was only after the fall of Carthage that such evils flourished to the point of driving plebeians and patricians into open conflict: "The way was clear for pursuing rivalries, [and] there arose a great many riots, insurrections, and in the end, civil wars."[43]

Most Roman historians saw a different wellspring of social strife: the reform program of the Gracchus brothers, Tiberius and Gaius, in the first century B.C.E. From their tutor, the Stoic philosopher Blossius of Cumae, the Gracchi had apparently learned a Greek-influenced vocabulary for dividing Roman politics into factions of "aristocrats" and "democrats," with the result that later students of Rome would see this cleavage as the basis of the city's fatal susceptibility to civil war. Cicero, Velleius Paterculus, Appian, and Florus would all take the murder of Tiberius Gracchus in 133 B.C.E. as Rome's first fatal rift, while Varro would settle on the death of the younger brother in 121 B.C.E. as the crux, saying it was Gaius who had "made the citizen body two-headed—the origin of the civil discords."[44] These troubles among the tribunes of the people, Tacitus writes in his *Histories*, were "trial runs for civil war."[45] And, as Cicero notes, it was the division between those who supported the aristocracy (*optimi*) and those who took the side of the people (*populares*) that sowed the seeds of treachery and discord into the Roman republic.[46] These explanations are not incompatible, of course; strung together, they could tell a compelling story, encouraging a later historian like Augustine in his own account of Rome's fatal flaws.

In fact, the various analyses of civil wars in the Roman historical canon did not so much compete as accumulate. The myth of Romulus and Remus explains the most fundamental cause of the city's propensity toward conflict. Sallust's moralistic assault on the luxury and corruption that followed the defeat of Carthage suggests the preconditions. The recollections of Cicero and others of divisions under the Gracchi prefigure the splits that would later result in outright factions and deeper divisions within the body politic, ultimately leading Romans to take up arms against fellow citizens.

This is how a sequence turned into a cycle. Explanations turned into justifications. And events settled into a narrative stretching deep into Rome's past—to its very beginnings—projecting a shadow onto its future, to rise up again at moments of political strain. In this mode, Tacitus describes the anxieties of the common people after the murder of Galba during the Year of the Four Emperors: "They recalled the memory of civil wars and how many times the city had been captured, of the devastation of Italy, the plundering of provinces, of [the Battles of] Pharsalus, Philippi, Perusia and Mutina, names famous for public disaster."[47] That cycle of civil wars would be played out again and again: indirectly, as in a poem like Statius's *Thebaid* (92 C.E.), which narrates the primal, fratricidal competition at Thebes between the two sons of Oedipus, Eteocles and Polynices, with the Roman civil wars of the first century C.E. as backdrop;[48] and also directly in those who, like Tacitus and Florus, structure Roman history around the experience of civil war—to say nothing of later accounts of civil wars across time, well into the eighteenth century, until the American and French Revolutions.

By far the most comprehensive narrative depicting a Roman propensity to civil war was the Christian version authoritatively retailed by Augustine in *The City of God*. He would write his theological and historical masterwork in the wake of the barbarian invasion of Rome in 410 C.E., composing its twenty-two books from 413 to 426 C.E. Among its many purposes is to explain why Rome had fallen. Christianity's opponents claimed that the new religion had been the cause: if only the pagan gods could have been appeased, the city could have fought off its attackers. To rebut the charge that Christianity had sapped Rome and left it vulnerable to the Goths, Augustine argues that the empire's moral debility and susceptibility to division existed long before the birth of Jesus; he ascribes it to precisely that sequence of events adduced by his predecessors among Rome's historians of civil war. But there is an evident paradox here. Had Rome not been a vehicle of salvation, carrying the gospel across the known world, wherever its empire? Might there, then, be a divine purpose behind the sack of the city, just as with its earlier success? Augustine follows his predecessors in tracing the city's moral history back to its very founding and through its interminable subsequent episodes of turbulence and self-destruction to its collapse. How could the rage of barbarians or the conquest of foreigners compare with the horrors of citizens killing citizens?

Augustine had the benefit of a thorough education in Roman literature and a period teaching rhetoric in Milan, the empire's cultural capital in his youth. He was steeped in the works of Cicero, Sallust, and Virgil and knew many of the books of Livy's comprehensive history of Rome that are now lost.[49] This erudition enabled him to compile a comprehensive history of Rome's internal disturbances from Romulus and Remus—whose fratricide "showed the extent to which the earthly city is divided against itself"— all the way to his own times. If he could show that its moral decay preceded by a very long while the birth of Jesus, then Christianity could hardly be the cause of its decline and fall. Sallust provides just the evidence Augustine needs "in his History, where he shows how the bad morals which came forth from prosperity [after the defeat of Carthage] led at last to civil wars." From the Gracchi to Sulla, Rome's seditions "proceeded even to civil wars," without the city's gods doing anything to prevent them; indeed, the gods themselves were sometimes seen to incite the citizens against one another and give them an excuse for their contentions. The Romans erected a temple to the goddess Concord, Augustine noted ironically, "but Concord abandoned them, while Discord cruelly led them even into civil wars."[50]

Augustine's account of pagan Rome was a catalog of "those evils which were more infernal because internal," a series of "civil, or rather uncivilized, discords."

"How much Roman blood was shed, and how much of Italy was destroyed and devastated," he laments, "by the Social War, Servile War and Civil Wars!" Here he follows Florus in telling Roman history as a succession of wars, each building on the moral instability of its predecessor to shake the foundations of the commonwealth again. The intervals between open fighting were no less bloody than the battles themselves as, after Sulla's first victory, "peace vied with war in cruelty, and conquered." The first civil wars, of Marius and Sulla, led inexorably to all Rome's other internal wars until the advent of Augustus, the civil warrior (according to Augustine) in whose reign Jesus was born: "But those wars began long before the advent of Christ, and a chain of causes linked one crime to another."[51]

While in the middle of writing *The City of God*, Augustine encouraged Paulus Orosius, a Spanish priest who had migrated to North Africa, to undertake his own history "against the pagans" in response to the barbarian sack of Rome. Orosius's *Seven Books of History Against the Pagans* (417–18 C.E.) was truly universal, spanning the more than 5,618 years since the creation of the world down to the author's own time. The priest sets Rome's catalog of civil wars into the much longer story of the crimes, wars, and natural disasters humanity had suffered since the beginning of recorded time,[52] even as he traces Rome's civil wars in sequence, much as his predecessors (and sources) among the earlier Roman historians had done. He sees the crime of "parricide," of murders within families, as a recurring symptom of civil war, at least from the time of the Persians, who "fought a civil war, or rather *a war more than civil*"—there was that line from Lucan again!—after the death of their king Darius II led to a succession battle between his sons, Artaxerxes and Cyrus. Orosius follows the conventional chronology of Rome's civil wars, beginning with Sulla, but sees the cycle as continuing even down to his own times. Here he parts company with Augustine, who holds that these worst of wars were fought only among pagans, not between pagans and Christians. Orosius answers those who claimed there were no such contemporary "civil" wars by arguing "that it would indeed be more accurate to call them wars against allies, but it will be to our advantage"—that is, to the benefit of Christians— "if they are called civil wars." Why? Because they were *just* wars, fought for the praiseworthy cause of Christian victory and ameliorated by Christian forgiveness: "Who can doubt that the so-called civil wars of today are fought with more mildness and mercy, or indeed suppressed rather than fought?"[53]

Augustine, for one, doubted it. He never mentions Orosius by name and seems to have been disappointed by his follower's history, which was constructed around the optimistic idea that the Roman Empire was and would remain the vehicle divine providence had chosen to spread Christianity.[54] As he brought his own *City of God* to completion, Augustine maintained a firm separation between pagans and Christians—that is, between those who inhabited the Earthly City (symbolized by Rome) and the believers of the Heavenly City. As Augustine reminds his readers, the Romans had ceaselessly found reason to fight each other, with ever more destructive effects for the entire Roman world: "The very breadth of the Empire has produced wars of a worse kind: that is, social and civil wars. By these, the human race is made even more miserable, either by warfare itself, waged for the sake of eventual peace, or by the constant fear that conflict will begin again." The contrast with that other city, the City of God, a *civitas* whose citizens were never at war with one another, could hardly have been greater.[55]

*

Rome's canon of civil wars, from Caesar to Augustine, generated three enduring—and enduringly influential—narratives. The first was what might be called the republican story; sympathetic to the supposedly selfless civic values of the Roman republic, it portrayed the endless repetition of civil wars as springing from the very roots of Rome itself. By this account of Roman history, to be "civilized" at all was to be prone to civil war; to suffer only one civil war seemed impossible, because others would inevitably follow so long as Roman civilization itself lasted. Then there was an imperial narrative that followed much the same trajectory but reached a very different conclusion. Civil war was a persistent disease of the body politic, and it had only one cure: the restoration of monarchy or the exaltation of an emperor. This was a story that culminated in the creation of the Roman Empire under Augustus Caesar. "In this way," wrote the Greek-speaking historian Appian, "the Roman polity survived all kinds of civil disturbance to reach unity and monarchy," "an evident demonstration," agreed his late sixteenth-century English translator, "that peoples rule must give place, and Princes power prevayle."[56] Finally, there was a Christian narrative, in which civil war was the besetting sin of a city or commonwealth dedicated to the things of this world rather than to the glory of God. This worldliness was the source of its self-destruction and ensured it could not ultimately be a fit vehicle for salvation. All these narratives would be applied to later sequences of political and military disturbance throughout Europe and its empires until well into the eighteenth century.

Later generations would ratify by adoption the Roman orators', poets', and historians' conception of what civil war looked like, how it was fought, and what its consequences would be. Readers of these classical texts would understand their own internal power struggles in terms inherited from the Romans. They would learn the meaning of civil war from the Latin they read in school and at university, ensuring the inherited view formed their thinking from the earliest opportunity. They would write poems inspired by Lucan and compile histories of their own dissensions under the spell of Sallust, Tacitus, and the other Roman chroniclers of civil strife. And major political thinkers in the seventeenth century—among them, Hugo Grotius, Thomas Hobbes, and John Locke—would use Roman language to debate sovereignty and treason, rebellion and revolution. These efforts would put traditional conceptions of civil war to the test for the first time, but only by carrying on a dialogue with ancient forebears. So long as Rome's poets and historians were remembered, forgetting could not be a feasible defense against civil war.

PART II

Early Modern Crossroads

3

Uncivil Civil Wars

The Seventeenth Century

Roman accounts of civil war were central to the classical tradition handed down through educational institutions in Europe and the Americas, equipping later generations with a vocabulary and a set of narratives they could apply to their own troubles, if not always availing much reassurance. As Thomas Hobbes remarked in 1642, just after the onset of England's first civil war, "The famous deeds and sayings of the Greeks and Romans have been commended to History not by Reason but by their grandeur and often by that very wolf-like element which men deplore in each other; for the stream of History carries down through the centuries the memory of men's varied characters as well as of their public actions."[1] Hobbes had begun his publishing career in 1629 with his translation of Thucydides; in 1670, close to the end of his life in 1679, he produced a history of England's civil wars inspired in part by Roman models. Although deeply skeptical of the political effects of classical learning—for example, he thought Greek and Roman republican ideas to be one of the root causes of England's troubles—Hobbes was, like his contemporaries, as we shall see, deeply indebted to the Roman canon of civil war.

That canon would not—could not—be forgotten. Rome's writers, from Cicero and Caesar to Lucan and Augustine, continued to be read and imitated as long as they were taught and published. After the revival of classical learning that we call the Renaissance in the fifteenth and sixteenth centuries, pupils, almost invariably boys, learned poetry and rhetoric from Latin textbooks. They crowned their studies with history and philosophy by reading the works of Caesar, Sallust, Tacitus, and Cicero. The same texts were not always in continuous use, but many of the works Augustine had studied in North Africa in the fourth century C.E. would have been familiar to the young William Shakespeare (1564–1616) at his grammar school in Stratford-upon-Avon over a thousand years later.[2] And the reputations of Roman writers on civil war closely tracked the prevalence of internal conflict in Europe. Between 1450 and 1700, editions of these historians greatly outpaced printings of their Greek predecessors, so that five of the top ten best sellers of classical historians were histories of civil war. Sallust's histories were the two most frequently reprinted texts, with Caesar, Tacitus, and Florus not far behind.[3]

Though he is forgotten now, Florus became a mainstay of school and university curricula, shaping views of Roman history among generations of young scholars, some destined to reflect critically on the Roman experience.[4]

Hobbes would have read Florus's *Epitome* as a schoolboy and later used it as a textbook when he tutored the young aristocrats William Cavendish II in 1608 and William Cavendish III in the 1630s; significantly, he called *Behemoth*, his history of England's upheavals in the mid-seventeenth century, an "Epitome" of the English Civil Wars.[5] When the first professorship of history was created at Oxford in 1622, the incumbent's main task was to lecture on Florus. (The first to hold the chair, Degory Wheare, was perhaps excessively zealous; after eight years and 154 lectures, he still had not progressed past the historian's first book.)[6] In 1636, according to Oxford's new statutes, all undergraduates had to attend lectures on Florus twice a week; this is the curriculum John Locke would have followed as a student at Oxford in the 1650s.[7] Editions of Florus continued to appear almost annually until his stock fell at the end of the eighteenth century, along with that of his fellow epitomist the fourth-century historian Eutropius, whose Roman history Adam Smith, for one, studied at school in Scotland in the 1730s.[8]

Roman histories of civil war shaped perceptions of conflict well beyond Europe, too. There was, for example, plentiful evidence that a sequence of civil wars was being played out in recognizably Roman colors in the Americas after the Spanish conquest. In the 1530s and early 1540s, conquistadors in Peru, led by Francisco Pizarro and Diego de Almagro, fast friends who had turned into bitter enemies, fought a series of wars for the spoils of conquest, ensnaring families and followers. In the following decades, the Spanish historians Gonzalo Fernández de Oviedo, Agustín

de Zárate, and Pedro Cieza de León narrated the struggles
of the Pizarros and the Almagros, their Spanish armies and
indigenous allies, in terms drawn from Sallust, Plutarch,
Livy, and Lucan. Oviedo alluded to Lucan in describing
"this war, worse than civil war, and no less hellish," while
Cieza de Léon mordantly noted that "the wars that are
most feared and that are fought with the greatest cruelty
are civil wars."[9] And writing a few decades later, in the
early seventeenth century, the indigenous historian the
Inca Garcilaso de la Vega likewise described "the civil wars
that took place between the Pizarros and Almagros" in
the second volume of his chronicle of Peruvian history.[10]
Europeans had evidently exported civil war to a wider
world as a distinguishing mark of their civilization even if
they generally did not use the term to describe the contentions of indigenous peoples in the Americas. Nevertheless,
to be civilized was to be capable of—but also fatally susceptible to—civil war.

The Roman sequence of civil wars was the inspiration
for some of the most creative political thought and literature in late medieval and early modern Europe. In his *Discourses on Livy* (ca. 1517), Niccolò Machiavelli anatomized
Rome's tumults in search of lessons for his own times.
Michel de Montaigne viewed the French civil wars of the
late sixteenth century from a defensive distance: "Civill
warres have this one thing worse than other warres, to
cause every one of us to make a watch-tower of his owne
house."[11] France's turmoils also lent topical bite to Christopher Marlowe's play *The Massacre at Paris* (ca. 1592).
The theme of civil war is central to Shakespeare's entire

body of work, in the Roman plays from *Julius Caesar* (1599) to *Antony and Cleopatra* (1606–7) as well as in his English histories, including *King John*, but especially in the three *Henry VI* plays and *Richard II*.[12] But the most popular English tragedy in the seventeenth century was not any of Shakespeare's—not *Hamlet*, not *King Lear*, not *Macbeth*—but instead Ben Jonson's *Catiline* (1611), based on Sallust's account of Catiline's conspiracy.[13]

Lucan's poem on the Roman civil war between Caesar and Pompey provided a particularly flexible template for framing the later civil wars. For example, in the 1590s the English poet Samuel Daniel (1562–1619) composed a history in verse of the fifteenth century battles for the English Crown known as the Wars of the Roses, *The First Fowre Bookes of the Civile Wars Between the Two Houses of Lancaster and Yorke* (1595). Shakespeare certainly fell under the spell of Lucan as he drew on Daniel's poem to write *Richard II* (Daniel in turn would plunder Shakespeare's *Henry IV* plays for a revised version of his poem in 1609).[14]

Daniel took the shape of his narrative along with many details from Lucan to tell what he called "our last" (meaning latest) "Civile Warres of England." The opening lines of the poem would have been a clear signal to his classically educated readers of his debt to the Roman model:

I sing the civil warrs, tumultuous broyles,
And bloudy factions of a mighty land:
Whose people hauty, proud with forain spoyles,
Upon themselves, turne back their conquering
    hand:

Whilst Kin their Kin, brother the brother foyles,
Like Ensignes all against like Ensignes band:
Bowes against bowes, the Crowne against the
    crowne,
whil'st all pretending right, all right throwen
    downe.[15]

Lucan's javelins (*pila*) become English bows, and imperial eagles are now the contested "crownes." The armies of Lancaster and York otherwise replay the pathologies of Caesar and Pompey's expansive yet self-destructive polity as immortalized by Lucan.

In early modern England, at least, Lucan was the "central poet of the republican imagination," the one who most inspired those skeptical of monarchy as the best constitution for a commonwealth and, later, those who would support Parliament against the Crown in the British civil wars of the mid-seventeenth century.[16] In the fifty years before the outbreak of those wars, the poets Christopher Marlowe (1564–93), Arthur Gorges (d. 1625), and Thomas May (ca. 1596–1650) all translated at least parts of Lucan's *Civil War*.[17] May extended his version beyond the truncated, ten-book version Lucan had left to include the rest of Julius Caesar's life, shortly before writing the first history of England's troubles amid what he, echoing Lucan, called "a War indeed . . . much more then civill."[18] It has even been plausibly argued that at least one reason why the republican John Milton (1608–74) originally cast his *Paradise Lost* in ten books—rather than in twelve, after Virgil's *Aeneid*—was as a tribute to Lucan.[19] These works can all be seen as part of an accumulating body of "the poetry of civil war . . . with its own characteristic and recurrent figures of speech, images, and themes."[20]

Yet Lucan was not simply the property of those who were critical of, or even hostile to, the political form of a monarchy, as Milton was. Among defenders of the rule of kings in seventeenth-century Britain, Sir Robert Filmer (1588–1653) placed on the title page of his *Patriarcha* (1680) lines from Lucan as a warning against the dangers of unfettered liberty, and two years later the first authorized edition of Hobbes's *Behemoth* adapted the Roman poet's opening lines for that title page.[21] In the eighteenth century, Lucan returned as a republican symbol when Jean-Jacques Rousseau quoted him in his *Discourse on the Origin of Inequality* (1755) and on the title page of his essay on perpetual peace (1761).[22] And there were further appropriations during the French Revolution, when the swords of the Garde Nationale allegedly carried a motto from Lucan's poem.[23] The Romantic poets Samuel Taylor Coleridge and Percy Bysshe Shelley would be among his last major admirers in the nineteenth century. Thereafter, not until after World War II would interest in the poet decisively rebound. Nevertheless, the vicissitude of interest in Lucan has tracked the currency of Roman ideas of civil war for some eighteen hundred years.

Historians have hotly debated whether books made revolutions in the seventeenth and eighteenth centuries, but there is little doubt that civil wars made books.[24] The conceptions of history found in Lucan and his early modern imitators view the present as the product of past struggles and the future as likely to emerge from a similar progression of "bloody factions" and "tumultuous Broyles":

> Intestine strife, is fearefull moste of all,
> This, makes the Sonne, to cut his fathers throate,
> This, parteth frendes, this brothers makes to
>   bralle,
> This robbes the good, and setts the theeves a
>   floate,
> This, Rome did feele, this, Germanie did taste,
> And often times, this noble Lande did waste.[25]

This tendency to look back to earlier civil wars and to project their consequences forward would grow more pronounced during the course of the seventeenth century in Britain. By the 1630s, the history of Europe in general, and of England in particular, appeared to be founded on the primal contentions of the Romans, distinguished as it was by an accelerating and compounding series of internal conflicts. Rome's historians and poets kept alive the memory of the wars of Sulla and Marius, Pompey and Caesar, but more recent history, across northern Europe especially, also sustained the memory of those earlier moments. In the 1640s and 1650s, an avalanche of writings, many in translation, about past civil wars, in Rome, but also in France, England, and Spain, were published to help Britons make sense of their own troubles.

Early modern Europeans saw their own internal troubles as the culmination of a cycle of similar wars that had played out across Europe since the fall of the Roman Empire and which seemed to follow the pattern of Rome's civil wars.[26] England alone had been through the Barons' Wars of the thirteenth century, the Wars of the Roses in the fifteenth century and then the civil wars of the mid-seventeenth century. Italy had had its civil wars in the fifteenth century, followed by the French Wars of Religion and the Dutch Revolt against the Spanish Monarchy in the late sixteenth century, the latter a conflict that Hugo Grotius thought "might not improperly be called *Sociall*, or a warre of Confederates . . . nor wanteth Reason why it may not be termed a Civil War," according to his account, published posthumously in 1657.[27]

After the British constitutional crisis of 1640–41 broke out into armed arrays across England, the strife was often seen in light of the Dutch and French civil wars and as the continuation of English strife in the thirteenth and fifteenth centuries. To take one prominent example, John Corbet, historian of the English city of Gloucester, declared the stakes in 1645 to be even higher than in those prior disputes:

The Action of these times transcends the Barons Warres, and those tedious discords betweene the Houses of *York* and *Lancaster*, in as much as it is undertaken upon higher Principles and carried on to a nobler end, and effects more universall.[28]

Histories of civil war proliferated. The Earl of Monmouth translated the Italian Giovanni Francesco Biondi's *History of the Civill Warres of England* (1641), on the Wars of the Roses. Enrico Davila's Tacitean *Historie of the Civill Warres of France*—the subject of an acerbic anonymous commentary by the U.S. vice president John Adams later in the eighteenth century—appeared for the first time in English in 1647.[29] The Royalist poet Richard Fanshawe accompanied his 1648 translation of Guarini's *Il pastor fido* with "a short Discourse of the Long Civill Warres of Rome" dedicated to Charles, the Prince of Wales, in which he affirmed the Roman distinctions between social war, servile war (which he called "a *Mutiny*"), and conspiracies, like that of Catiline, in favor of those conflicts that were "properly *Civill warres.*"[30] In 1650, Sir Robert Stapylton published a translation of Famiano Strada's "history of the Low-Countrey Warres" (*De bello Belgico*), and in 1652 an English version appeared of Sandoval's history of the Spanish civil wars of the early sixteenth century, accompanied by the commendation that no one would find the French Wars of Religion strange who had read of England's Barons' Wars—or, presumably, find England's troubles odd who had learned of Spain's a century earlier.[31]

All these works affirmed the place of England's "civill uncivill warres" within larger historical patterns.[32] Charles I is alleged to have remarked of his opponents, after reading Davila, that "the Truth is, their Swords had already transcribed it in *English* Blood, before [the translator's] pen had done it in *English* Inke."[33] The sheer variety of publications—classical and modern; English and continental European—shows how far the range of available historical models extended beyond republican Rome or the Barons' Wars of medieval England.[34]

*

Discussions of civil war in early modern Europe might have begun with poetry and history, as the humanist education of most participants in the mid-century crisis would lead one to expect, but over the course of the seventeenth century the subject fell increasingly into the domain of law and civil science—or what we would now call political and legal philosophy. Here, too, Roman conceptions set the terms of debate. In 1604, for example, drawing on Roman legal thought, Hugo Grotius argued that war in itself was neither just nor unjust. It was not a normative term at all but a descriptive one, signifying only "armed execution against an armed adversary." It was the nature of the cause that determined whether it was just: if prosecuted merely to injure, it was by definition unjust, or against right; if to execute a right, it could be justified. Grotius then divided wars into two kinds: public, if waged by the will of the state, and private, if by some other.[35] There his definition of public war stood in his original formulation, but at some point he added a further qualification: "Public war may be either 'civil' (when waged against a part of the same state) or 'foreign' (when waged against other states). What is known as a 'war of allies' is a form of foreign war."[36]

Private wars could, likewise, be civil or foreign, Grotius added in another postscript, but he did not develop the implications of civil war that lacked public authority on at least one side. He was clearer on the more immediate question of whether booty might be seized: it could be taken as justly in a civil war as in any other legitimate kind. Here he was answering his opponents, notably the sixteenth-century Spanish legal writer Fernando Vázquez de Menchaca (1512–69), who had argued that prizes could not properly be taken in civil wars. This was to bar plunder in all wars among Christians, because, the Spaniard argued, every such war was a civil war. Grotius was incredulous: "Who will acquiesce in [the] assumption that the wars of Christians are civil wars, as if to say, forsooth, that the whole of Christendom constitutes a single state?"[37] Similar arguments about the extent of the commonwealth or community—whether Christian, European, regional, or global—within which a war might be called "civil" would recur later in the eighteenth and nineteenth centuries, as we shall see. Nonetheless, for Grotius, whether a war was civil or foreign, or fought among Christians or against non-Christians, was irrelevant to the legitimacy of prize taking; that depended solely on whether the war was just or unjust.

When Grotius got around to writing his most extensive and enduring answer to these questions in his major work *The Rights of War and Peace* (1625), civil war was not a major category. His crucial distinctions are among three kinds of wars:

> The most general and most necessary Division of War is this, that one War is private, another

publick, and another mixed; that is a publick War, which is made on each Side by the Authority of the Civil Power. Private War is that which is made between private Persons, without Publick Authority. Mixed War is that which is made on one Side by publick Authority, and on the other by mere private Persons.[38]

So firmly is Grotius set against private war and its cost of engaging a "Country in dangerous Troubles and bloody Wars" that he counsels the wisdom of Plutarch and Cicero, even when one is faced with a usurper: *"A Civil War is worse than the necessity of submitting to an unlawful Government . . . Any Peace is preferable to a Civil War."*[39] Conservative sentiments like these would later earn Grotius the contempt of Jean-Jacques Rousseau, who saw him as little more than a defender of tyranny and slavery.[40]

Grotius had dedicated his whole book to arguing that war could be just, on the Roman grounds of self-defense in a just cause. He left unanswered the knottier problem whether a civil war, either private or mixed, could be justified on *both* sides at the same time: For how could each side claim self-defense, when one or the other had to have begun the hostilities? For those who came after Grotius, the answer to that question turned on establishing which party could legitimately be held to be the public authority and hence which could be held to be upholding legal authority against private insurrection.

In thinking about these matters in the language of natural law, Grotius's most rigorous successor (and critic) was the English humanist, historian, and student of civil science Thomas Hobbes. The very purpose of civil philosophy, according to Hobbes, was, in the bluntest terms, to prevent "confusion and Civill war; for the avoiding whereof, all Civill Government was ordained" (*Leviathan*, 1651).[41] Merely parsing the rights of war and peace in the abstract, as Hobbes believed Grotius had done, was not enough; it was essential to know why wars happened. Hobbes would locate the reason in a want of understanding. As he notes in *De Corpore* (1655), "All such calamities as may be avoided by human industry, arise from war, but chiefly from civil war; for from this proceed slaughter, solitude, and the want of all things . . . The cause, therefore, of civil war is, that men know not the causes neither of war nor peace, there being but few in the world . . . that have learned the rules of civil life sufficiently." Because "from want of moral science, proceed civil wars," Hobbes took it upon himself to teach his fellow citizens the philosophy that might save them from these supreme calamities.[42]

For Hobbes, the defining task for any properly constituted internal authority is to secure peace for all its citizens. In his first major political work, *De Cive*, he defines peace negatively, as the absence of war, and war as "that time in which the will to contend by force is made sufficiently known by words or actions."[43] Apart from war between states, Hobbes isolates two further forms: civil war and the competition between individuals in the state of nature. Civil war could, by definition, exist only after a commonwealth (*civitas*) had been created. What existed before then, in "the condition of men outside civil society (the condition one may call the state of nature) is no other than a war of all men against all men [*bellum omnium contra omnes*]; and in that war all men have a right to all things."[44] As a struggle between disorganized individuals, who might make contingent agreements with allies (*socii*) this was possibly a *social* war, but certainly not a civil one. There would be no drums, no trumpets, and no standards, because no armies and no generals, and of course no formally armed citizens, or *cives*—none of the elements, definitive or decorative, of a civil society. Hobbes's famous war of all against all was not a civil war at all.

According to Hobbes, civil war arises when the public authority itself had become divided. As he explained to his former pupil William Cavendish, 3rd Earl of Devonshire in 1645, "Experience teaches . . . that the dispute for [precedence] betwene the *spirituall* and *civill power*, has of late more then any other thing in the world, bene the cause of *ciuill warres*, in all *places of Christendome*."[45] That might have been correct at the time (and it would be central to Hobbes's account of the motivation for creating a unitary sovereign later in his *Leviathan*), but it was only one contingency of a more fundamental phenomenon. In *De Cive*, Hobbes writes that the "*sovereign power* in a commonwealth . . . always exists and is exercised, except in times of sedition and civil war; at those times the one *sovereign power* becomes two"—or, in Florus's formulation of what had happened under the Gracchi, which Hobbes would have recalled, a two-headed commonwealth is created out of one. Faction, of whatever kind, would be the most likely origin of such division, especially when "they try to get by arms what they could not get by eloquence and intrigue; and a civil war is born." A faction was actually "like a commonwealth within the commonwealth [*civitas in civitate*]." Any prince who allowed faction within his commonwealth was thus "as good as admitting an enemy within the walls."[46] The inevitable consequence would be a war in which citizens became enemies of citizens: hence, in the idiomatic Roman sense of the term, a true *civil* war.

By the time Hobbes published a second and more widely distributed edition of *De Cive* in 1647, England had been long immersed in what he called "his country's present calamity."[47] The pivotal moment in that crisis came when King Charles I was charged by his prosecutors in January 1649.[48] His capital crime would be treason. As one historian has recently noted, however, "What constituted treason and therefore merited punishment was a matter of partisan judgement" when both Charles and Parliament claimed to represent the sovereign authority.[49] Indeed, to put an anointed monarch on trial, it was necessary to redefine the location of sovereignty, and hence the object of treason as Parliament rather than the Crown.[50] With that reversal of perspective, it became possible to conceive of the king as waging war against the English people, a war that was, by definition, civil because directed within the commonwealth and against its citizens.

Parliament passed its "Ordinance Erecting a High Court of Justice for the King's Trial" on January 6, 1649. The two major "high and treasonable Offences" with which Charles was charged were, first, that he "had a wicked Design totally to subvert the Ancient and Fundamental Laws and Liberties of this Nation, and ... to introduce an Arbitrary and Tyrannical Government" and, second, "that besides all evil ways and means to bring this Design to pass, he hath prosecuted it with Fire and Sword, *Levied and maintained a cruel War in the Land, against the Parliament and Kingdom*, whereby the Country hath been miserably wasted, the Publick Treasure Exhausted, Trade decayed, thousands of People murdered, and infinite other mischiefs committed."[51] Arbitrary government was the end, "cruel war" the means. But against what law would this have been an offense worthy of trial and even execution?

Before January 1649, it had been impossible for the Crown to declare war on its own subjects; it could act defensively against rebels, but war against its own people was legally inconceivable. Even before it had declared itself to be the locus of sovereignty, then, the House of Commons had to rewrite the law of treason. The Rump Parliament announced itself to be "the supreme power in this nation" on January 4, 1649, but already on January 1 it had asserted "that by the fundamental Laws of this Kingdom, it is treason in the King of *England*, for the Time being, to levy War against the Parliament and Kingdom of *England*."[52] In so doing, they crucially altered what had been English law since the fourteenth century, which had included among its list of offenses the crime of "levying war" against the king. That definition of treason was of Roman origin, derived from the *Digest* of Roman law, where it was described in part as waging war without the command of the emperor.[53] Thus, whichever body had the legitimate authority to levy war was, by definition, the sovereign.

It was in the aftermath of this debate that Thomas Hobbes elaborated his own general theory of sovereignty in *Leviathan*. Though agnostic on the question of whether the sovereign should be a single person or an assembly, he left no room for the possibility of resistance against sovereignty, however constituted. For Hobbes, its constitution was the alternative not to *civil* war but to the condition of war *outside* civil society:

> It is manifest, that during the time men live without a common Power to keep them all in awe, they are in that condition which is called Warre; and such a warre, as is of every man, against every man. For WARRE, consisteth not in Battell onely, or the act of fighting; but in a tract of time, wherein the Will to contend by Battell is sufficiently known ... So the nature of War, consisteth not in actuall fighting; but in the known disposition thereto, during all the time there is no assurance to the contrary. All other time is PEACE.[54]

The sovereign power is instituted precisely to secure peace and prevent war. Any division of sovereignty would lead to confusion and contention as to the "common Power"; it was therefore essential to maintain the indivisibility of the sovereign's rights, including "the Right of making Warre, and Peace with other Nations, and Common-wealths." "For," he argued, "unlesse this division precede, division into opposite Armies can never happen. If there had not first been an opinion received of the greatest part of *England*, that these Powers were divided between the King, and the Lords, and the House of Commons, the people had never been divided, and fallen into this Civill Warre." He argued in chapter 18 of *Leviathan* against vain objections that one might suffer under a tyrant or popular government: "The estate of Man can never be without some incommodity or other; and that the greatest, that in any forme of Government can possibly happen to the people in generall, is scarce sensible, in respect of the miseries, and horrible calamities, that accompany a Civill Warre."[55] Such a condition marked the dissolution of sovereignty and the return to the pre-civil state of nature where life could be solitary, poor, nasty, brutish, and short. In this sense, civil war was for Hobbes strictly an oxymoron, though bound he was by the contemporary parlance for describing a time without consensus about who, or what, constituted the common power over the people.

Hobbes had been born in 1588, the year of the Spanish Armada, and lived an extraordinarily long life, which spanned almost all of England's seventeenth-century troubles, just long enough for him to contribute to the Exclusion Controversy, which aimed to remove the Catholic James, Duke of York, from the succession to the English throne, before his death in 1679.[56] He would, however, have had to have lived a full century to have witnessed the Glorious Revolution of 1688–89 and to have read John Locke's *Two Treatises of Government* written in the wake of the Exclusion Controversy but subsequently revised and only published in 1689 "to establish the Throne of our Great Restorer, Our present King *William* . . . And to justifie to the World, the People of *England*."[57] Locke had been a pupil at Westminster School when Charles I was executed nearby in Whitehall.[58] He became an attentive student of the history of civil wars, from those of Rome's long experience to the ones his father took part in on the side of Parliament in the 1640s. Over the course of his life, Locke would own the Inca Garcilaso's history of the civil wars in Peru, the Tacitean histories of Davila and Strada, and many accounts of the Dutch Revolt, as well as several copies of Florus, Lucan, and Caesar's commentaries, among other works on civil war.[59] Yet his account in the *Two Treatises* of tyranny and the legitimate response to it echoes the charges made against the allegedly malevolent monarch at his trial.

Locke denied that the state of nature was a state of war, which he defined as "not a passionate and hasty, but a sedate setled Design upon another Mans life," and hence quite different, in conscious intent and precise direction, from Hobbes's abiding condition of insecurity amid the passions of others.[60] There is no reason to believe that Locke was responding specifically to Hobbes; his sole reference to "Civil Wars" shows how far his political theory is from those of both Hobbes and Grotius. Yet as if replying to the passage from Grotius quoted earlier, Locke argued, "But if they, who say it [the right of resistance to a tyrant] *lays a foundation for Rebellion*, mean that it may occasion Civil Wars, or Intestine Broils, to tell the People they are absolved from Obedience . . . and that therefore this Doctrine is not to be allow'd, being so destructive to the Peace of the World. They may as well say upon the same ground, that honest Men may not oppose Robbers or Pirates, because this may occasion disorder or bloodshed." Humans enter civil society in order to escape the state of nature; the greatest threat to their security once in the commonwealth, however, is not their own passions, or even foreign enemies, but the illegitimate use of force by their rulers, which it is indeed proper to resist: for these rules, "so destroying the Authority, which the People did, and no Body else can set up, and introducing a Power, which the People hath not authoriz'd, they actually *introduce a state of War*, which is that of Force without Authority . . . and so they putting themselves into a state of War with those, who made them the Protectors and Guardians of their peace, are properly, and with the greatest aggravation, *Rebellantes* Rebels."[61] The immediate object of concern here was Charles's son James, Duke of York; during the Exclusion Crisis, Locke, like many contemporaries, feared a reversion to Stuart absolutism and with it a return to the cycle of civil wars that had begun in 1641. At the same time, we can also see him entering into the long-running discussion of the meaning and nature of civil war that had drawn in Grotius and Hobbes earlier in the seventeenth century.

Locke understood civil war as being what Grotius might have called a "mixed" war, having "publick Authority" on one side, but that authority would be on the side of the people, not the ruler. It was, thus, a species of war that could never be just on both sides. In this sense, even more radically than Hobbes, Locke repudiates the Roman tradition of civil war as taking place within the *civitas*, between armed groups of fellow citizens. For Locke, civil war entailed the extinction of the commonwealth, the collapse of civil society—an exit from civility itself—until just authority could be restored. Locke clearly thought such a restoration had taken place in 1688 with what he called "our delivery from popery and slavery from the arrival of the Prince of Orange"—that is, James II's brother-in-law William of Orange, who came to the throne with his wife, Mary, in the political maneuver known for its alleged bloodlessness as the Glorious Revolution.[62]

Would Locke have judged the Glorious Revolution to be seventeenth-century Britain's last civil war, or even a civil war at all? It seems highly unlikely. It was relatively brief, was rapidly resolved, and did not recur, unlike the civil wars of republican Rome or medieval and early modern Europe. More recent historians have seen the Glorious Revolution as the English, or British, Civil War that never was: "There was indeed no civil war in 1688; no battle, that is to say, very little bloodshed, and no general relapse into a condition of epidemic armed violence such as had obtained in England between 1642 and 1646." If the events constituted a "Fourth" English Civil War, after the three others conventionally counted between 1641 and 1649, then it was "over before it started" in the closing months of 1688.[63] The Glorious Revolution might then have been the English, or British, civil war to end all civil wars: a factional struggle in which both sides had armies but claimed no territory and engaged in no military conflicts (at least, on English soil). Instead, they bloodlessly arranged for the transmission of authority from one faction to another: a "civil" process, perhaps, but hardly a war.

A bleaker view of the inevitability of civil war came from Locke's contemporary the aristocratic English republican thinker Algernon Sidney (1623–83). Sidney, like Hobbes and Locke, had been actively engaged in the Exclusion Controversy, but he turned from the theory of political resistance to its practice and was executed in 1683 for his role in a plot against the life of the king. He might have seen such conspiracy as unavoidable, indeed even preferable to the greater conflicts that kingly regimes produced by their very nature. "All monarchies are subject to be afflicted with civil wars," he wrote in his posthumously published *Discourses Concerning Government* (1698). "But commonwealths are less troubled with those distempers." Indeed, as the title of his chapter on the subject put it, "Popular Governments are less subject to Civil Disorders than Monarchies; manage them more ably, and more easily recover out of them." He argued that this was in large part because non-monarchical regimes did not suffer from the same destructive disputes over inheritance and the succession as monarchies.[64]

Sidney showed this distinction by a detailed breakdown of all the violent disturbances across history: in Israel under its kings, in the Persian monarchy, in Rome, France, Spain, and Britain. For example, the succession caused "many Revolutions" in France, where, as in Rome, "the end of one Civil War has bin the beginning of another." As if the pages of evidence from the Mediterranean and northern Europe were not enough to convince his readers, Sidney concluded with a litany of the civil wars that had ravaged England since the Norman Conquest. "The Miseries of *England* on the like occasions," he wrote, "surpass all." From the contested succession after the death of William the Conqueror to the troubles of the Tudors, English history appeared to have been an almost continuous time of troubles for five centuries.[65]

Sidney's history was clearly indebted to the Roman historians and their imitators. As he had noted in his earlier *Court Maxims* (1664–65) regarding the ferocity of wars over the royal succession, "Of this truth England, France, and Flanders give undeniable testimony; each of which has lost more blood than was shed in all the cruel wars of Marius and Sulla, Caesar and Pompey, and all the others that happened in Rome from the expulsion of the kings to the establishment of the caesars." What more than all these histories could be needed to demonstrate that it was monarchy that bred war, and republicanism that brought peace, in the ancient world as in the modern? The Augustan argument that commonwealths, or "free states," "wearied with civil dissensions, have sought monarchy as their port of rest" was as dangerous as it was absurd: "We may as well conclude death better than life because all men doing what they can to preserve life do yet end in death. That free states by divisions fall often into monarchy only shows monarchy to be a state as death unto life."[66]

Sidney clarified the Roman meaning of civil war by discriminating it from the other kinds of wars the Romans had faced: the name of "Civil Wars," he thought, was "most absurdly applied to the servile and gladiatorian Wars; for the Gladiators were Slaves also, and Civil Wars can be made only by those who are Members of the Civil Society, which Slaves are not. Those that made the *bellum Sociale* [Social War], were Freemen, but not Citizens; and the War they made could not be called Civil."[67] Sidney was disputing his predecessors and contemporaries who used Roman history to argue that republican government led straight to anarchy and instability. He argued instead that "all Monarchies are subject to be afflicted with Civil Wars . . . But Commonwealths are less troubled with those distempers."[68]

The Roman republic—the period when neither kings nor emperors ruled the Roman people—was the best illustration of that correlation. In particular, Sidney was refuting the staunch monarchist Sir Robert Filmer regarding "the Imperfection of Popular Government" in his *Patriarcha* of the late 1620s. Filmer portrayed Rome's "Democratie" as turbulent and short-lived: a mere 480 years, from the expulsion of Rome's last king, Tarquinius Superbus, to the rise of Julius Caesar. Conflict between the nobility and the people led to seditions that then spawned a destructive sequence of "civil" wars: "The *Social* War was plainly Civil; the Wars of the Slaves, and the other of the Fencers; the Civil Wars of *Marius* and *Sylla*, of *Cataline*, of *Caesar* and *Pompey* the *Triumvirate*, of *Augustus*, *Lepidus* and *Antonius:* All these shed an Ocean of Blood within *Italy* and the Streets of *Rome*." Contradicting those, like Florus, who saw Rome's greatest achievement—the expansion of its empire—as the fruit of "*Democratical* Government," Filmer argued, "Even at those times, when the *Roman* Victories abroad, did amaze the World, then the Tragical Slaughters of Citizens at home, deserved Commiseration from their vanquished Enemies." These wars continued even while Rome expanded as its citizens turned their conquering arms upon themselves, until the "Civil Contentions at last settled the Government again into a Monarchy."[69]

To prove the necessity of monarchy and the instability of republican government, Filmer had turned the republican narrative of civil war on its head in the service of an Augustan account of the benefits of monarchy for securing peace. Sidney's rebuttal of Filmer was equally polemical. He argued, as Sallust had, that the spoils of empire were like an infection that ravaged the body politic: " 'Twas hard, if not impossible, to preserve a Civil equality, when the Spoils of the greatest Kingdoms were brought to adorn the Houses of private men."[70] It was not adherence to a republican constitution that had caused Rome's seditions and ultimately its civil wars; it was straying from that constitution. And it was not citizens without monarchs who caused war, but a hostile band of other enemies. Nonetheless, his terms, and not Filmer's, would have been recognized by Roman thinkers as an accurate description of the enemies they faced during many of the wars of the republic. "Civil Wars can be made only by those who are Members of the Civil Society": this was an idiomatically Roman understanding of this form of conflict.

*

If the Roman writers on civil war had taught anything, it was that the cycles of civil war, once begun, were likely to continue unbroken. " 'Tis in vain to seek a Government in all points free from a possibility of Civil Wars, Tumults, and Seditions," Sidney warned. "That is a Blessing denied to this life, and reserved to compleat the Felicity of the next."[71] It seemed that, as heirs to Rome, the European nations that gradually emerged could not shake off Roman habits of organized violence or Roman ways of understanding them. Civil war was one of the distinguishing marks of civilization, for there could be no civilization without *civitates*, that is, cities or states, and it was the natural fate of these to be riven by civil strife. The French jurist and political thinker the baron de Montesquieu (1689–1755) captured the dilemma in his 1734 reflections on the grandeur and decline of the Roman Empire: "Whilst Rome was conquering the world, a hidden war was carrying on within its walls: these fires were like those of volcanos, which break out the instant they are fed by some combustible substance."[72] That would be one unforgettable lesson of Rome's history of civil war until the late eighteenth century and even beyond.

Beginning in that period, a new narrative gradually emerged in Europe, also comprising a succession of political upheavals and likewise linking past and future, yet now in a way ripe with utopian possibilities. In this vision of history, a sequence of revolutions rather than a series of civil wars would form the central story not of congenital strife but of modern emancipation, starting with the American and French Revolutions and developing throughout history. The creation of this narrative would entail its own act of forgetting. The nascent category of revolution was designed, in part, to repress memories of civil war and to replace them with something more constructive, more hopeful, and more forward-looking. As the early nineteenth-century French philosopher Théodore Jouffroy (1796–1842) argued in the wake of the French Revolutionary and Napoleonic Wars, "The civil wars of Europe are over."[73] That revolutionary hope could be sustained only by overlooking both the similarities between civil war and revolution and the considerable overlap in the concepts used to understand them. But the Roman conception of civil war would not go quietly; the age of revolutions was also to be an age of civil wars.

4

Civil War in an Age of Revolutions

The Eighteenth Century

That civil wars and revolutions must always be distin
guished from each other is a fundamental assumption of
modern politics. The usual view—that revolution is driven
by high ideals and transformative hopes while base motives
and senseless violence animate civil war—can be traced to
the late eighteenth century, in the era of the American and
French Revolutions, when conceptions of revolution first
emerged. And that view has persisted, even after the fall of
Communism in 1989, after the Arab Spring, and into our
present age of civil wars. In November 2013, for example, *The Guardian* published an interview with a Syrian
businessman forced into exile in Turkey by the ongoing
crisis in his homeland. He lamented that the high ideals
of the uprising against the Syrian president, Bashar al-
Assad—freedom, some kind of equality, the protection of
Islam—had been replaced by sectarian violence and fighting among various militias, jihadis, and foreigners. "This

is not a revolution against a regime any more, this is a civil war," he said.[1]

On the surface, there do seem to be compelling reasons to keep revolution and civil war conceptually distinct. Civil wars have generally been assumed to be sterile, bringing only misery and disaster, while revolutions have often been seen as fertile ground for innovation and improvement. Civil wars hark back to ancient grievances and deep-dyed divisions, while revolutions point the way toward an open and expansive future. Likewise, civil wars are local and time-bound, taking place within particular, usually national, communities, at particular moments.[2] By contrast, revolution seems almost a contagion, occurring when it does across the world, at least the modern world, which in a sense it defines, as an unfolding progress of human liberation. Since at least the collapse of Communism, however, it has been much harder to view revolutions without an acute awareness of the violence and human devastation that attend them too. As a result, after 1989, the comparative study of that noble creature, revolution, declined rapidly even as the study of that rough beast, civil war, boomed. Thus a repressed truth was rediscovered: the heart of most great modern revolutions was civil war.

It has been a bitter pill to swallow. Civil wars, by the conventional understanding, betoken the blighting and collapse of the human spirit, while revolutions affirm and actualize it. How disturbing, then, to realize that a force so definitively modern, novel, and forward-looking might owe so much to one so archaic, traditional, and backward facing. Not that there wasn't something new about revolution. As the political theorist Hannah Arendt (1906–75) noted in 1963, "Revolutions, properly speaking, did not exist prior to the modern age; they are among the most recent of all major political data." She contrasted them with the enduring category of wars—including civil wars—which, she thought, were "among the oldest phenomena of the recorded past."[3]

The opposition between revolution and civil war has deep historical roots. According to the towering German historian of political concepts Reinhart Koselleck (1923–2006), revolution emerged across the course of the eighteenth century "as a concept in contrast to that of civil war." At the beginning of the century, by contrast, the two expressions "were not interchangeable, but were not at the same time mutually exclusive." With its associations of destructive religious conflict across Europe in the sixteenth and seventeenth centuries, civil war was the very sort of calamity that proponents of enlightenment hoped to prevent in the future. By contrast, revolution was synonymous with the leading edge of useful transformation across all domains of human activity: in education, morality, law, politics, science, and, not least, religion. The irrational, atavistic, and destructive weed of civil war would wither away, never to find favorable soil again. This was one of the very goals of the Enlightenment. The absence of any entry for "civil war" (*guerre civile*) in that great summation of enlightened knowledge, Diderot and d'Alembert's *Encyclopédie* (1751–65), was itself a small but significant indication of how successful the *philosophes* thought their age had been at eradicating the problem.[4] At the same time, the practical desire to abolish civil war gave way to a visionary program for promoting revolution. The result by the late eighteenth century was the relatively sharp duality with which we are familiar. "In many respects, then," as Koselleck concluded, "'civil war' had now acquired the meaning of a senseless circling upon itself, with respect to which Revolution sought to open up a new vista."[5]

But that would take time. Meanwhile, it should be clear by now that the page on which self-consciously modern revolutionaries rewrote the script of political change was in fact a palimpsest—underneath the new version, still very much visible, was the one transmitted by the historians of Rome's civil wars. That new script, no less than the old, was an act of will. It too would feature contestations over sovereignty and be likewise shadowed by the specter of recurrence. Still, the synoptic accounts of Roman conflicts inspired a new genre of European historical writing in the seventeenth and eighteenth centuries, one that presented the histories of particular nations or peoples as narratives of their "revolutions"—meaning their experiences of invasion, their disputes over the succession to the throne in monarchies, and their civil wars.[6]

The Romans and their descendants had concatenated specific internal struggles into larger narratives that, for the most part, assumed that civil wars would form a destructive sequence of events. Monarchists and writers favoring empire would depict that cumulative horror as the disease for which autocratic rule would be the cure.

But the story of successive violent upheavals leading to fundamental changes in authority and sovereignty was never abandoned, only transformed by European historians. It would endure as a history of revolutions stretching across the centuries and bit by bit effacing the blight that was civil war. Eventually, a modern genealogy of revolution was re-created, in which civil war was the inconvenient ancestor that had to be suppressed but never quite seemed to go away.

Historians in the late seventeenth century reconstructed a sequence of disruptive "revolutions" by which Rome had moved over the centuries from its early monarchy to its empire via the period of the republic.[7] For example, the English cleric Laurence Echard (1672–1730) composed *The Roman History from the Building of the City to the Perfect Settlement of the Empire by Augustus Cæsar* (1695, and later editions) along these lines and followed it by translating the work of the French scholar Pierre Joseph d'Orléans as *The History of the Revolutions in England Under the Family of the Stuarts, from the Year 1603, to 1690* (1722), while Vertot himself capitalized on the success of his own *Histoire des révolutions arrivées dans le gouvernement de la république romaine* (1719, and later editions) to treat the more recent "revolutions" in Portugal and Sweden.[8] Imitators would anatomize revolutions throughout European history and in the wider world of Europe and Asia. Throughout the life span of this genre, civil wars were included in the rosters of revolutions, and revolutions could not be distinguished conceptually from civil wars. "Revolutions" also became the standard European description for violent upheavals in Asia, including the fall of the Ming dynasty in China in 1644. Only toward the end of the eighteenth century did Europeans cease to call these Asian struggles "revolutions," as they jealously reserved that term for their own political transformations.[9]

By that time, contemporary European thinkers could distinguish at least three forms of civil war: what might be called "successionist," "supersessionist," and "secessionist" civil wars. Successionist civil wars were the besetting sin of monarchies. They arose from those disputes over the succession to the thrones of Europe that had plagued royal regimes since the Middle Ages, as Algernon Sidney, among others, mercilessly pointed out. In the 1680s—when the thrones of the Three Kingdoms of Britain and Ireland were under dispute between two branches of the Stuart family—Sidney had written that such successionist struggles were like the civil wars of the Romans. They were repetitive and potentially unending because they sprang from the very nature of monarchy itself: "the violence of those who possessed the Crown, and the Ambition of such as aspired to it," always meant "that the end of one Civil War has bin the beginning of another."[10] This was the Roman model of recurrence transposed to a post-Roman world of both monarchies and republics.

Supersessionist civil wars were those in which opposing parties battled for authority over a single territory. In these, the state did not have two heads, as the Roman metaphor had painted it, but it had become effectively two bodies, each trying to supersede the other. Division alone was not the distinguishing feature of this species; the

Romans and their heirs knew that well enough. It was the elevated status of both sides in a civil war—the incumbent sovereign, whether a monarch or a republican assembly, for instance, and the rebels—as "constituting, at least for a time, two separate bodies, two distinct societies" that marked this as novel.[11] This conception was a matter of law, not fact. Indeed, the legal construction of civil war that originated in the mid-eighteenth century would shape arguments with decisive effect during both the American and the French Revolutions. It would also remain operative in the context of international law well into the nineteenth century. But this is getting ahead of the matter.

Secessionist civil war, by contrast, was a relatively new fact in the late eighteenth century. Secession had been a Roman category but with a much more specific meaning than it would later acquire. On three occasions, in 494, 449, and 287 B.C.E., the lower classes of Rome— the plebs—went on strike and retreated to spaces outside the city, actions known as the "secessions of the plebs." These did not lead to civil wars and indeed happened long before those conflicts the Romans would recognize as wars among their citizens. The modern usage of "secession" referred more generally to the attempt by part of a political community to break away from the existing political authority and assert its own independence, or, in the words of the American Declaration of Independence of 1776, when "one People . . . dissolve the Political Bands which have connected them with another, . . . to assume among the Powers of the Earth, the separate and equal Station to which the Laws of Nature and of Nature's God entitle them."[12] There were few precedents before the late eighteenth century for such an action, most notably the Dutch Revolt from the Spanish monarchy in the 1580s; it was only after the success of Britain's North American colonies in exiting from the empire in 1776 that this model began to proliferate and to gain legal recognition. Thus, the Americans provided a truly revolutionary conception of civil war that would be imitated across the world in the following two centuries.

*

The great innovator in modern conceptions of civil war was the Swiss writer Emer de Vattel (1714–67). Little known today, except by scholars, he was for almost a century probably the most influential contemporary legal thinker in the world. Vattel was born in the Swiss canton of Neuchâtel and aspired to a diplomatic position. He had been thoroughly schooled in what contemporaries knew as the law of nature and nations—that is, the intellectual tradition originating ultimately in Roman law and philosophy that treats the norms governing the behavior of individuals and states as being inherent in the rational nature of humans themselves. Vattel's major work would be a summation of natural law as it applied to the conduct of states or nations, a compendious work titled *The Law of Nations* (1758). The book secured him political preferment from the elector of Saxony in Dresden. It also put him on the map as a great legal authority, not least for the use

Thomas Jefferson and others made of his work when writing the Declaration of Independence in 1776.

The subject of Vattel's *Law of Nations* was what we would now call international law, though Vattel looked broadly to the law of nature, not simply to the behavior of states. For the American founders, it would serve almost as a bible of international conduct in the era of the American Revolution. Widely translated from its original French, it would inspire a new generation of revolutionaries in Latin America and in southern Europe a few decades later. And it could be found in the libraries or on the desks of lawyers, politicians, and administrators across the world at least until the 1830s. What made Vattel appealing to so many was his blend of realism and morality. He wrote within the robust ethical framework of natural law, but he also evinced a pragmatic understanding of international politics. His work was furthermore so wide-ranging and comprehensive that it could supply arguments for almost any position, whether submission or resistance, colonialism or anticolonialism, for instance. He artfully combined existing arguments and traditions while seeking to clarify and invent where the rules of international conduct were unclear or lacking. Civil war was just one subject in which his innovations would be profoundly influential as he sought to bring it within the scope of the law of nations for the first time.

Vattel wrote self-consciously within a tradition that included many of the seventeenth-century thinkers we have already encountered, particularly Hugo Grotius,

Thomas Hobbes, and John Locke. From Locke, he took a cautious theory of resistance to unjust rulers. "We seldom see such monsters as Nero," he wrote. From Hobbes, he inherited a theory of the sovereignty of free and independent states within the international realm. And from Grotius he derived much of his interest in the definition of war and the laws designed to regulate it, whether the justifications for going to war (or what is known technically as the *jus ad bellum:* the right to go to war) or the rules governing its conduct (what is known as the *jus in bello,* or the rights during a war). Vattel's own definition of war was "that state in which we prosecute our right by force." He nonetheless disagreed with Grotius that there could be any such thing as a private war, confining its exercise to states alone, as Jean-Jacques Rousseau, writing four years later, would in his *Second Discourse.* This was, in his definition, "public war . . . which takes place between nations or sovereigns and which is carried on in the name of the public power, and by its order."[13] On the face of it, Vattel's definition would seem to exclude any chance that rebels against a sovereign or "public power" could be recognized as legitimate belligerents. But his crucial innovation was to argue that they could, thereby opening the way both to the application of the laws of war to civil conflicts and to a potentially radical doctrine by which outside powers could intervene in the affairs of other sovereign states.

Vattel's argument had begun from the "question very much debated" as to whether sovereigns should treat rebellious subjects according to the laws of war. One consideration was empirical; there were various forms of disturbance that could afflict a state, among them a tumultuous "commotion," a more violent "sedition," or an "insurrection" covering a whole city or province, challenging the sovereign authority itself. None of these could be called legitimate, he thought: "every citizen should . . . patiently endure evils which are not insupportable" unless they are denied justice, in which case resistance might be justified "if the evils be intolerable, and the oppression great and manifest."[14] This had been Locke's argument in his *Second Treatise;* it would also be a central contention of the American Declaration of Independence. In that document, Thomas Jefferson had even gone back to the language of the charge against Charles I in 1649, which had accused him of levying "cruel and unnatural wars." In one passage excised from the final version of the declaration, Jefferson accuses George III of personally promoting the slave trade across the Atlantic as the basis for charging him with the same crime his ancestor had allegedly committed: that he had "waged cruel war against human nature itself" by depriving Africans of their liberty and transporting them across the ocean. His waging such a "cruel war" against "a distant people who never offended him"—in this case, African people—was justification for the colonists to cast off the king's sovereignty.[15]

But what if the sovereign's demands become intolerable, causing his own people to rise up in arms against them? Then, Vattel stated in a groundbreaking definition, we have a case of civil war: "When a party is formed in a state, who no longer obey the sovereign, and are possessed of sufficient strength to oppose him,—or when, in a republic, the nation is divided into two opposite factions, and both sides take up arms—this is called *civil war*." This could be distinguished from a mere rebellion by the fact of the insurgents having justice on their side; if the cause of opposition is just, then the sovereign (or divided authority in a republic) must wage formal war against the opposition: "Custom appropriates the term of *'civil war'* to every war between the members of one and the same political society."[16]

Vattel then backed into one of the most revealing paradoxes about civil war: that the apprehension of fragmentation sharpens the awareness of affinity. The sides in a civil war can recognize each other as parts of "the same political society" at the point they have splintered into separate and hostile factions, because "it produces in the nation two independent parties, who consider each other as enemies, and acknowledge no common judge," and who become "two separate bodies, two distinct societies." (Nowhere does he consider the possibility that more than two parties might fight a civil war within the same society.) Vattel's novel move was the inference he then drew from the fact of this stark division: "They stand therefore in precisely the same predicament as two nations, who engage in a contest, and, being unable to come to an agreement, have recourse to arms." It followed that if the two independent bodies were now, in effect, two nations, the law of nations should regulate their contentions; a "civil" war thereby became an international war. If rebel subjects had just cause and had raised arms, sovereigns should treat them according to the law of war, for by this point the unitary nation or state has already ceased to exist. The conflict has become "a public war between two nations." It therefore no longer falls under internal domestic law.[17]

But who was to judge whether the conditions for civil war had been met? The shift in jurisdiction and perspective that Vattel proposed had startling implications for external powers. Under normal circumstances, the integrity of a sovereign state was sacrosanct; no outside authority could interfere in its affairs. But in the case of a state split into two "nations," other powers could try to restore peace, for example by mediation. If that failed, Vattel went on, they may "assist the party which they shall judge to have right on its side, in case that party requests their assistance or accepts the offer of it," as they would in the case of a war between two states.[18] This opened up the possibility of intervention, on humanitarian grounds or others, at the discretion of foreign parties regarding the internal affairs of other states.[19] Vattel's key example of such a civil war from recent European history was the Glorious Revolution. "The English justly complained of James II" in 1688, he argued, and then appealed to the Dutch for help, which William of Orange duly gave before taking the throne as King William. Because the resistance was justified and had thus made the English people and the monarchy of James II "distinct powers," William's intervention was legitimate: "Whenever therefore matters are carried so far as to produce a civil war, foreign powers may assist that party which appears to them to have justice on its side."[20]

In 1758, this was still an earthshaking view of civil war; its full potential would become evident only in the revolutions after Vattel's death in 1767.

*

Shortly after the Battles of Lexington and Concord in April 1775 and of Bunker Hill in June of that year, the Dutch-born surveyor and cartographer Bernard Romans (ca. 1720–84) published a chart of Massachusetts with a teasing caption: "Map of the Seat of Civil War in America."[21] A few weeks earlier, he had issued a proposal for subscribers to buy his planned publication, "Shewing the Seat of the Present Unhappy Civil War in North-America." The map itself contained detailed vignettes of Boston and of the battle lines constructed across the city "by the Ministerial Army."[22] Romans sympathized with the colonial cause and had fought as an engineer and troop commander in the years before issuing his snapshot of occupied Boston. As if his political allegiances were not clear enough, he dedicated his 1775 map to John Hancock, then president of the Continental Congress and whose house, occupied by British troops, appeared in the illustration of Boston. Romans would be best known for his *Concise Natural History of East and West Florida* (1775), but later in the conflict he published another kind of history, an account of the Dutch Revolt of the sixteenth century as a "proper and seasonable mirror for the present Americans" in 1778–82.[23]

The meaning of the title "Map of the Seat of Civil War" might not now be obvious. Surely this was a revolution, not a civil war? Otherwise, what conception of war could possibly describe the events leading up to 1775? Traditional histories of the American "Revolution" would resist calling it a civil war.[24] There were surely many reasons for this among future generations of American historians and the wider public in the United States. The most obvious was the wish to avoid confusing or conflating the event with the much more divisive American civil war that took place between 1861 and 1865. By the mid-nineteenth century, the designation "civil war" implied, not least, slaughter on an industrial scale by modern armies waging huge pitched battles, with the entire society on a war footing—a total war, in fact. By contrast, the military encounters of the American Revolution appeared relatively small-scale, with casualties, of course, but little spillover into the society at large—nothing like the violence visited on civilian populations in, say, the French Revolution. The American Revolution was also assumed, again in popular mythology, to have been cohesive rather than divisive, with a population broadly united behind the cause of independence. By these lights, the Revolution was an act of liberation by self-identified Americans who felt their distance from Britain and demanded self-determination as recompense for just grievances. "Every thing that is right or natural pleads for separation," Thomas Paine argued in January 1776. "The blood of the slain, the weeping voice of nature cries, 'TIS TIME TO PART."[25]

If American nationalist histories of the Revolution portrayed it as a crisis of disintegration, more recent historians have seen it as a crisis of integration, sparked by the similarities, not the differences, between British subjects on either side of the Atlantic. Owing to the pressures of war with France, the connections created by more integrated communications, and their place in a burgeoning transatlantic consumer economy, American colonists had grown closer to Britons in the metropolis over the course of the eighteenth century. In the aftermath of the Seven Years' War—that titanic struggle between Britain and France for imperial dominance in North America and South Asia— the British Parliament's will that colonial subjects cover their share of the costs of their defense and of the wartime deficits led to a series of revenue-raising measures that aroused opposition in North America. The resulting controversy split the empire, and not simply between colonial and metropolitan subjects but between those in the colonies who joined colonial resistance, mostly from the thirteen British colonies along the Eastern Seaboard of North America, and those that did not—in Nova Scotia, Quebec, and the British Caribbean, for instance. A divided empire was the battleground for a war among fellow citizens—a civil war.[26]

As for the Revolution, recent historians, less enthralled to pious narratives of American destiny, have reconsidered it a civil war, too. After substantial numbers of British troops had arrived in North America, it took on the characteristics of a full-scale war, with generals, trumpets, and standards (as the Romans might have noticed), and it was uniquely wrenching precisely because it was fought against domestic kindred rather than identifiably foreign enemies, not least in local conflicts in bitterly divided colonies like New York and South Carolina. But the conflict also split families and the wider population into so-called Patriots (supporters of resistance against Great Britain) and Loyalists, who, at the very least, retained their allegiance to the Crown but were otherwise politically and ethnically diverse. They included British colonists, Native American groups like the Cherokee and Mohawk, and an estimated twenty thousand enslaved persons who liberated themselves from their masters by crossing British lines during the course of the war. The best estimates for the total number of white Loyalists suggest that about 20 percent of the population, or roughly half a million colonists, remained loyal to the Crown by the end of the war in 1783; some sixty thousand of them, along with fifteen thousand slaves, left the United States as part of a global diaspora that reached Canada, East and West Florida, the Bahamas, Sierra Leone, British India, and Australia. The proportion of the population of British North America in arms was, in fact, comparable to those fighting during the U.S. Civil War.[27] "This, then," concludes a leading historian of the Atlantic world about the American Revolution, "was a civil war as much as a revolution."[28]

Civil war had not been the first Roman model used during the course of the British imperial crisis of the 1760s and 1770s. Initially, another had come to hand: the Social War, which had concerned metropolitan relations and the rights of allies to be recognized as full citizens. For example, in 1766, the London-based agent for the Massachusetts Bay Colony, William Bollan (d. 1776), charged that British ministers "seem to delight in blood, and are . . . sollicitous to introduce a *social war*, whereby after so narrowly escaping the sword of our enemies we should employ our own swords in destroying ourselves." Bollan's accusation came with a warning from Roman history: "*Rome* when in her flourishing estate was brought to the brink of ruin by the social war, occasioned by her refusal to communicate the *Roman* right." Could Britain meet the same fate if it likewise failed to extend the full range of its rights to its "allies" within the empire?[29] Ten years later, the English dissenting minister and pamphleteer Richard Price (1723–91), in one of the most widely reprinted polemics on the political controversy in the British Atlantic, likewise recalled the contribution of Rome's allies to the success of its wars, their claim to equal rights, and the disasters that followed Roman rebuffs: "A war followed, the most horrible in the annals of mankind, which ended in the ruin of the Roman Republic." He too wondered whether Britain might suffer the same calamity, should it refuse to enfranchise its "allies" within the empire.[30]

The most prominent analysis of the transatlantic conflict as a social war came in the longest pamphlet of the revolutionary controversy: Adam Smith's *Wealth of Nations* (1776). Smith was not as alarmist as Bollan or Price, but he did adduce Rome's belated response to the Social Wars as a possible solution to the present conflict:

> Towards the declension of the Roman republick, the allies of Rome, who had borne the principal burden of defending the state and extending the empire, demanded to be admitted to all the privi-

leges of Roman citizens. Upon being refused, the social war broke out. During the course of that war Rome granted those privileges to the greater part of them, one by one, and in proportion as they detached themselves from the general confederacy . . . If to each colony, which should detach itself from the general confederacy, Great Britain should allow such a number of representatives as suited the proportion of what it contributed to the publick revenue of the empire, in consequence of its being subjected to the same taxes, and in compensation admitted to the same freedom of trade with its fellow-subjects at home . . . a new method of acquiring importance, a new and more dazzling object of ambition would be presented to the leading men of each colony.[31]

By the time *The Wealth of Nations* appeared in the autumn of 1776, however, American independence had already been declared in July. Smith's proposal of an imperial parliament, with representatives from the American colonies, came too late. Any federal solution was unlikely to be adopted by either side, and the conception of the American war as a social war disappeared along with the idea of equal rights and representation for Britons on both sides of the Atlantic.

The idea of the transatlantic conflict as a "social war" implied that those Britons who inhabited the western side of the Atlantic Ocean differed from those in metropolitan Britain in their status and their rights. They were "allies," or as the Romans would have said, *socii*, but not equal citizens, or fellow *cives*.[32] The language of civil war implied much closer kinship among all parties, as well as the existence of a common polity, of which all were fellow members. That polity was the British Atlantic empire, and it was even more expansive than Rome's Mediterranean empire at its zenith; to assume otherwise would have reinforced the suspicion of war hawks in Britain that the colonists had been set on secession and independence for months, if not years, before July 4, 1776. As in the case of Rome, it was at the moment of internal fragmentation and collapse that the boundaries of community—and the contested bonds of fraternity—could become most painfully evident.

After British troops had opened fire on colonial militiamen at Lexington and Concord in April 1775, contemporary commentators began freely to use the language of civil war. On April 24, 1775, *The Newport Mercury*, a newspaper in Rhode Island, noted the change that had taken place in the conflict with the use of military force: "Through the sanguinary Measures of a wicked Ministry, and the Readiness of a standing Army to execute their Mandates, has commenced the *American Civil War*, which will hereafter fill an important page in history."[33] Other writers in 1775–76 also called it a "civil war," a "civil war with America," and an "American civil war."[34] In 1780, a historical novel appeared that was inspired by "some recent circumstances" in America titled *Emma Corbett; or, The Miseries of Civil War*, which represented the traumas of the American civil war through family division and images of gender confusion and disguise.[35] Fifty years later still, the American novelist James Fenimore Cooper reflected on the implications of calling the Revolution a civil war, with the benefit of hindsight and after a nationalist narrative of the dispute as a movement for Americans' self-determination had already coalesced:

> The dispute between England and the United States of America, though not strictly a family quarrel, had many of the features of a civil war. Though the people of the latter were never properly and constitutionally subject to the people of the former, the inhabitants of both countries owed allegiance to a common king. As the Americans, as a nation, disavowed this allegiance, and as the English chose to support their sovereign in the attempt to regain his power, most of the feelings of an internal struggle were involved in the conflict.[36]

At the very least, calling it a "civil war," American or otherwise, placed the imperial crisis into a sequence of British civil wars, stretching back (by some definitions, at least) through the Glorious Revolution via the three English Civil Wars of 1642–45, 1648–49, and 1649–51 to the Middle Ages, as Paine did. Later historians would also see this transatlantic civil war as part of a series of "British revolutions" in the seventeenth and eighteenth centuries.[37]

In July 1775, the same month that Bernard Romans's "Map of the Seat of Civil War in America" appeared, the Continental Congress issued its first declaration, almost exactly a year before the much more famous Declaration of Independence. Also drafted by Thomas Jefferson, the "Declaration . . . Seting Forth the Causes and Necessity of Their Taking Up Arms" justified the move to armed resistance against British forces. The members of Congress tried to reassure "the minds of our friends and fellow subjects in any part of the empire . . . that we mean not to dissolve that Union which has so long and so happily subsisted between us, and which we sincerely wish to see restored." Their stated aim was "reconciliation on reasonable terms, . . . thereby to relieve the empire from the *calamities of civil war.*"[38] The July 1775 declaration accompanied the Olive Branch Petition to George III requesting conciliation with the colonists, but both arrived in Britain after the British ministry had already perceived a fundamental change in the nature of the conflict; Lord North wrote to King George III on July 26, 1775, that "the war is now grown to such a height, that it must be treated as a foreign war."[39] In August 1775, the king duly declared the mainland colonies to be in open rebellion and no longer under his protection, and Parliament confirmed the royal proclamation with legislation in December 1775. The British American rebels became the first to face the dilemma of transforming struggles within an empire to a conflict outside it.

Writing in Philadelphia in January 1776, Thomas Paine (1737–1809) presented the case for American independence according to the contemporary "custom of Nations" in the closing pages of his incendiary pamphlet *Common Sense*. He argued that only independence would permit a mediator to negotiate peace between the United States and Great Britain. Foreign alliances could not be secured without it. Charges of rebellion would persist if it were not declared. Moreover, it was essential for a "manifesto to be published, and despatched to foreign courts"; until it was, "the custom of all courts is against us, and will be so, until by an independance, we take rank with other nations."[40] In order to become legitimate belligerents outside the British Empire rather than rebels within it, the colonists had to transform themselves into bodies recognizable within the prevailing norms of the international realm. Only then could they declare war and enter into agreements with other independent sovereign states. The first American civil war would end; the first Anglo-American war could begin.

Paine bolstered his larger argument in favor of independence from Great Britain with a historical account of civil war. He reached back to the Roman narrative of sequential civil wars as it had been reimagined by Algernon Sidney to present an argument in favor of nonhereditary government on the grounds that it was a better safeguard of peace. He contrasted his own attachment to republicanism with what he called the "most plausible plea, which hath ever been offered in favour of hereditary succession," in a passage that hewed closely to Sidney's arguments from almost a century earlier. The traditional justification for monarchy, he recalled, was supposedly that it preserves a Nation from civil wars; and were this true, it would be weighty; whereas, it is the most barefaced falsity ever imposed upon mankind. The whole history of England disowns the fact. Thirty kings and two minors have reigned in that distracted kingdom since the [Norman] conquest, in which time there have been (including the [Glorious] Revolution) no less than eight civil wars and nineteen Rebellions. Wherefore instead of making for peace, it makes against it, and destroys the very foundation it seems to stand on . . . In short, monarchy and succession have laid (not this or that kingdom only) but the world in blood and ashes.[41]

Paine's antimonarchical mathematics are worth pausing over. It is not clear how many civil wars Paine would have discerned during the Wars of the Roses, or even amid the mid-seventeenth-century troubles, nor does he suggest how to distinguish "rebellions" from "civil wars." What is striking, however, is that he seems to include the Glorious Revolution among the roster of England's civil wars; 1688–89 was a year of two monarchs, James II and William (and his consort, Mary), and thereby no doubt only half as bad as the Year of the Four Emperors chronicled by Tacitus in his *Histories*. For Paine, the Glorious Revolution was simply one more example of how a contested succession could lead to national instability, setting citizens against citizens in their quest to affirm their monarchical subjecthood. The cure for civil war was not, as the pro-

Augustan writers and their heirs asserted, the imposition of monarchy but rather the installation of government without kings.[42] This would be the solution implicit in the Declaration of Independence when it severed the tie between British American colonists and the British Crown by declaring that the former colonies were now "United States."

In July 1776, the Declaration of Independence publicly presented facts to a "candid World" to prove that "the United Colonies are, and of Right ought to be, Free and Independent States . . . and that all political Connection between them and the State of Great-Britain, is and ought to be totally dissolved."[43] In the eyes of the declaration's proponents, Britain was now on one side of an international conflict, the United States of America—in the plural, of course—on the other. They were no longer conceived of as being part of the same political community, and hence their inhabitants were not fellow citizens or members of what Algernon Sidney called the same "Civil Society." The American war was no longer what Paine might have reckoned to be the ninth British civil war since 1066.

The Declaration of Independence had informed the great powers of Europe that the United States was (or, in fact, were) now open for business and available for alliances. It did so in the language of the contemporary legal norms, drawn directly from Vattel's Law of Nations. Vattel had been the first major proponent of the natural law tradition in Europe to identify independence with external sovereignty, or statehood in the international realm.[44] It was for this reason that Benjamin Franklin sent the latest edition of Vattel's work to the Continental Congress in 1775, because "the circumstances of a rising state make it necessary frequently to consult the law of nations."[45] Vattel's repeated and characteristic description of states as "free and independent" featured prominently in the declaration as a means of ensuring recognition from "the Powers of the Earth" for the American struggle against Great Britain, as did his arguments (derived from Locke) that the camel's back had been broken after a "long Train of Abuses and Usurpations" had justified not merely rebellion but secession from the British Empire.[46] With this act, what had begun as a typical early modern provincial tax revolt and then turned into a British civil war became "the American War."

Transforming rebellious struggles within empires to legitimate conflicts outside them was a problem faced by insurgents throughout the Americas in an age of imperial revolutions that were also civil wars.[47] Moving from internal to external conflicts shifted the source of relevant norms and sanctions from domestic law to the laws of war and to the law of nations. For example, facing viceregal charges of rebellion in New Spain in 1812, José María Cos sought to transform a "war between brothers and citizens" into a war of independence by asserting the legitimate equality of New Spain with Spain and by subjecting their contentions to the "laws of nations and of war." Later, in 1816, José de San Martín in Argentina likewise protested, "Our enemies, and with good reason, treat us as insurgents, while we declare ourselves vassals. You can be sure no-one will aid us in such a situation": an almost exact echo of Thomas Paine's argument forty years earlier.[48]

In all these struggles, independence, in the sense promoted by Vattel of autonomy from interference by outside powers, was only one solution among many to imperial crisis; in most cases, it was not the first, but in fact often the last, option embraced by Americans, North and South, in their struggles for sovereignty. The hemisphere's multiple transitions from empire to state (and, in some cases, like Mexico and Brazil, from one empire to another) were never smooth or uncontested, in part because the legal and political sources of sovereignty were eclectic and plural. Sovereignty was less a source of jurisdictional certainty than a site of ferocious contestation because empires, not states, were the communities in the Americas within which civil wars were fought in this alleged age of "revolutions." As in the case of Rome, it was only at the moment of internal fragmentation and collapse that the boundaries of community—and the contested bonds of fraternity—could become most painfully evident.

*

The great test case for the mutual implication of revolution with civil war is the French Revolution. Historians have located the origins of the modern vision of revolution precisely in France in 1789. This was the moment when, we are told, the concept of "revolution was revolutionised." It was novel because in that year "the French imagined a radical break with the past achieved by the conscious will of human actors, an inaugural moment for a drama of change and transformation projected indefinitely into the future."[49] Before 1789, revolutions were often conceived as unavoidable feats of nature, as predetermined astronomical cycles, or as eternal recurrences in human affairs.[50] One of the characters in Hobbes's dialogue on the English Civil Wars, *Behemoth*, had classically expressed this view with regard to the events of 1649–60 in Britain: "I have seen in this revolution a circular motion, of the Soveraigne Power through two Usurpers Father and Son [Oliver Cromwell and Richard Cromwell], from the late King [Charles I] to this his Son [Charles II]." This was a revolution in the sense of returning, not overturning.[51]

After 1789, revolutions in the plural became revolution in the singular. What had been natural, unavoidable, and beyond human control became instead voluntary, calculated, and repeatable. Revolution as an occurrence gave way to revolution as an act. With that daring feat of collective imagination, it became irreversibly political, encompassing primarily (but not exclusively) those fundamental changes in the distribution of power and sovereignty. In the years after 1789, revolution also developed into an authority in its own right, in whose name political violence could be legitimated. Taken together, these features made up "the script for modern politics invented in 1789," a script designed in part to expel civil war to the wings of the historical stage and put a new cast of actors in its place.[52]

These elements constituted a novel conception of revolution as a process by which the world could be made over again. It was an idea very different from the compulsive repetition of civil war in the Roman narratives and reflected a larger movement toward new ideas of historical time in the last eighteenth century, one that led away from assumptions of recurrence inherited from antiquity.[53] "Every revolution," noted the French historian François Furet, "and above all the French Revolution itself, has tended to perceive itself as an absolute beginning, as ground zero of history." By this logic, it was a paradox that the uniqueness of each successive revolution indicated its universality.[54]

Since its composition in 1789, the modern script of revolution has been frequently reenacted on stages around the world. The later revolutionaries adapted it to their purposes and added new properties for each performance. Their dramas borrowed lines and gestures, symbols and costumes, from previous productions. Such borrowings could constrain the actors, as Karl Marx classically noted in *The Eighteenth Brumaire of Louis Bonaparte:* "Thus Luther donned the mask of the Apostle Paul, the Revolution of 1789 to 1814 draped itself alternately as the Roman republic and the Roman empire, and the Revolution of 1848 knew nothing better to do than to parody, now 1789, now the revolutionary tradition of 1793 to 1795."[55] But they invariably justified the effort, because each attempt to overthrow tradition contributed to the creation of a new tradition. In this manner, after 1789, a consciously accumulating repertoire of revolutions came to form the scarlet thread of modernity.

Given such a potent reputation, it might appear that looking for the civil war at the heart of any revolution is downright *counter*revolutionary. Opponents of revolution have often attempted to deny its legitimacy by calling attention to the violence and destruction attending any effort to overturn the existing social and economic order, a cost that no such transformation could ever justify. And with civil war having now acquired such retrograde connotations, to tag a revolution as such could be seen as undermining its potential for liberation and opening up a new future. Yet there can be no innovation without tradition. As Marx pointed out, even the primal revolutionaries of 1789 cast their eyes back to the Romans, as their successors would in turn look back to 1789 for their inspiration.

The French Revolution was not a secessionist process, in the manner of the American Revolution. Nor was it a successionist one, because there was no dispute about the legitimacy of the Bourbon claim to the French throne—just the legitimacy of placing sovereignty in the figure of a monarch rather than the nation. Was it then a supersessionist civil war, in the sense that Vattel had defined it? Did France, at some point after the storming of the Bastille, break into two parts, even two nations, battling each other for authority and supremacy? One contemporary who thought so was Edmund Burke (1729–97). The Irish-born politician and thinker made his name through both his political writings and his speeches in the British Parliament. Like Thomas Paine, but for very different reasons, he had supported the cause of American independence, as he also approved the cause of other downtrodden peoples, in Ireland and India, for example. Yet he became a prophetically skeptical commentator, and an increasingly aggressive antagonist, in the British debate on the course and consequences of the French Revolution.

Burke agreed with Paine not only about the essential justice of the American Revolution. He also concurred with him that the Glorious Revolution had been a civil war. In *Common Sense*, Paine had sought to shake his colonial readers out of their complacent British monarchism by reminding them of the warlike tendencies at the heart of monarchy itself, not least by including the Glorious Revolution in the litany of civil wars since 1066. Burke's depiction of the events of 1688–89 as a civil war was meant, by contrast, to defend monarchy against the incipient tendencies of the revolution to strip the royal family of their legitimacy, perhaps even their lives. In his *Reflections on the Revolution in France* (1790), he notes acidly that the "ceremony of cashiering kings"

> can rarely, if ever, be performed without force. It then becomes a case of war, and not of constitution. Laws are commanded to hold their tongues amongst arms, and tribunals fall to the ground with the peace they are no longer able to uphold. The Revolution of 1688 was obtained by a just war, in the only case in which any war, *and much more a civil war*, can be just. *Justa bella quibus necessaria.*[56]

Why did Burke call the Glorious Revolution a "civil" war? It is possible that he wrote here as an Irishman rather than as an English politician and that recalling the armed conflict between James II and William III on his native soil

brought to mind its enduring consequences for his homeland. (The Battle of the Boyne in 1690, at which "King
Billy" was victorious, is still commemorated annually by
Protestants in Northern Ireland.) In light of this experience, he would argue two years later that the Glorious
Revolution was "not a revolution, but a conquest; which
is not to say a great deal in its favour."[57] Or Burke might
have remembered the English side of the revolution as
an invasion by one claimant to the thrones of the Three
Kingdoms, backed by force and by his English supporters,
against another. He certainly seemed to agree with Vattel
that William had intervened justifiably into English affairs
to assist the English people, who had been wronged and
had appealed for his help. England, and perhaps by implication, the other British kingdoms, had become internally
divided to the degree that a state of civil war existed; only
its people, oppressed by a tyrant, had justice on their side;
therefore, it was into a just war on their behalf that William had entered. In any case, Burke was arguing that
what had happened in 1688 was exceptional and not to be
repeated. Dethroning a monarch could not be regulated
by law or determined by right; it was a question of armed
necessity and hence of war. And because it was fought
between members of the same political community, it was
by definition civil.

Behind Burke's argument about 1688 in the light of
1789 lay a history stretching back through Vattel to ancient
Rome. The quotation with which he ended this passage—
"*Justa bella quibus necessaria*," or in English, "Those wars
are just to those whom they are necessary"—comes from

a famous exchange in Livy's *History of Rome*, wherein one of Rome's enemies justifies offensive war on the grounds that the Romans had rejected an overture of peace. Burke could well have remembered the line from Livy, but he was also surely aware that Vattel had quoted it in *The Law of Nations*. There, Vattel imagines circumstances in which a nation fights against an invader with just cause for making war. If the invader does not accept terms of submission, however, then the balance of justice tips in favor of the nation invaded, "and his hostilities now becoming unjust . . . may very justly be opposed." Citing the incident from Livy, Vattel concludes the paragraph quoting the passage at greater length.[58] While the specific context in Vattel is a war between nations, or states, Burke was well aware that the author meant all such justifications to apply as well when a state had divided into two "nations" as a result of civil war.

Rejecting the very notion of the Revolution, Burke saw the French after 1789 as having instead fissured into two warring nations, each of which claimed sovereignty, one in the name of the king, the other on behalf of the people. He took this analysis from "the latest and best [account of the law of nations], and whose testimony he preferred"— that is, from Vattel, who had used it to legitimate external intervention in a formerly sovereign nation's affairs.[59] Following suit, as early as 1791, Burke argued that Britain and its allies could—indeed, should—intervene in France on the side of the king and his supporters. He used Vattel explicitly to prove that "in this state of things (that is in the case of a divided kingdom) by the law of nations, Great

Britain, like every other Power, is free to take any part she pleases."[60] "Revolutionary" France was in actuality a divided nation in a state of civil war; indeed, it was effectively two nations, and Britain was free to judge which had justice on its side. For all Vattel's insistent caveats, in the absence of any external tribunal, the judgment of which side's cause was just remained discretionary.

The debate concerning foreign intervention in civil war, encapsulated by Vattel and joined by Burke, is a reminder that conflicts within national borders cannot be wholly distinguished from international ones. The success or failure of one faction may depend on foreign aid or recognition, and such intervention can readily transform the hostilities into external war with geopolitical consequences well beyond the borders of the community in which the conflict first arose. To be sure, Vattel did not want to see his "maxim" abused, to "make a handle of it to authorise odious machinations against the internal tranquility of states," but hardheaded arguments in such circumstances might easily support any act of intervention, so long as a revolution had been conscientiously redefined as a civil war.[61]

It was reasons of state like this, soothing as they were to established rulers, that led Immanuel Kant in his *Perpetual Peace* to include Vattel among the "sorry comforters," the proponents of natural law who, with their expedient ethics, encouraged amoral political action. Nonetheless, Kant's own rather more restrictive grounds for intervention could have been taken straight out of Vattel:

If a state, through internal discord, were to split into two parts, each putting itself forward as a separate state and laying claim to the whole; in that case a foreign state could not be charged with interfering in the constitution of another state if it gave assistance to one of them (for this is anarchy). But as long as this internal conflict is not yet critical, such interference of foreign powers would be a violation of the right of a people dependent upon no other and only struggling with its internal illness; thus it would itself be a scandal given and would make the autonomy of all states insecure.[62]

In the context of the French Revolutionary Wars, such a doctrine could nonetheless become a license for perpetual war rather than for perpetual peace. A year after Kant had written, Burke argued in his "Second Letter on a Regicide Peace" (1796) that the French proponents of popular sovereignty had turned their *armed doctrine* against the rest of Europe and that for these Jacobins the ensuing conflict "in it's spirit, and for it's objects, . . . was a *civil war;* and as such they pursued it . . . a war between the partizans of the antient, moral, and political order of Europe against a sect of fanatical and ambitious atheists which means to change them all."[63] All states were now undoubtedly insecure, Burke believed, for what had begun as a revolution had mutated first into a civil war confined to France and then into one engulfing all the inhabitants of Europe.

*

Burke was an unsympathetic observer of the course of the French Revolution. His conflation of revolution and civil war was meant to undermine the legitimacy of the revolutionaries, not to make any subtle historical point about confusion of categories. In an odd way, he did anticipate some recent historians of the Revolution, who have seen it as a civil war in multiple dimensions—for instance, in the executions of the Terror and in the military suppression of counterrevolutionary activity in the Vendée, in western France, in 1793–95, which claimed more than 150,000 lives.[64] More is the pity, then, that this political and social cataclysm would most determine the script of revolution for the future. At the same time, it would also be the one perhaps most amply to confirm the suggestion that civil war is a "common form of collective violence which fires the Furies of revolution, all the more so if it should interlock with quasi-religious foreign war."[65] *Pace* one leading historian of the French Revolution, every revolution was not a "war of independence"; each might instead be considered a civil war.[66]

Revolutionaries rebottled what in other circumstances—or by other ideologues—had been labeled rebellions, insurrections, or civil wars. Indeed, one sure sign of a revolution's success is precisely that retrospective rebranding. It can happen relatively quickly; for example, the transatlantic conflict of the 1770s that many contemporaries saw as a British "civil war" or even "the American Civil War" was first called "the American Revolution" in a speech by the chief justice of South Carolina as early as October 1776, though the term did not appear officially until the Continental Congress issued its *Observations on the American Revolution* in 1779.[67] The rebranding can also come more slowly, as when the French historian François Guizot became the first in 1826 to call the mid-seventeenth-century crisis in Britain the "English Revolution"; as he explained, "the analogy of the two revolutions is such that [the English] would never have been understood [as one] had not [the French] taken place."[68]

To uncover the modern script of revolution from these mystifications, we need to be alert to the scripts of civil war that revolutionaries have followed and subsequently attempted to efface or deny. In *The Communist Manifesto*, Marx and Engels note that "in depicting the most general phases of the development of the proletariat, we traced the more or less veiled civil war, raging within existing society, up to the point where that war breaks out into open revolution."[69] Just over twenty years later, in *The Civil War in France* (1871), Marx remarks how the conservative French government joined forces with the Prussians, who had just defeated France to crush the Paris Commune in 1871: "The highest heroic effort of which old society is still capable is national war; and this is now proved to be a mere governmental humbug, intended to defer the struggle of classes, and to be thrown aside as soon as the class struggle bursts into civil war."[70] Writing in 1916, in the middle of World War I, not long after he had emerged from a careful reading of Clausewitz's *On War*, Lenin argued that following the victory of the proletarian revolution, at least three kinds of wars would remain: wars of nationalist self-determination; wars of bourgeois suppression, fought against emergent socialist states; and civil wars.[71]

As "a professional revolutionary of global civil war," Lenin would continue to maintain that the oppressed could liberate themselves only by violent means.[72] For peoples beyond Europe, war would be the tool for national liberation against imperialism; to argue otherwise was simply European chauvinism. Socialism would not eliminate war. Its victory could not be instantaneous or universal. It would take many blows to vanquish the hydra of capitalism. And insofar as socialist revolution itself could not be divorced from war, it would be bound up with civil war: "He who accepts the class struggle cannot fail to accept civil wars, which in every class society are the natural, and under certain conditions inevitable, continuation, development and intensification of the class struggle. That has been confirmed by every great revolution."[73] Looking back on the Russian Revolution, Joseph Stalin would agree with Lenin's analysis: "The seizure of power by the proletariat in 1917 was a form of civil war."[74] For revolutionary actors, then, civil war was integral to evaluating the causes, course, and consequences of modern "revolutions." In light of this, when tracing the genealogy of modern revolutions, we should seriously consider the hypothesis that civil war was the genus of which revolution was only a species.[75]

PART III

Paths to the Present

5

Civilizing Civil War

The Nineteenth Century

The address by Abraham Lincoln (1809–65) at the dedication of the Soldiers' National Cemetery on November 19, 1863, may be the best-known speech in American history. Lincoln located his words precisely in time and space: eighty-seven years after the Declaration of Independence, he delivered them on a "great battlefield" at Gettysburg, Pennsylvania, from which they have always been called the Gettysburg Address.

> Fourscore and seven years ago our fathers brought forth, on this continent, a new nation, conceived in liberty, and dedicated to the proposition that all men are created equal. Now we are engaged in a great civil war, testing whether that nation, or any nation so conceived, and so dedicated, can long endure.[1]

Lincoln's plangent eloquence and hard-won brevity on that day have inspired more commentary than has any

other text in American history except the declaration itself
and the U.S. Constitution. Almost all of the address's 272
words have been inspected minutely, except for the most
chilling, his description of the ongoing conflict in which
the dead had fallen at Gettysburg as "a great civil war."[2]
The speech may be familiar, perhaps even too familiar, but
the meaning of all its words is not as clear as it might at
first seem.

Lincoln could not have known that he was speaking at
almost the midpoint of what would be the most costly military struggle fought on North American soil. The conflict
had begun two and half years earlier in April 1861 with
the Confederate bombardment of Fort Sumter in South
Carolina; it would grind on almost as long to its formal
conclusion with the surrender of the Confederate general Robert E. Lee at Appomattox Court House in April
1865, though that act hardly brought hostilities to an end.[3]
The war was surely "great" in terms of the lives lost, the
costs endured, and the stakes for each side, for the African
Americans caught between them, and for the wider world.
No one, enslaved or free, participant or observer, North-
erner or Southerner, Unionist or Confederate, could dis-
agree about that. But that this great struggle was a "civil"
war was less certain when Lincoln spoke at Gettysburg
than it is now, in the long aftermath of the Union victory.

Only six months before the Gettysburg Address, the
Union army had received copies of *General Orders No.
100*, the legal code for the conduct of war drafted by the
Prussian-born American lawyer Francis Lieber (1798–
1872). That document was not produced in the context

of a conventional war between nations, but it still carried the marks of traditional conceptions of war and of civil war. This was especially true of Lieber's definition of civil war in the *Code*. He was mindful that Vattel had thrown down a challenge, over a century earlier, for any such legal description, a challenge that his own superior, the Union general (and international lawyer) Henry Wager Halleck (1815–72), had later taken up in refuting Vattel. Lieber's own legacy on the question of civil war is distinctly ambiguous: the *Code* would endure, in U.S. military circles and in the foundations of international humanitarian law in the twentieth century. At the same time, however, his conception of civil war was internally contradictory and inapplicable to the conflict at hand. It was also irreconcilable with Lincoln's implicit understanding of a "great civil war," uttered amid a struggle that would become a paradigm of the relationship between secession and civil war.

We should be suspicious by now that the words "civil war" could ever be used without political intent or ideological baggage. Following the age of revolutions, civil war was supposed to have become an illegitimate form of struggle, a throwback to the turbulent rule of kings or to the recurrent instability of republican Rome—an ancient curse that enlightened modern times had lifted. Some did not think so. For example, the mid-eighteenth-century French republican the abbé de Mably (1709–85) has an English "Milord" in his dialogue *The Rights and Duties of the Citizen* (1758) shockingly state that "civil war is sometimes a great good," for it can act as a surgery to remove a gangrenous limb that could destroy the body politic.[4] The early Spanish liberal politician Juan Romero Alpuente (1762–1835) likewise argued in a speech of 1821 that "civil war is a gift from heaven," offering a chance for national renewal—a phrase that would echo through Spanish history into Spain's civil war in the twentieth century.[5] And in 1830, the French politician and memoirist the baron de Chateaubriand (1768–1848) mocked those "lovers of humanity who, in armed quarrels, distinguish species and faint at the very name of *civil war:* 'Compatriots who kill each other! Brothers, fathers, sons confronting one another!' All this is no doubt very sad; however, a people is often strengthened and regenerated by internal discords."[6] Civil war might still be just in the eyes of those for whom it is necessary. But as ever, the question was who decides it is necessary and when to call it a civil war.

If civil war was not yet obsolete, it was also, perhaps anachronistically, unregulated. Thinking about it had not kept pace with the age's systematic approach to so many other phenomena. Between the mid-eighteenth century and the mid-nineteenth century, the moral and political questions raised by revolutionary civil wars made ever starker the lack of a theoretical—and, especially, a juridical—framework for restraining and ultimately civilizing it. This was largely because civil war had for so long been written about by historians and poets rather than by philosophers or social theorists.[7] Civil war challenged some of the most basic definitions of war, because the modern definition of war was a conflict *between* established sovereign entities—states—not a conflict *within* them. Jean-Jacques Rousseau offered this classic definition

in his *Social Contract* (1762): "War is . . . not a relationship between one man and another, but a relation between
one State and another . . . any State can only have other
States, and not men, as enemies." Individuals, in other
words, cannot be the enemies of states, because they "are
enemies only by accident, not as men, nor even as citizens,
but as soldiers"; if they are inimical to one another, they
cannot be engaged in war.[8] By these lights, civil wars were
not "wars" at all, because the parties were not confined to
states and the combatants could not all be soldiers, that is,
legitimate belligerents authorized to fight by a sovereign.

The greatest of all modern works on warfare, Carl von
Clausewitz's *On War* (1832), never mentions civil war.[9] As
mentioned earlier, there is no great work of strategy titled
On Civil War, even as a parallel to Mao Zedong's or Che
Guevara's works on guerrilla warfare.[10] Clausewitz's contemporary rival in the theory of war Antoine Henri Jomini
(1779–1869), a Swiss officer who had served with the
French army, does admit civil wars and wars of religion.
But he concedes, "To want to give maxims for these sorts
of war would be absurd." This was because he viewed these
as wars of "opinion"—or, as we might now say, wars of
ideology—and as such more destructive and cruel than wars
of policy, because they are more irrational.[11] Such attitudes
prevented the extension of the original Geneva Convention (1864) to civil wars: "it goes without saying international laws are not applicable to them," asserted one of the
Convention's original drafters, Gustave Moynier in 1870.[12]
The challenge facing Lincoln and Lieber, then, was to do
what Jomini and Moynier initially thought impossible: to

lay down "maxims" for the conduct of civil war by applying international law, thereby bringing civil war within the
pale of civility.

*

Abraham Lincoln's decision to pronounce the conflict in
the United States "a great civil war" was, as suggested,
contestable even in 1863. For to do so was to presume the
Union's interpretation of the Confederacy's actions. It was
to affirm that combatants on both sides had been, and still
remained, members of the same political community: the
United States of America. The label also highlighted what
was at stake in the conflict: the unity of the nation and the
inviolability of the Constitution, as well as the illegitimacy
of unilateral secession. To term it "the Civil War" at any
time after 1865 has been to accept the victory of that interpretation and of the principles the Union had sought to
protect and defend. That conclusion was hard-won, and
still the term would remain a source of friction well into
the twentieth century. But it would prove futile to seek to
change the accepted name for the defining cataclysm of
American history. It would also become morally unaccept-
able to challenge the logic of the term "Civil War," implying as it did unity as much as division and, as so often in the
history of ideas of civil war, recognition of commonality
amid rupture. This paradox would remain especially acute
in the North American case as the conflict became the test
case for the legitimacy of secessionist civil war everywhere.

For supporters of the Confederacy, it was not a war

between fellow citizens or members of the same "Civil Society," as Algernon Sidney might have said. It was a secessionist civil war, fought to establish among other things the right to secede and ignited by a series of acts of secession from the Union. This made it, from the Confederate vantage point, not an *intra*-national conflict but an *inter*national one, a war between polities, not within the bounds of a single community. The Confederate states argued that they had exercised their constitutional right to secede from the Union and believed they had now formed a new union, the Confederate States of America, which was entitled to conduct its own affairs, including its own military defense, as an independent entity. By contrast, the logic of the Union, and of Lincoln, rendered the Confederacy's secession an act of "rebellion" and the conflict to suppress it a "civil war," and yet Lincoln himself used the term "rebellion" almost six times as often as "civil war" during the conflict.[13] The larger historical context may suggest why.

The import of the term "civil war" was under particular pressure in the middle of the nineteenth century. This was a period of thickening global connections, which rendered the ancient boundedness implied by "civil" war moot. Eighteen months before the Gettysburg Address, the French novelist Victor Hugo (1802–85) had a central character in his masterpiece *Les Misérables* (1862) contemplate the changing implications of civil war in a cosmopolitan world. (Hugo was a great admirer of Lincoln's; after his assassination in 1865, the French author helped to organize a subscription for a commemorative medal to be sent to Mary Todd Lincoln in honor of the greatest victim of a great civil war.)[14] *Les Misérables* got around rapidly in English translation in New York in 1862 and then the following year in Richmond, Virginia, as "almost the only fresh literary food of those engaged in a slaveholders' rebellion," in the dismissive assessment of a Rhode Island newspaper.[15]

Hundreds of pages into Hugo's masterpiece, Lincoln's contemporaries could have read the reflections on civil war of Marius Pontmercy, son of a noble veteran of Waterloo. (That the name Marius recalls Sulla's adversary in Rome's first civil war could hardly have been accidental.) As Marius heads toward the barricades in Paris to battle against the restored Bourbon monarchy, he knew "he was to wage war in his turn and to enter on the field of battle, and that that field of battle which he was about to enter, was the street, and that war which he was about to wage, was civil war!" He shudders at the thought, wondering what his heroic father might have made of his actions, even as he expresses some philosophical doubt about the very category:

> Civil war? What does this mean? Is there any foreign war? Is not every war between men, war between brothers? War is modified only by its aim. There is neither foreign war, nor civil war; there is only unjust war and just war . . . War becomes shame, the sword becomes a dagger, only when it assassinates right, progress, reason, civilization,

truth. Then, civil war or foreign war, it is iniqui-
tous; its name is crime.[16]

The action of the novel at this point is set in 1832, but
Pontmercy's musings reflect Hugo's own apprehensions of
the blurred boundaries between civil war and other kinds
of conflicts. Within the broader setting of "the whole
great family of man" (to take a pointed phrase from Lincoln), any distinctions between civil war and foreign war
had begun to collapse.[17]

The U.S. Civil War took place at the heart of a global
capitalist economy built on cotton and the labor of the
enslaved, with ramifications felt in the Caribbean, Europe,
Egypt, and South Asia.[18] It also occurred amid a global
explosion of violence in the mid-nineteenth century. This
period began with what were, in proportion to population,
the century's two bloodiest wars—the Taiping Rebellion
in China (1850–64) and the War of the Pacific (1879–84),
which saw Peru and Bolivia aligned against Chile; it also
included the Crimean War (1853–56), the Indian Rebellion or "Mutiny" of 1857, Mexico's Reform War (1858–61),
Japan's Boshin War (1868–69), the Franco-Prussian War
(1870–71), and Spain's successionist Third Carlist War
(1872–76).[19] For the Americas, the interval marked the last
among a great run of upheavals since the mid-eighteenth
century, during which efforts at imperial reconstruction
had led to independence movements, revolutions, and civil
wars, often with the result, if not always the original aim,
of making smaller states out of larger ones and empires.[20]

Nor was the violence of the Civil War an exceptional response to the circumstances. From the Dutch Revolt of the 1580s to the American Revolution, and from the United States in 1861 to Yugoslavia in 1991, secession has routinely led to civil war. A group within a state, exasperated by what it sees as the suppression of its right to self-determination, asserts that right as a claim to independent statehood. In response, the existing state asserts its right to territorial integrity and authority over all its inhabitants, resisting the group's claim with coercive violence. Secession—the attempt to create a new state—thereby leads to civil war: armed conflict within an established state. To be sure, there have been some peaceful secessions—for example, Norway's from Sweden in 1905, Iceland's from Denmark in 1944, Singapore's from the Malaysian Federation in 1965, Montenegro's from Serbia in 2006, and Kosovo's, also from Serbia, in 2008—but these have been the exceptions.[21]

The logic of history seemed as impeccable as it was implacable: secession causes civil war, just as civil war was until recently the most likely outcome of attempted secession. The most comprehensive recent tally of warfare around the world counts 484 separate wars between 1816 and 2001; 296 of those were typed as "civil" wars, of which 109 were fought to create a new state rather than take control of an existing one. Secessionist conflicts thus constituted more than a fifth of all wars in the past two centuries accounting for a substantial portion of the civil wars in that period. They tended to occur most often "during the two institutional transformations that have shaped the landscape of the modern world"—that is, imperial expansion and the process of state creation, especially after decolonization. Furthermore, the likely onset of such wars "show[s] a dramatic peak immediately before nation-state formation," while "the odds of civil war onset are more than five times higher in the first two years after independence than in the other post-independence years."[22] In this *longue durée* perspective, the American Revolution looks typical and the U.S. Civil War anomalous, again if only for its belatedness, not for its violence.

*

The global violence of the Civil War era raised a question that would be faced repeatedly in the nineteenth and twentieth centuries, with consequences down to our own time: Was it possible to *civilize* civil war? Nothing could soften its trauma, of course: the sundering of the political community, antagonism within families, the death to kinship, the fear of recurrence, the shame of both victory and defeat. But while perpetual peace was an ever-receding hope, there was some evidence war could be tamed if not abolished. Since the seventeenth century, European powers and their heirs in the Americas had striven to regulate the conduct of their conflicts, bringing them under the rule of law. Alas, the treatment of non-European peoples became quite another matter; a toxic by-product of this effort was an opening gap between those who were to be dealt with humanely and those who were not, the latter not even considered human. The difference corresponded to the line being drawn between civility and incivility, between the realm of civilization and the barbarism that lay outside.

As far as the law was concerned, civil war was one thing; wars between states quite another. So long as states were left to police actions within their own borders, it would be up to their discretion to decide whether to treat rebels as criminals rather than as belligerents. The horrors of warfare on the battlefields of mid-nineteeth-century Europe did lead to the most famous humanitarian response to the inhumanity of war, the foundation of the Red Cross in 1863, but even this institution originally excluded civil wars from its remit. At only the second meeting to discuss creating an organization to aid the wounded, the founding committee moved that "no action should be contemplated during civil wars," though it reserved the right to extend its operations in the future.[23] In similar fashion, the original Geneva Convention of 1864 did not explicitly extend its protections to combatants in civil wars, though within a decade the founders of the Red Cross and framers of the Convention would have second thoughts on the matter.[24]

Until that change of heart, the question remained of how civil war could be brought within the emergent global framework of law. One possible answer had come on the eve of the U.S. Civil War from the English liberal philosopher John Stuart Mill (1806–73). Mill used the case of intervention in civil wars to illuminate the new geography of civilization and barbarism; during the conflict itself, he would redraw the frontiers of barbarism to include the Confederacy. In "A Few Words on Non-intervention" (1859), he mapped Great Britain's ethical responsibilities in an unstable world divided between self-preserving sovereign states, "members of an equal community of nations, like Christian Europe," and "parties . . . of a very low grade of social improvement"—that is, peoples potentially subject to empire. The advance of European empires across the globe had grown only more urgent since a century earlier, when Vattel had addressed "the disputed question . . . whether a nation is justified in taking part, on either side, in the civil wars or party contests of another: and chiefly, whether it may justifiably aid the people of another country in struggling for liberty." Mill argued for two grounds on which it would be legitimate for outside powers to intervene: if the aim was to help a people throw off a foreign ruler rather than a native government, and when there is "a protracted civil war, in which the contending parties are so equally balanced that there is no probability of a speedy issue" and outside force is needed to end the conflict.[25]

These conditions drastically restricted the possibilities for intervention imagined by Vattel, but Mill thought them compatible both with contemporary practice and with international morality. On this basis, Mill vehemently supported British neutrality in the American Civil War and equally strongly opposed any concession to the Confederacy, a "Power professing the principles of Attila and Genghis Khan as the foundation of its Constitution." Peace, then, was not the answer, but rather "war to protect other human beings against tyrannical injustice; a war to give victory, to their own ideas of right and good, and which is their own war, carried on for an honest purpose by their free choice—[this] is often the means of their regeneration." While his thinking could not justify intervention, Mill nonetheless saw the war as a crusade for four million enslaved persons who had not consented to secession but were "human beings, entitled to human rights."[26]

As Mill was well aware, the modern international order rests on two fundamental but incompatible principles. The first is sovereign inviolability or independence. Within its own borders, each state has primary authority and jurisdiction, with which no outside power may interfere. The second is the idea that human rights must be respected and the international community has the power to intervene on behalf of those who seek to exercise their rights or find them to be violated. The two principles are enunciated in the 1945 charter of the United Nations, but they both have much deeper roots. In fact, Vattel might have been the first to articulate them together, in his repeated axiom that states—though his term, in French, was "nations"—are "free and independent."[27] These words would find their way without acknowledgment into the U.S. Declaration of Independence, which announced that the former colonies were now "Free and Independent States" while also affirming the natural equality of human beings and their rights of resistance. The early stages of the conflict in North America would show that these two foundational principles could be detached from each other and that each alone could be the spark for civil war.

One of the few observable regularities in world history since 1776 is that any state that has declared its independence will resist attempts by any section of its population or territory to become independent in turn. That is so notwithstanding the would-be secessionists invoking the same principles, even in the same language, that informed the original Declaration of Independence. Thus, for example, in December 1860, South Carolina's secession convention approved a declaration that said in part,

> South Carolina has *resumed* her position among the nations of the world, as a separate and independent State; with full power to levy war, conclude peace, contract alliances, establish commerce, and to do all the other acts and things which independent States may of right do.[28]

(The South Carolina declaration, like those of other Confederate states, studiously avoided any mention of human equality and the rights of all human beings, focusing on the rights of states.)

To the nation that had begun with its own Declaration of Independence, the only response to this challenge could be military action: war. In his address to Congress on July 4, 1861, Lincoln argued that the Confederate attack on Fort Sumter three months earlier had starkly presented not just to the United States but "to the whole great family of man the question, whether a constitutional republic, or a democracy—a government of the people, by the same people—can or cannot maintain its territorial integrity against its own domestic foes." By their preemptive strike, the Confederates themselves had made the choice one of "'Immediate dissolution, or blood.'" Yet Lincoln rejected his enemies' description of their action as secession; he mocked "the seceded States, so called," and rebuffed their "position that secession is *consistent* with the Constitution—is *lawful* and *peaceful*"—by means of a reductio ad absurdum. If it were agreed that secession was constitutional, he reasoned on, then logically the Confederate states should retain a right of secession in their own constitution, even at the cost of self-destruction: "The principle [of secession] itself is one of disintegration, and upon which no government can possibly endure."[29]

Lincoln implied that in the American case secession and civil war were joined both sequentially and causally—sequentially because the "so called" secession of South Carolina and the other states of the Confederacy had required the Union to defend its integrity; because the armed response took place within the borders of the United States, it led to a domestic, or civil, war. And they were linked causally because without the assertion of a right to secede, there would have been no need for formal hostilities: no secession, no civil war. For Lincoln, these connections were hardly accidentally or exclusively American. These inevitabilities could, he thought, be felt by "any nation," any member of "the whole great family of man," whose statehood was grounded in its territorial integrity. With the benefit of a further 150 years' experience, which has seen the global proliferation of states, we inevitably hear Lincoln not just as the great emancipator and champion of popular government but also as the defender of indivisible sovereign statehood itself.

Lincoln acknowledged that the very term "secession" was almost as incompatible with a constitutional order as the act itself. In 1861, he would insist to Congress that the withdrawal of the Confederate states from the Union was in fact not a secession but a rebellion. This was Lincoln's own view, but he argued that the distinction was not his alone: "It might seem, at first thought, to be of little difference whether the present movement at the South be called 'secession' or 'rebellion.' The movers, however, well understood the difference. At the beginning, they knew they could never raise their treason to any respectable magnitude by any name which implies *violation* of law." Accordingly, he went on, the Confederates had "sugar coated" rebellion with the argument that secession was compatible with the Constitution and thereby succeeded in "drugging the public mind of their section for more than thirty years."[30]

Lincoln recognized that secession could be legal only if it was consensual; otherwise "no State, upon its own mere motion, can lawfully get out of the Union . . . *resolves* and *ordinances* to that effect are legally void; and . . . acts of violence within any State or States, against the authority of the United States, are insurrectionary or revolutionary, according to circumstances."[31] He was apparently untroubled by what is now the most pressing question in contemporary legal discussions of secession—that is, whether or not international law acknowledges a norm in favor of the practice.[32] He implicitly assumed that it did not and asserted instead the proposition that it was incompatible with current American constitutionalism. As he argued in the Gettysburg Address, the basis of that constitutional order was the principle "that government of the people, by the people, for the people, shall not perish from the earth." That principle had to be defended, even at the cost of a great civil war to coerce the breakaway states back into the Union.[33]

*

Within a few weeks of the bombardment of Fort Sumter, all sides—Northern and Southern, American and foreign—had recognized the existence of a war within the borders of the United States.[34] But the question of just what kind of conflict it was, and hence what rules should apply to its conduct, remained controversial. In the eyes of supporters of the Confederacy, President Lincoln had prejudged the issue when in April 1861 he had ordered ports from Chesapeake Bay to the mouth of the Rio Grande to be blockaded on the grounds that the states of the Confederacy had raised "an insurrection against the Government of the United States." This meant, among other things, that Union forces could capture neutral ships attempting to supply the Confederate states on the grounds they were illegally supplying an enemy in time of war.[35]

In February 1863, the Supreme Court heard four cases, collectively known as the Prize Cases, on appeal from courts in Boston, New York, and Key West. The plaintiffs argued that the blockade, and the subsequent use of prize law to distribute the proceeds from four captured ships, applied the laws of war where no war had been declared, and hence such laws could not operate. The main question before the Court was, therefore, whether a state of war existed that would justify the president's invocation of the laws of war. Justice Robert Grier, writing for the majority in March 1863, was persuaded by the government's lawyers that a war was indeed in progress. To call the action of the Confederacy an "insurrection" did not preclude that fact, nor could the absence of a declaration of war prevent the government from treating its adversaries as belligerents: "A civil war always begins by insurrection against the lawful authority of the Government. A civil war is never solemnly declared; it becomes such by its accidents—the number, power, and organization of the persons who originate and carry it on." The president was bound to face this conflict "in the shape it presented itself, without waiting for Congress to baptize it with a name," but Grier himself did not hesitate to call it the "greatest of civil wars."[36]

Vattel's epoch-making definition of civil war lay behind Grier's judgment, even though he did not follow Vattel's analysis of the consequences of that description. Vattel had offered a factual description of when a civil war had broken out and of what would allow all sides to recognize that two warring nations had emerged within the same territory. The existence of a war would be clear to all: by the "number, power, and organization" of those who prosecuted it. It needed no declaration, but once it was evident as war between two nations, domestic law no longer applied. Rather, the law of nations, including the laws of war, was operative.[37]

The U.S. Army officer Henry Halleck attacked Vattel's account of civil war at length in his *International Law* (1861) early in the course of the hostilities. His arguments were hardly abstract; they could be said not only to apply to the situation at hand but even to arise directly from it. While agreeing with Vattel that the two parties in a civil war are entitled to treat each other according to the laws of war, Halleck rejected the claim that foreign powers may regard both as independent states and assist whichever they decided had the just cause: "Such conduct would be a direct violation of the rights of sovereignty and independence." He no doubt had the American Revolution in mind when he went on to say that foreign states may recognize "the independence and sovereignty of a revolted province ... when that independence is established in fact," even before the former sovereign has acknowledged it. (On these grounds, France and other powers had entered into diplomatic and military relations with the United States long before Great Britain had formally recognized American independence by the Treaty of Paris in 1783.) Yet he strongly condemned Vattel's view that "a foreign state may take part in the civil wars of its neighbors." This was a charter for international chaos, because "there would be no limits to its right to interfere in their domestic affairs."[38]

In this dispute, as so often, much depended on what was meant by civil war. Halleck offered his own factual and historical definition later in his work. He distinguished civil wars from what he called (following Jomini) "wars of opinion"—whether these were "political wars," such

as the wars of the French Revolution, or religious conflicts, like the Crusades or "the wars of Islamism"—and
from national wars of liberation or revolt against oppression.[39] His first definition was narrowly successionist—
that is, confined to those wars, whether monarchical or
republican, "which result from hostile operations, carried
on by different parts of the same state, as the wars of the
roses in England, of the [Catholic] league in France, of
the Guelphs and Ghibellines in Italy, and of the factions
in Mexico and South America." Civil wars, he continued,
could also include "wars of insurrection and revolution,"
when they involve different factions fighting for ascen-
dancy or a change of government—that is, what I have
earlier called supersessionist civil wars. However, "mere
rebellions . . . are considered as exceptions to this rule,
as every government treats those who rebel against its
authority according to its own municipal laws." To accord
every rebel group the full panoply of protections guaranteed by international law to legitimate sovereigns "would
be both unjust and insulting to the government of the state
against which the rebellion or revolution is attempted."[40]
According to Halleck, then, rebellion and civil war were
quite different beasts. The question in 1861, as in 1863
and later, was whether a rebellion or a civil war was taking
place within the territory of the United States.

    This collision of perspectives was a problem not only
for politicians but even more acutely for military com-
manders, especially on the Union side. Under what rules
of engagement would the Union army treat the rebels?
Did the laws of war apply, and would bringing them to

bear imply that the conflict was, indeed, one between the forces of separate states? Could such an irregular form of conflict be constrained by any rules of combat? If one side saw the other as rebels or insurgents, could there be any limits on their behavior toward such outlaws? And why might it matter if this was not an international war but a civil war? Another of Lincoln's advisers, the Maryland anti-secessionist and pamphleteer Anna Ella Carroll (1815–94), answered such questions defiantly in 1861 with support from Vattel: "This is a civil war; and, therefore, the Government may employ all the Constitutional powers at its command for the subjugation of the insurrectionary forces in the field. But while it is enabled to employ all the powers, it is obliged to observe at the same time, all the established usages of war. For the same enlightened maxims of prudence and humanity are as obviously applicable to a civil war as to any other."[41]

The Supreme Court's decision in the Prize Cases—deeply divided though it was at 5–4—opened the way for legally defining the difference between civil war and kindred concepts like rebellion and insurrection, as well as applying "the usages of war" to the present situation. What followed would in fact be the first-ever attempt to define civil war, in response to centuries of contestation and confusion. By no coincidence, the instigator of the search for a lawyer's definition had been Halleck, an international lawyer as well as an army general. The person he recruited for this delicate task was Francis Lieber, the lawyer who had probably thought longer and harder about the legal significance of civil war than anyone at the time. Alas, even he would find the responsibility almost too great, and the result was only more perplexity.

Lieber had fought at the Battle of Waterloo (where he was left for dead on the battlefield) and, after immigrating to the United States, later became the first American professor of political science. Having begun his career teaching at the University of South Carolina, he was increasingly appalled by the institution of slavery, not least at his own college, and in 1857 he moved to New York, where he taught law and politics at Columbia College (now Columbia University).[42] Lieber's main claim to fame would be his authorship of the *General Orders No. 100* of the Union army in 1863. Better known as the Lieber Code, it remains famous as the first attempt to codify the laws of war, and therefore as the direct ancestor of the Geneva and Hague Conventions and the foundation of the modern laws of war.[43] Lieber's qualifications to create it were more than academic. As well as having experience of living on both sides of the sectional divide, between North and South, he knew the division even more personally. Three of his sons were in uniform, two fighting for the Union and one for the Confederacy. "Behold in me the symbol of civil war," he lamented in May 1861.[44]

Lieber had been reflecting on the issues of rebellion, revolution, and, crucially, civil war for many years before drafting his Code, but under the pressure of the job he was forced to change his mind on his definitions. In some early notes from around 1850, he ran through the various terms that could be used to describe different species and degrees of revolution—"Rising," "Revolt," "Riot," "Insurrection," "Sedition," "Rebellion," and so on—and included among them both "Secession" and "Civil War."[45] Around the same time, he reflected at length on the question of secession, especially in relation to South Carolina, where he was then living and teaching. He viewed the prospects of a successful secession dimly: "No peacible secession is possible . . . theory or no theory, right or no right, the Union will say: We must keep you; we cannot afford one of the south to cave in; the Union *shall* continue."[46] And so, of course, it would transpire a decade later. Success, or the prospect of success, was for him a major criterion for distinguishing the different kinds of collective antistate actions: "A State can resist, can rebel and if the rebellion be successful it will be called revolution. But . . . [l]et us call things by their right names. The right of secession is one thing and that of rebellion another." His example of a successful "rebellion" in this case was the American Revolution, in which "the Declaration of Independence gave . . . a national existence" to what, until July 4, 1776, had been British colonies.[47]

Early in the war between the North and the South, Lieber had again grappled with the definition of civil war. Only a few months after the hostilities began, between October 1861 and February 1862, he gave a series of lectures to his Columbia College students titled "Laws and Usages of War." He began by noting that he and his listeners were living in the "most martial period of our race" and, more specifically, that they were "in the midst of a bitter civil war in this country, while all Europe is preparing for war on a gigantic scale . . . We live in a grave age." He alluded to other conflicts, including the Crimean War and the Taiping Rebellion, and showed that he was well aware that the mid-nineteenth century was a moment of peculiar global instability. "Rebellion in China and here" made the relevance of the laws of war to civil war especially urgent but hardly clear. He followed thinkers like Rousseau in defining war as a contention between "political societies," not among individuals; only formal combatants could be accounted enemies. This led him to a distinction between "war" and civil war, the closest he would come to hazarding a definition of the latter before his work on the Code: "In international law we mean, as a matter of course, by war the contest between nations or independent governments, acknowledged as such by the family of nations. By civil war we mean the protracted state of active hostility of one portion of a political society against another portion."[48]

Lieber argued that the laws of war applied in civil war as in "true war or contentio justa [just conflict]" (a notable distinction) but only while also recognizing the continuing force of domestic law over those opposing the legitimate government:

But there is this difficulty shrouding all civil war, that on the one hand the rebel or insurgent is besides being a warfarer, a belligerent, a criminal, that is to be punished or at any rate punishable by the lawful government, and that on the other hand the large number of the insurgents (without which they would not have entered the civil war) precludes the lawful punishment and leads to those amnesties which are proclaimed while the criminality of the rebel may indeed be the greater.

At this point, Lieber did not distinguish as clearly as Halleck would in his *International Law* between rebellion and civil war. A civil war could have the features of both a "true war or contentio justa" and a domestic police action against insurrection, but not all insurgents could be punished as if they were common criminals: "It is a question of *expediency*, and not of law or morality."[49] How to overcome this double nature of civil war—as the conduct of both true war and mere criminality—presented a dilemma that Lieber could not resolve. His lecture notes include a fragment reflecting on the various principles underpinning the laws of war as the prelude to an account of their application in civil war. They tail off inconclusively: "Now in Civil War &c &c." Likewise, when, later in 1862, Lieber would publish a pathbreaking short treatise titled *Guerrilla Parties: Considered with Reference to the Laws and Usages of War*, he would deliberately not "enter upon a consideration of their application to the civil war in which we are engaged."[50]

That would have to wait until Henry Halleck invited him, in August 1862, to present his views to the public "on the usages and customs of war." Halleck's request came at a poignant moment. In his reply to the general's request, Lieber revealed that he had just received news of his son Oscar's death in Richmond, Virginia, after fighting in the Confederate army at the Battle of Williamsburg. "Civil war," he said mournfully, "has thus knocked loudly at our own door."[51] He soon began work on a short text on the laws of war, which he had been contemplating for some time—his Columbia College lectures were probably a preparation—but which now gained added impetus from Halleck's invitation and the tragedy hanging over his family. The problem, he confided to the U.S. attorney general, Edward Bates, was the lack of authoritative precedents in the legal literature. "Civil war has been little treated by the authors on the Law of War. Nor has there ever been a Civil War with the peculiar characteristics which signalize ours." He would, he told Bates, have to rely instead on "the authority of common sense."[52]

The correspondence between Halleck and Lieber revealed just how little guidance common sense could offer at such a fraught moment. Lieber's draft had deliberately not distinguished among civil war, rebellion, insurrection, and invasion, but Halleck asked for each to be delineated in the Code. The war was not quite into its second year when Lieber circulated what he thought was a complete draft of the Code in February 1863. A handful of copies had been printed to allow a select group of readers to annotate and comment on Lieber's work. On one remaining copy, Henry Halleck notes a striking absence from the list of the laws of war: "To be more useful at the present time it should embrace civil war as well as war between states or *distinct* sovereignties."[53] Lieber might have deliberately omitted civil war in an effort to dodge difficulties he could already perceive it would create. Yet, ever the keen lawyer, after Halleck's nudge, he did intend to offer his political masters in Washington, D.C., a precise definition. But it was easier said than done. "I am writing my 4 sections on civil war and 'invasion,'" Lieber wrote to Halleck in March 1863. "Ticklish work, that!"[54]

The account of civil war Lieber had provided to his students in New York—"the protracted state of active hostility of one portion of a political society against another portion"—was too inexact for the formal purpose of codification, particularly this one. After all, the paragraphs on civil war and its analogues would be the culmination of the Code, the final set of distinctions its readers in the Union army would take away with them. How, then, did Lieber define civil war? He distinguished it both from "insurrection" and from "rebellion," in ways that reflected the specific political conditions under which he wrote in the spring of 1863:

> 149. Insurrection is the rising of people in arms against their government, or a portion of it, or against one or more of its laws, or against an officer or officers of the government. It may be confined to mere armed resistance, or it may have greater ends in view.
> 150. Civil war is war between two or more portions of a country or state, each contending for the mastery of the whole, and each claiming to be the legitimate government. The term is also sometimes applied to war of rebellion, when the rebellious provinces or portions of the state are contiguous to those containing the seat of government.

151. The term rebellion is applied to an insurrection of large extent, and is usually a war between the legitimate government of a country and portions or provinces of the same who seek to throw off their allegiance to it and set up a government of their own.[55]

The context since 1861 had clearly shaped Lieber's distinctions. The difference between "insurrection" and "rebellion" was one of degree, with the latter approaching the condition of interstate conflict, or war, if undertaken for "greater ends," such as throwing off allegiance and setting up an independent government—that is, a self styled secessionist movement such as the Confederacy.[56]

Lieber presented two distinct definitions of civil war, one traditional and one novel. The first—"war between two or more portions of a country or state, each contending for mastery of the whole"—could be traced back to the Roman tradition and corresponds to what I have called a "supersessionist" model. The second conception— "sometimes applied to war of rebellion, when the rebellious provinces or portions of the state are contiguous to those containing the seat of government"—was unprecedented, both legally and historically. Lieber had made it up out of whole cloth, tailoring it to the needs of the moment. The U.S. Civil War might have been fought between two portions of the country, but only the Union aimed at recovering overall mastery or claimed to be the legitimate government over the whole territory. The Confederate states professed some moral continuity with the original rebellious colonies of the American Revolution, but that amounted to no claim on the territory of the states remaining in the Union. And yet, in Lieber's construction, the boundary between rebellion and civil war collapsed; the one ("war of rebellion") could be redescribed as the other ("sometimes applied . . .") when the circumstances were right—that is, when the "rebellious provinces" abutted "the seat of government," as, of course, they did in North America in 1863, with the U.S. capital of Washington, D.C., placed within the state of Virginia.

By Lieber's second definition, the Civil War was therefore not a civil war at all; it was in fact a rebellion. This validated the Union's response, because the U.S. Constitution provided for the means to "suppress Insurrections," including the suspension of habeas corpus "in Cases of Rebellion," which Lincoln had done (with Lieber's advice and support) in 1861. After the war, the Fourteenth Amendment to the Constitution (1868) would refer accordingly to "engage[ment] in insurrection or rebellion" as a disqualification for public office.[57] And, as we have seen, the official history of the conflict would be titled *The War of the Rebellion*, to drive home the Unionist account of the war as an uprising against a legitimate government.[58] In public and in private, however, both Lieber and Lincoln referred to it variously, usually as a "rebellion," sometimes as a "civil war," making a mockery of the lawyer's fretful efforts at precision in distinguishing them.

Lieber's definition nonetheless had an afterlife. As the *Code*'s leading historian has written, "The document was instantly influential" after Lieber had sent copies to

Europe, with translations and imitations appearing across the continent from the Netherlands to Russia between 1866 and 1896.[59] Two years after the Italians had adopted a parallel code, *General Orders No. 100* was reissued verbatim by the United States in 1898, this time in the context not of a civil war but of an "insurrection" in the Philippines.[60] Lieber's *Code* would still be studied by the U.S. Army in the aftermath of the terrorist attacks of September 2001; it was reprinted in 2007 as part of a study of a "masterpiece of counterguerrilla warfare" in the archipelago in 1901–2.[61] Since the *Code*'s first appearance, U.S. Army field manuals had made no attempt to revise Lieber's definition of civil war, only updating the rubric somewhat after the Geneva Conventions of 1949 to cover "armed conflicts not of an international character."[62]

In the intervening years, the naming of the most divisive war in American history continued to be controversial. During the conflict, there could be no agreement on what to call it. Although in its early stages even Southerners referred to it as a civil war, they generally came to prefer other terms: "the war," "the War for Independence," and even "the Revolution," to suggest continuity with an earlier struggle for self-determination led by white slaveholders from the South such as George Washington and Thomas Jefferson.[63] Northerners meanwhile called it "the Rebellion," "the War of Secession," and "the Civil War." It was only after the end of formal hostilities that other names proliferated—"the Late War," and "the Late Unpleasantness," for instance. (One assiduous collector has discovered 120 different terms.) "The War Between the States" was mostly a postwar designation, and it gained special prominence in 1899 when the United Daughters of the Confederacy approved a resolution that it replace all references to the Civil War, the War of Secession, and the War of Rebellion. As one implacable Confederate woman argued, "Don't allow the War of the States to be called a Civil War. If we allow this, we own that we were one State, not many, as contended."[64]

It was not until 1907, while debating a bill to provide pensions for veterans of the Mexican War and the Civil War, that the U.S. Congress agreed that the official name would be the "Civil War." A Democratic senator had protested that it had been a "War of Secession": "It was a war to establish the right of secession . . . The war was in the nature of a rebellion, and to a certain extent it was a civil war, but in the broad sense, in the full sense, it was a war of secession." A Mississippi senator likewise protested, "It was not a civil war and it was not a war of rebellion. It was a war between sovereign States."[65] But these protests, like those of other sympathizers of the Lost Cause, were in vain. "No more is to be heard of the 'war of the rebellion' nor the 'war between the States,'" a Washington, D.C., newspaper reported the morning after the debate. "What Gen. Butler once called in derision 'the late unpleasantness' is henceforth to be known as 'the civil war.' The Senate so decided yesterday."[66] The United Daughters of the Confederacy was undeterred and continued to campaign for changes to school textbooks and to press Congress for recognition of "the War Between the States," on the grounds that "'Civil War' is defined by the best authorities as a war between the citizens of a 'common country,' 'citizens of the same nation,' etc. Now for four years we maintained an entirely separate government from that of the United States, being an entity known the world over as the Confederate States."[67] These efforts were a relatively minor part of the enduring battle over the memory of the Civil War and had strikingly little relevance to the African American population of the United States. For them, the war had been the motor of emancipation—"the Abolition War," in Frederick Douglass's phrase—the origin of both profound hope and equally deep disappointment, yet still a great good, perhaps even a gift from heaven.[68]

*

During the U.S. Civil War—as a conciliatory consensus now agrees to call the conflict in the United States—the category of civil war came firmly under the authority of lawyers for the first time. Beginning with Francis Lieber, they were the first professional group to claim competency to define the undefinable and its precise determinants and empirical benchmarks. Vattel and Halleck had led the way in attempting to describe civil war in the context of the law of nations (or what, by Halleck's time, had become known as international law). But Lieber was the first to try to discriminate civil war from its near neighbors "insurrection" and "rebellion," however arduously, as he complained, and with limited success, as we have seen. The meanings of civil war would continue to grow, the urge to restrain the proliferation eventually peaking during the latter years of the Cold War. But it originated a century earlier, finding its agent in a man who almost perished at Waterloo. That history of European battlefields haunted Lieber as much as the personal and national tragedy of the war of 1861–65.

Another history would continue to haunt memories of the U.S. Civil War, both in the short and in the long terms: the history of Rome. Liberated from the Roman narratives about the natural recurrence of civil war, supporters of both the Union and the Confederacy nonetheless reached back to the ancients for analogues of their struggle and its aftermath. The novelist and poet Herman Melville (1819–91), for one, affirmed the importance of the Roman past even in the act of repudiating it in the poem he wrote to commemorate the surrender at Appomattox on Palm Sunday, April 9, 1865:

> The warring eagles fold the wing,
>   But not in Cæsar's sway;
> Not Rome o'ercome by Roman arms we sing,
>   As on Pharsalia's day.
> But Treason thrown, though a giant grown,
>   And Freedom's larger play.
>   All human tribes glad token see
>   In the close of the wars of Grant and
>   Lee.[69]

With its allusions to Caesar, Pompey, and Lucan, Melville's lines are almost an epitaph to the Roman conception of civil war in the era of industrialized slaughter.

Almost, but not quite: in June 1914, the United Daughters of the Confederacy unveiled a monument to the Confederate dead at Arlington National Cemetery outside Washington, D.C., that carried on with the Roman tradition. On the plinth is the seal of the Confederate States of America with the motto "To Our Dead Heroes by the United Daughters of the Confederacy Victrix Causa Diis Placuit Sed Victa Catoni" ("the conquering cause pleased the gods, but the conquered [pleased] Cato").[70] The line is from the first book of Lucan's *Civil War*, and the ambivalence was Lucan's own. It implies that a civil war could not be just on both sides but that there could still be moral consolations, however illusory, even for the defeated. Friedrich Engels had said as much to Karl Marx in a letter of May 1862: the Confederates, he thought, "abide by *the outcome of the big battles* and console themselves with *victrix causa diis*, etc."[71] What Lincoln had called "a great civil war" at one cemetery in Pennsylvania was transmuted by the Roman allusion into an emblem of the Lost Cause at another American burial ground. As so often, progress toward perpetual peace entailed a march through the graveyards filled by civil wars.

Worlds of Civil War

The Twentieth Century

"All European wars, said Voltaire, are civil wars. In the twentieth century his formula applies to the whole earth. In our world, which shrinks progressively as communications become swifter, all wars are civil wars: all battles are battles between fellow-citizens, nay more, between brothers."[1] The words are those of Jaime Torres Bodet (1902–74), the Mexican scholar, poet, and diplomat who served as the second director general of the United Nations Educational, Scientific, and Cultural Organization after World War II. He was speaking in 1949, soon after the foundation of the UN and its sibling organizations and in the wake of the momentous events of 1947–48, among them, Indian independence and partition, the foundation of the State of Israel and the first Arab-Israeli conflict, and the promulgation of the Universal Declaration of Human Rights: a pivotal moment that one of his contemporaries, the émigré German political scientist Sigmund Neumann (1904–62), called—with the addition of the Chinese civil war and burgeoning anticolonial nationalism in the Middle East and Southeast Asia—both "the age of revolutions" and "the international civil war."[2]

The title as well as the message of Torres Bodet's speech, delivered in Paris at the United Nations Day ceremony on October 24, 1949, was "Why We Fight": not in the sense of the global military conflict that had ended four years earlier, but in a different struggle—the fight for peace. On this occasion, Torres Bodet's sentiments about civil war were sounder than his scholarship. Although Voltaire did famously argue that Europe was a "kind of great republic divided into several states," all with "the same principle of public law and politics, unknown in other parts of the world," he did not stretch his vision of European community to imagine its wars as *civil* wars.[3] That leap was taken instead by Voltaire's more courtly predecessor the French Catholic archbishop and political writer François de Salignac de la Mothe Fénelon (1651–1715). In his immensely popular work of advice for a young prince, the *Dialogues of the Dead* (1712), Fénelon has the character of Socrates offer an eloquent pacifist argument based on the cosmopolitan principle of common humanity:

All Wars are properly Civil Wars [*Toutes les guerres sont civiles*], 'tis still Mankind shedding each other's Blood, and tearing their own Entrails out; the farther a War is extended, the more fatal it is; and therefore the Combats of one People against another, are worse than the Combats of private Families against a Republick. We ought therefore

never to engage in a War, unless reduced to a last
Extremity, and then only to repel our Foes.[4]

All such wars are not just civil wars; they are, as Lucan
might have said, *worse* than civil wars, precisely because
they ensnare ever larger circles of humanity.[5] It was one
of the many paradoxes of the civil war's intellectual history
that as the world came closer to the cosmopolitan ideal of
universal humanity, the more intimate would international
and even global wars become. More acute pain, not more
assured peace, might be the unintended outcome of the
world's progressive shrinkage as cosmopolitan empathy
and interaction grew.[6] Enlightened thinkers like Fénelon
who believed in Europe's cultural unity feared that all wars
between Europeans would become civil wars, because they
were fought within the bounds of a community of fellow citizens who recognized one another as such. Under
Immanuel Kant's later conception of cosmopolitan right in
"Toward Perpetual Peace," the realm of mutual recognition itself became global, because "the (narrower or wider)
community of the nations of the earth has now gone so
far that a violation of right on *one* place of the earth is felt
in *all*."[7]

Over the century of near-constant warfare that was
Europe's "Second Hundred Years' War" (1688–1815),
European civil war had, rather ironically, come to sig-
nify, both on the Continent and in its imperial outposts,
a degree of cultural unity as well as civilizational difference from the rest of the world. In his own *Project for
Perpetual Peace* (1761), Jean-Jacques Rousseau judged the

wars between the powers of Europe to be "much the more deplorable, as their combinations are intimate; . . . their frequent quarrels have almost the cruelty of civil wars."[8] Four decades later, in 1802, Napoleon reportedly told the British minister Charles James Fox, during the negotiations for the Anglo-French Treaty of Amiens, that "Turkey excepted, Europe is nothing more than a province of the world; when we battle, we engage in nothing more than a civil war."[9] And in 1866, the French historian Henri Martin saw no end to these European civil wars, which for him included the recent Crimean War (1853–56), because he viewed Russia, too, as part of the same civilization.[10] The saying that all European wars were civil wars would again become popular in the moment between the twentieth century's two great wars, when it was usually attributed to Napoleon, perhaps recalling his bon mot of 1802.[11]

The second half of the twentieth century would indeed witness the globalization of civil war, but not quite in the form Torres Bodet or his predecessors in the Enlightenment might have anticipated. This new world of civil war emerged with three overlapping features. First, civil war (now technocratically rebranded as "international conflict of a non-international character") gradually came under the jurisdiction of international institutions, especially international humanitarian law, in the wake of World War II, but with subsequent modifications during the age of decolonization and then during the internal conflicts of the 1990s. Second, and closely related to the first, civil wars became seemingly ubiquitous, distributed across most parts of the world (especially Africa and Asia, but in the 1990s in an otherwise pacified Europe as well), and then gradually came to supplant wars between states as the world's most common and widespread form of large-scale organized violence. And third, the communities within which civil wars were imagined as taking place—the polities, *civitates*, or spheres of human commonality—became ever wider and more capacious, until the idea of "European civil war" gave way to various conceptions of "global civil war" in the present century.

At the same time, the era's great transnational conflicts, from World War I to the Cold War and then on to the "Global War on Terror" early in the twenty-first century, were often seen as civil wars in the realms of political and legal argument. But as we shall see, by the 1960s and 1970s social scientists and philosophers had begun to take a more focused interest in civil war as a topic of analysis, speculation, and definition. Traces of all these arguments endure in ideas of civil war today and are likely to linger into the future.

*

Shortly before Torres Bodet delivered his speech in October 1949, a humanitarian conference aimed precisely at ameliorating the ever-expanding effects of war concluded its deliberations in Geneva in August 1949. The Diplomatic Conference, as it was known, drew representatives from across the world to revise the Fourth Hague Convention of 1907 and the 1929 Geneva Convention with particular regard to the status of civilians in time of war.

The most pressing issue on the minds of many of the assembled delegates was how to extend the protections guaranteed to recognized combatants in conventional international warfare to "the victims of conflicts not of an international character." Not all of them could agree that this was necessary or desirable; some, including the British delegation, thought the incursion of international law into domestic disputes was an infringement of national sovereignty. (Recall that it was, in fact, on just such grounds that the original Geneva Convention of 1864 had not been extended to civil wars.) Others, however, argued successfully that "the rights of the State should not be placed above all humanitarian considerations" because "civil war was more cruel than international war." The result of these deliberations was Common Article 3 of the Geneva Conventions (1949), now finally applied to what was precisely termed "armed conflict not of an international character" (later compressed to "non-international armed conflict" or, still more succinctly, "NIAC").[12]

The 1949 discussions leading to Common Article 3 built on proposals set forth in Stockholm in 1948 by the International Committee of the Red Cross to make application of the existing Geneva Conventions "obligatory on each of the adversaries" in "cases of an armed conflict which are not of an international character, especially cases of civil war, colonial conflicts, or wars of religion." After much discussion, the revised draft presented in Geneva in 1949 omitted the last qualifying clause and specified only "armed conflict not of an international character." That became the preferred formulation thereafter among international lawyers and international organizations, despite early objections that it could cover too wide a range of violent acts within the frontiers of a single state: not just "civil" wars, but any enemies of the state, whether legitimate freedom fighters, brigands, or even common criminals—in fact anyone engaged in riots or coups d'état rather than actions recognizable as wars. Did they all deserve the protection of the Geneva Conventions, even if their actions were illegal under domestic law?[13] Most civil wars were wars "not of an international character"; however, only some wars "not of an international character" were civil wars. Trying to draw a line between the two overlapping categories would remain a continuing source of controversy and confusion up to the present.[14]

As finally adopted, Common Article 3 of the Geneva Conventions was minimalist in its ambitions. It provided that civilians and members of armed forces who were no longer combatants (for instance, because they were wounded or ill) were "in all circumstances to be treated humanely"; that "the wounded and sick shall be collected and cared for"; that the Red Cross would be permitted to minister to anyone involved in the conflict; and that the parties to the conflict should endeavor to apply as many remaining provisions of the Geneva Conventions as possible.[15] The article permitted great latitude of interpretation, not least because no attempt was made to define more exactly what constituted an "armed conflict not of an international character," thus avoiding "the dangers of under- and over-inclusivity." What resulted was not so expansive that it might encompass a range of internal police actions (or the threats to national sovereignty provoking them), for example, yet not so restrictive that too many conflicts might be excluded from any regulation or amelioration. On the other hand, it gave states ample discretion to decide whether or not conflicts crossed the threshold from rebellion to civil war and therefore to decide for themselves whether their own actions against rebels would be subject to Common Article 3 and the rest of the Geneva Conventions. That latitude seemed especially precious to states with overseas colonies that might demand self-determination. So it was for Portugal, which in 1949 "reserve[d] the right not to apply the Provisions of Article 3, in so far as they may be contrary to the provisions of Portuguese law, in all territories subject to her sovereignty in any part of the world."[16]

Common Article 3 was drafted and approved in 1949 largely in response to concerns about the inadequacy of the existing Geneva Conventions during recent conflicts such as the Spanish Civil War (1936–39). In the decades after World War II, the heightened incidence of "noninternational" conflicts demanded greater precision in the application of the conventions. Amid the proxy wars of the Cold War, and the wreckage of disintegrating empires, intervention into internal conflicts became more common, tarnishing the luster of the Long Peace then emerging in Europe. These pressures led to a program of updating and revising the Geneva Conventions between 1974 and 1977. In this context, the Institute of International Law (Institut de Droit International)—the leading professional body of the global community of international lawyers—met in

1975 in the German city of Wiesbaden to draft a document titled "The Principle of Non-intervention in Civil Wars." This Wiesbaden protocol noted "the gravity of the phenomenon of civil wars and of the suffering they cause" and expressed concern that such conflicts could readily escalate into international conflicts if any side sought foreign involvement, thereby triggering the opposing side to do likewise. External parties were urged not to intervene, except to offer humanitarian, technical, or economic aid "not likely to have any substantial impact on the outcome of the civil war." In the course of setting conditions for noninterference, the institute sought briefly to define "civil war" as "any armed conflict, not of an international character, which breaks out in the territory of a State" and in which either an insurgency aiming to take over the government, or to secede, opposes the established government; or two or more groups vie to control the state when no government exists. Crucially, the Wiesbaden Protocol also set limits specifying what was *not* a civil war; "local disorders or riots," "armed conflicts between political entities separated by an international demarcation line," and "conflicts arising from decolonization" were all beyond the pale.[17]

The outcome of these discussions was a set of further protocols, of which the second—Additional Protocol II (1977)—applied to conflicts of a non-international character. The limits set at Wiesbaden continued to apply, because AP II excluded riots and also wars of decolonization, these being covered instead by Additional Protocol I, which first brought international humanitarian law to bear directly on anti-imperial struggles. The second Additional Protocol expanded the protections and prohibitions relevant to civil wars, remaining today the chief component of humanitarian law relevant to them.[18] The application of those protections depends on the judgment that a conflict "not of an international character" is in progress. If the conflict is held to be "international"—that is, between two independent sovereign communities—then the full force of the Geneva Conventions applies. If it is "non-international," then it will be covered by Common Article 3 and Additional Protocol II.[19] But if the violence has not been deemed a conflict of either kind— perhaps because it is a riot or an insurgency—it remains within the scope of domestic jurisdiction and hence subject to police action. In these cases, a great deal hangs on the determination of whether a conflict is "not of an international character" or, in plain speech, whether it is a "civil" war.

The legal boundaries of what is or is not a civil war have continued to be flexible and dynamic.[20] The institute's next major resolution concerning non-international conflicts (1999) reflected the experience of the Balkan Wars: "*Considering* that armed conflicts in which non-State entities are parties have become more and more numerous and increasingly motivated in particular by ethnic, religious or racial causes," with especially devastating consequences for civilian populations, the institute recommended that international humanitarian law should apply to "internal armed conflicts between a government's armed forces and those of one or several non-State entities, or between several non-State entities."[21] This shift in turn reflected the jurisprudence of the International Criminal Tribunal for the Former Yugoslavia, or ICTY, which, over the course of the 1990s, had attempted to apply international humanitarian law to internal conflicts.

In 1996, the ICTY ruled that the Bosnian war had mutated from an international war into a civil war at the point in 1992 when the former Federal Republic of Yugoslavia had withdrawn its support from the ethnic Serbs. This shift was of special significance because the defendant before the tribunal, the Bosnian war criminal Duško Tadić, claimed it had no jurisdiction over his actions because the statute creating the tribunal applied only to international armed conflicts. The tribunal's 1996 ruling was later reversed on appeal, but it revealed how much can hang on the definition of a conflict as civil war—in this case, whether or not Tadić could be held liable for breaches of the Geneva Conventions.[22] The ICTY Appeals Chamber made the stakes very clear in its ruling on the *Tadić* case:

Why protect civilians from belligerent violence, or ban rape, torture or the wanton destruction of hospitals, churches, museums or private property, as well as proscribe weapons causing unnecessary suffering when two sovereign States are engaged in war, and yet refrain from enacting the same bans or providing the same protection when armed violence erupted "only" within the territory of a sovereign State?[23]

The international institutions created in the last decade or so have tried to answer such questions convincingly, building on earlier efforts, like those of the Red Cross, to apply the constraints increasingly standard in conventional warfare to civil wars.[24] The 2004 revision of the British Ministry of Defence's manual on the laws of war for military personnel, for example, has served to bring civil wars within the theoretical reach of war.[25] The U.S. Army's groundbreaking *Counterinsurgency Field Manual* of 2007, written with events in Iraq and Afghanistan very much in mind, likewise recalled the need to apply the relevant provisions of the Geneva Conventions and acknowledged that "although insurgencies can occur simultaneously with a legal state of war between two nations, they are classically conflicts internal to a single nation."[26]

Yet recent efforts to bring civil war within the pale of civility remain frustratingly and lethally incomplete; as the ICTY put it, there has been no "full and mechanical transplant" of the laws of war to civil warfare, nor could there be until all parties to such conflicts agree to be bound by international humanitarian law. The ICTY nonetheless laid down a vital principle for effecting the desired "transplant": "What is inhumane, and consequently proscribed, in international wars, cannot but be inhumane and inadmissible in civil strife."[27] As that principle is put into legal operation, the world might come closer to the "civilization" of civil war.

But matters are never quite so simple. Take the case of Syria in 2011–12. Ordinary Syrians understood the contention with Bashar al-Assad's regime throughout 2011 and the first half of 2012 to be civil war. Outside Syria, however, interested parties considered the matter more debatable. In December 2011, the U.S. State Department's deputy spokesperson Mark Toner demurred when asked if he agreed with a UN official that Syria was experiencing civil war. "We think violence needs to end in Syria. And that includes among the opposition elements," he said. "But there's no way to equate the two, which, in my view, is implied in using the term 'civil war.'"[28] As for the Assad regime, it naturally saw only rebellion. The opposition said they were engaged in resistance. Meanwhile, powers like Russia and the United States held the threat of declaring a civil war over each other's head as they jousted over intervention and nonintervention.[29]

It took the International Committee of the Red Cross until July 2012—more than a year into the conflict, and after some seventeen thousand deaths—to confirm that what was taking place in Syria was, in fact, an "armed conflict not of an international character."[30] Only with that determination could the parties be covered by the relevant provisions of the Geneva Conventions.[31] The reluctance to call the conflict a civil war has become typical of international organizations in the twenty-first century because so much—politically, militarily, legally, and ethically—now hangs on the use or withholding of the term. Thus, a set of legal protocols designed to humanize the conduct of civil war—to bring to bear humanitarian constraints on its practice and to minimize some of the terrible human cost—may have served only to constrain international actors from any such effort. To see how this paradoxical situation arose, we need to review a brief genealogy of the treatment of civil war in the social sciences, beginning in the 1960s.

*

"When today's social science has become intellectual history, one question will almost certainly be asked about it: Why did social science, which has produced so many studies of so many subjects, produce so few on violent political disorder—internal war?"[32] Here is one of those rare moments when a historian can hear someone from the past talking to them directly from the sources. It is a little unsettling to imagine that the actor here was speaking in 1963 and already waiting for an intellectual historian to map his field, but the question of Princeton professor Harry Eckstein (1924–99) was—and remains—perceptive.

As Eckstein was aware, the academic consensus had long been that civil war was good for absolutely nothing. Accordingly, civil war had been a Cinderella subject, of apparently equal irrelevance across all the academic disciplines. Yet starting in the 1960s, and inspired first by the Cold War and then by the wars of decolonization, American social scientists, often with the backing of the RAND Corporation and similar institutions of the military-academic complex, became increasingly invested in scrutinizing what was called broadly "internal warfare," a category that encompassed everything from guerrilla warfare and insurgencies to civil wars, coups, and revolutions.[33] Eckstein's call was not heeded as quickly or as wholeheartedly as he might have wished, despite the efforts of a research group on internal war that he ran at Princeton University, which included political scientists, sociologists, and even the odd historian. Progress was slow. "The crucial conceptual issues about internal war are still in the pretheoretical stage," lamented one of its first systematic analysts in 1970. "Satisfactory theories of internal war have neither been compiled nor evaluated."[34]

The continuing confusion about the meaning of civil war could be seen publicly when, in the spring of 1968, the U.S. Senate Foreign Relations Committee held a remarkable series of hearings during the Vietnam War titled *The Nature of Revolution*. These were chaired by Senator J. William Fulbright and called distinguished academic witnesses, including the eminent Harvard historian of revolution Crane Brinton (1898–1968) and his younger colleague Louis Hartz (1919–86), the political scientist and student of liberalism. On the last day of the hearings, a young Princeton political scientist, John T. McAlister, tried to explain the intractability of the conflict by noting that the United States was not "fighting a civil war that is a purely internal matter" but had instead become embroiled in "a revolutionary war involving all of the Vietnamese people." Senator Fulbright immediately wanted to know if there was a distinction between a revolutionary war and a civil war. McAlister argued there was: "In civil wars, including our own, there are secessionist goals on the part of those who are fighting. In a revolutionary war, by contrast . . . the primary goal is unification . . . [and] there are very distinct political goals about the whole reconstitution of the

basis of political order involved." There then followed a
bizarre exchange between the two southerners, Fulbright
of Arkansas and McAlister of South Carolina:

> THE CHAIRMAN. Well, with that definition is our
> own War Between the States a civil war or a
> revolutionary war?
>
> DR. MCALISTER. I would say that was a civil war.
>
> THE CHAIRMAN. They were seeking to secede?
>
> DR. MCALISTER. We were seeking to secede; yes.
>
> THE CHAIRMAN. We were seeking to secede.
> [Laughter.] But we failed.
>
> DR. MCALISTER. That is right.
>
> THE CHAIRMAN. And since then it has been a revo-
> lutionary war as to who controls it?
>
> DR. MCALISTER. That is right.
>
> THE CHAIRMAN. Is that right?
>
> DR. MCALISTER. That is right.
>
> THE CHAIRMAN. All right.[35]

Such southern humor might have been awkward in the
era of the civil rights movement, but it did reveal a persistent confusion, even among political scientists, about the
definitions of civil war and revolution.

Even Harvard's preeminent political philosopher was
confused. In the spring of 1969, also during the Vietnam
War, John Rawls (1921–2002) gave an undergraduate lecture course titled Moral Problems: Nations and War.[36]
Two years later, he would publish *A Theory of Justice*,
the work usually credited with reviving Anglo-American

political philosophy in the late twentieth century. That work was notoriously reticent on matters of international justice, but in his Harvard lectures Rawls faced squarely the questions swirling around American campuses, including Harvard's, about the ethics of war, conscription, and civil disobedience. Discussions of just war—both the just causes of war (*jus ad bellum*) and the justice of actions in war (*jus in bello*)—bulked large in the lectures. Rawls distinguished between different types of wars in order to define the principles that would best apply in each case. The initial typology found in his lecture notes proposes nine kinds:

1. Wars between existing via states (WW I + II)
2. Civil wars (of social justice) within via states or society (French Rev);
3. Wars of secession of minorities within region: American Civil War.
4. Colonial Wars of secession (from Empire): Algerian War; American Rev War?
5. Wars of intervention (humane intervention)
6. Wars of national unification (War of Roses; Tudors)
7. Wars of conquest, of Empire (Wars of Rome).
8. Wars of Crusade, religious or secular
9. Wars of national liberation (in present sense); guerilla wars[37]

Rawls's categories are as revealing as his applications. Civil wars were to be distinguished *both* from wars between states *and* from wars of secession, and wars of secession were further divided between intrastate and anti-imperial secessions. By implication, a civil war could only be considered a just war if its aim was what Rawls called "social justice"—that is, comprehensive internal reform directed toward the well-being of all the inhabitants of a viable state or society, such as France after 1789. Wars of secession might be thought just on the grounds that they aimed at the relief of an oppressed population—for example, that of a minority within an established state or of a colonized people within an empire. In common with contemporary international lawyers and political scientists, he separated civil wars from "wars of national liberation" and guerrilla wars.[38]

Rawls's distinctions were lucid, but his examples were rather less clear-cut. Initially, he was not sure what kind of war of secession the American Revolutionary War had been. In the body of the lectures, he included both the American Civil War and the American Revolution under "wars of secession of minorities." This was not evidence that Rawls, who pointedly did *not* include the Civil War under wars of social justice, equated the two great conflicts but it was perhaps an indication that he did not want to assimilate American Patriots with Algerian *colons;* in the American Revolution, it was the European settler population that sought to escape from empire, not the indigenous population or the enslaved, for example. And as an example of a civil war of social justice, he cited not the French Revolution but the Spanish Civil War.

Later in his lecture series, as he treated the *jus ad bel-*

lum in more detail, Rawls briefly examined the question of whether intervention in a civil war might be justifiable, taking John Stuart Mill's "Few Words on Non-intervention" and the Vietnam War as his points of reference. Rawls was quite dismissive of what he called the "troublesome" faults in Mill's argument and noted "it would not justify our intervention in Vietnam," because none of the arguments Mill rehearsed for British intervention in the nineteenth century could be applied to American policy in Vietnam: "We have not intervened neutrally in a protracted civil war; nor have we intervened to help a people throw off a foreign despotism." Indeed, Rawls concluded, intervention in such a case could only be "under *international* auspices, where the intervention is *impartial* . . . and undertaken for *clear* reasons of humanity."[39]

For Rawls in these lectures, civil war was at least temporarily helpful for clarifying the limits of humanitarian intervention and for elucidating the differences between various instances of national liberation and revolution. For the French philosopher and historian Michel Foucault (1926–84) a few years later, civil war was even more useful in helping to define what he was just beginning to call the "physics" of power. Each year, Foucault had to deliver a course of public lectures on the research he had undertaken while holding a professorship at the prestigious Collège de France in Paris. In 1973, his lecture was titled "The Punitive Society" ("La société punitive"), a topic that would become central to his conception of modern regimes of power. Like many commentators in the 1960s and 1970s on both sides of the Atlantic, Foucault found civil war "philosophically, politically, and historically, a rather poorly developed notion," not least because most analysts viewed it as what he called "the accident, the abnormality . . . the theoretical-practical monstrosity."[40] With his characteristic theoretical dexterity and historical daring, Foucault proposed to bring civil war from the margins of analysis to the center by arguing that it was hardly marginal or irrelevant to the understanding of power; civil war, he would argue, was, in fact, the matrix of all power struggles.[41]

Foucault's dazzling account of civil war in the 1973 lectures executed three particularly illuminating volte-faces in relation to standard historical accounts. First, he showed that civil war could not be identified with Hobbes's war of all against all in the *Leviathan;* indeed, Foucault argued that civil war was the very opposite of the Hobbesian state of nature. Second, he confronted the assumption that civil war was the antithesis of power because it represented its dissolution and breakdown, arguing that civil war was in effect the very apotheosis of power; politics was *civil* war by other means. And third, he contended that civil war had, in fact, not gradually disappeared in Europe in the transition from the early modern period of wars of religion and monarchical succession to the more stable world of modernity. There had been no progressive movement from an era of civil wars to an age of revolutions; rather, civil war had endured as the fundamental characteristic of what Foucault famously called the "disciplinary society," in which the structures of power constantly shape human beings.

In accusing Hobbes and his followers of conflating civil war with the war of all against all (*bellum omnium contra omnes*), Foucault argued, to the contrary, that they could not be further apart, in their character (the one collective, the other individual), their motivation, or, crucially, their relation to sovereignty; the war of all against all was the condition that preceded, and indeed necessitated, the constitution of a sovereign in Hobbes's political theory, while civil war marked the collapse of sovereignty, the dissolution of the sovereign itself.[42] Civil war was directed at seizing or transforming power and therefore "unfolded in the theatre of power"; it haunts power, even to the point that the daily exercise of power can be considered as like a civil war. In this sense, Foucault concluded, with a twist on Clausewitz's famous dictum that the master of the art of war himself would never have approved, "Politics is the continuation of civil war."[43]

While Rawls and Foucault were worrying about the theory of civil war, social scientists, especially in the United States, had already begun a decades-long effort to come up with an operational definition. Its major crucible of innovation was the Correlates of War Project which was then based at the University of Michigan. This was the most systematic attempt by the empirical social sciences to measure the incidence of conflict across the globe by collecting and analyzing data on wars since 1816. Initially, the bulk of the work focused on interstate warfare, as had earlier research programs on conflict, such as *A Study of War* (1942) by the American political scientist Quincy Wright and *Statistics of Deadly Quarrels* (1960) by the eccentric British meteorologist Lewis Fry Richardson.[44] But bracketing internal war from international war could not continue indefinitely, because, as the leaders of the Correlates of War Project admitted, "civil wars, insurgencies, and foreign interventions have come to dominate the headlines in our generation and now play as important a role in the international community as traditional interstate war."[45]

Once the compass of the Correlates of War Project had expanded to include internal wars, the team needed to develop criteria for civil war—as against other forms of conflict—that could be used to sort the masses of data they had collected on conflicts stretching back to the Vienna Settlement in 1815. They sought a quantitative, rather than a qualitative, definition, as they put it, "to minimize subjective bias" and, more pointedly, to "facilitate the construction of a data set," as a means of getting out of what they saw as the conceptual morass of competing and inconsistent definitions. So the definition of civil war devised for the Correlates of War would have a numerical cutoff point, a set of boundary conditions, some empirical criteria, and a great many problems:

> sustained military combat, primarily internal, resulting in at least 1000 battle deaths per year, pitting central government forces against an insurgent force capable of . . . inflict[ing] upon the government forces at least 5% of the fatalities the insurgents sustain.[46]

This "deceptively straightforward" definition was designed to allow political scientists and others to create the large sets of data needed to analyze the incidence of civil war across time and around the world.[47] It also excluded many conflicts that would have blurred the analysis because they did not fit the procrustean definition.

The core of that definition was empirical, not experiential: combatants and victims might believe they were trapped in a civil war, but until the death toll reached a thousand or antigovernment forces had killed at least fifty people, social scientists could tell them they were wrong, at least for the purposes of comparative analysis. A conflict had to be militarized, to distinguish it from other forms of internal violence like riots and coups d'état; it was only "primarily internal" because it also had to encompass internationalized civil wars, into which outside powers or forces had intervened; a thousand battlefield deaths annually defined it as a "major" civil war; it had to have two sides (but possibly only two sides), one of which was the existing government; and it had to be militarized on both of those sides, to distinguish it from, say, massacres or genocide.

There were many difficulties that could be discerned in this definition.[48] The greatest, surely, was the number of conflicts it does not encompass. Consider the condition of being "primarily internal"—that is, internal to a sovereign state, recognized as such by the international community: this was specified as being "internal" to the *metropole*, in order, quite deliberately, to exclude postcolonial wars of national liberation, just as international legal protocols did at the time. Like those protocols, this stipulation would mean omitting a conflict like the Algerian War or, to go further back in time, the American Revolution as a civil war.[49] A second problem was that the emphasis on *metropoles* also implied the existence not just of states but of nation-states in the "Westphalian" mold of territorially bounded sovereignty; by these terms, there could not really have been proper civil wars before roughly the early nineteenth century—let alone in classical Greece or ancient Rome, for example—because there were few states of the kind International Relations scholars might identify.[50] Without unitary sovereignty and its external recognition, it seems, there can be no *civitas*, and hence no "civil" war.

Finally, the definition would exclude many conflicts thought of, by at least some of their participants and by external observers, as civil wars—for example, the Swiss Sonderbund War of 1847. One of the shortest and least bloody civil wars on record—it lasted only twenty-five days and claimed 93 lives by the best count—it was nonetheless thought to be, at the time, as it is now, a civil war.[51] Likewise, it would exclude the Irish Civil War of 1922–23 (in which an estimated 540 pro-treaty troops died, along with perhaps 800 members of the army and an unknown number of Republicans).[52] And it would not encompass the Troubles in Northern Ireland, for which the death toll was around 3,500 between 1969 and 2001, with a peak of 479 in 1972; indeed, the requisite total of 1,000 deaths was not reached until April 1974, five years into the conflict.[53]

The essential contestability of the Correlates of War Project's definition became starkly clear during the Second

Gulf War, when it was used in 2007–8 to prove both that there was a civil war taking place within the boundaries of Iraq—and that there was not. Vehement disagreement arose as to whether the category fit the facts on the ground. Representatives of the Bush administration and others, mostly neoconservative military strategists and political pundits, denied that the turbulence merited the name. Terrorism? Insurgency? Perhaps. But a civil war? Certainly not. Then, in July 2006, the Yale political scientist Nicholas Sambanis had announced in *The New York Times* that according to the standard social-science criteria Iraq was indeed experiencing civil war.[54] By late in that year, there was no doubt among many inside and outside Iraq what was happening. The UN's secretary-general, Kofi Annan, for one, told the BBC, "When we had strife in Lebanon and other places, we called that a civil war; this is much worse."[55]

At the same time, various sectors of the U.S. media, including the NBC television network and newspapers such as *The New York Times* and the *Los Angeles Times*, were also calling the conflict in Iraq a civil war.[56] Adel Ibrahim, a young Shi'ite sheikh, vehemently told the *Times*, "You need to let the world know there's a civil war here in Iraq. It's a crushing civil war . . . We don't know who our enemy is and who is our friend."[57] When Turkey's then prime minister, Recep Tayyip Erdoğan, was asked if he thought there was a civil war in Iraq, he replied, "Muslims kill each other just because they belong to different sects. This is a civil war, because I cannot make any other definition."[58] By the end of 2006, half of the American population agreed, according to a Pew Research Center poll in December

2006, which found that "more Americans said the current violence in Iraq was mostly a civil war than said it was an insurgency aimed at the United States and its allies."[59] A few months later, an analyst at Chatham House, the British think tank on international affairs, argued that there was not a civil war in Iraq; in fact, there were "several civil wars and insurgencies, between different communities and organizations": Shi'as versus Sunnis, Sunnis versus the United States, Shi'as versus other Shi'as, Sunnis versus other Sunnis, Kurds versus non-Kurds, and so on.[60]

In testimony before the U.S. Congress in September 2006, the Stanford political scientist James Fearon had no doubt that "the rate of killing in Iraq—easily more than 30,000 in three years—puts it in the company of many recent conflicts that few hesitate to call 'civil wars' (e.g., Sri Lanka, Algeria, Guatemala, Peru, Colombia)." Fearon defined a civil war as "a violent conflict, fought by organized groups that aim to take power at the center or in a region, or to change government policies." The violence in Iraq fit that mold, he argued. It had also passed a significant threshold of casualties and could be directly compared with other civil wars around the world since 1945—in Lebanon, Turkey, and Bosnia, for example.[61] Such comparison could then help one to imagine what the future held for Iraq and the coalition forces stationed there. The results were not encouraging: civil wars last longer than other wars, ten years, on average; they often end only with a decisive military victory by one side or the other; leaving too precipitately after an intervention can only make matters much worse; power-sharing agreements usually devolve into violence when external guarantors to the agreements leave.

Fearon later revised the casualty figures upward, to 60,000, making "Iraq the ninth-deadliest civil war since 1945 in terms of annual casualties," and noted that everything that could be learned from earlier civil wars suggested that the Bush administration's agenda for Iraq was deeply misguided and likely to fail disastrously.[62] These were grim prognostications; here was another costly effect of applying the category. Quite predictably, there was the equally adamant view that it did fit the facts in Iraq. In December 2006, the Iraqi prime minister, Nouri al-Maliki, briskly rejected characterization of the conflict as a civil war and accused Kofi Annan of "burnishing the image" of Saddam Hussein as a viable belligerent. What Fearon and others could see clearly, commentators on the other side hotly denied.[63]

Longue-durée history proved useful in rebutting those who wanted to discover civil war in Iraq. In March 2006, the conservative Iranian journalist Amir Taheri published a short but wide-ranging essay brimming with historical counterexamples. He denied that Thucydides had written about civil war and saw Cicero as the first to popularize the term. He boiled the Roman definition down to its chief feature: "that it pitted one group of Roman citizens against another, with no armed intervention by foreign powers." This fit the wars of Sulla and Marius and Caesar and Pompey but not any of the many revolts in Roman history, such as Spartacus's. Taheri inferred from the Roman example that civil war "must be fought on political, not religious and/or ethnic grounds," and that "the conflict must be over the control of the whole disputed state and not aimed at splitting it into smaller units." These stringent criteria denied the name of civil war to almost every conflict ever called one, including the U.S. Civil War and the Algerian Civil War (1992–2002), except for the Russian, Spanish, and Lebanese. His conclusion? "Iraq is not in a civil war" and would not be until the multiple overlapping conflicts in the country coalesced into a two-sided, secular struggle for control of the Iraqi state with no foreign assistance or intervention.[64]

Later in the year, the eminent British military historian and journalist Sir John Keegan and the American commentator Bartle Bull offered a similar and only slightly more expansive dismissal of the term "civil war" to describe the violence in Iraq. For any conflict to earn the designation "civil war," they argued, "the violence must be 'civil,' it must be 'war,' and its aim must be either the exercise or the acquisition of national power." That is, it must be fought within a state by organized bodies of combatants drawn from a single national population who use force either to grasp or to retain overall political authority within the territory. Like Taheri, Keegan and Bull discovered from history that instances of civil war were "extremely rare," and they counted only five: the English Civil War (1642–49), the American (1861–65), the Russian (1918–21), the Spanish (1936–39), and the Lebanese (1975–90). Because the clashing parties in Iraq were fragmented, partly made up of non-Iraqi insurgents, and fighting for ends more contradictory or simply opaque than seizing national authority, Keegan and Bull concluded that Iraq's troubles did not qualify as the modern world's *sixth* civil war. Instead, they proposed that "the disorders in Iraq . . . are nearer to a politico-military struggle for power." They also echoed Erdoğan's analysis of the sectarian division between Sunnis and Shi'ites by noting, "It might be said that Islam is in a permanent state of civil war."[65]

The Iraqi government and representatives of the Bush administration officially denied that Iraq was in the grip of civil war. For the Iraqi government, to acknowledge otherwise would have implied it had lost authority. For the U.S. coalition, the characterization would have entailed a bevy of strategic implications. It could mean deciding which side, Sunni or Shi'ite, the coalition should support as it made its bets on an internal struggle for dominance. It could also imply that the invaders had unleashed sectarian enmities that previously had no outlet and that events were spinning out of their control. If such instability continued, then much higher troop levels would be needed to prevent it from spilling over Iraq's borders. Alternatively, a rapid but undignified withdrawal might be necessary to avoid being drawn ever deeper into indigenous dilemmas, which an alien presence could inflame but not resolve.

David Patten, an American sergeant with the Third U.S. Infantry Division in Baghdad who also held a doctorate in philosophy, warned in the summer of 2007 that "premature withdrawal could lead to a self-fulfilling prophecy, creating the conditions for a civil war that does not exist." Loose talk about civil war was little more than posturing and inexactitude, he charged, as when the Democratic representative John Murtha announced in January 2006, "We're fighting a civil war in Iraq," or Iraq's former interim prime minister, Ayad Allawi, lamented in March of that year, "If this is not civil war, then God knows what civil war is." Yet, Patten warned, "debate should not be political. Precision matters."[66]

Patten cited the U.S. Army's 1990 field manual for low-intensity conflict:

> **civil war:** A war between factions of the same country; there are five criteria for international recognition of this status: the contestants must control territory, have a functioning government, enjoy some foreign recognition, have identifiable regular armed forces, and engage in major military operations.[67]

This definition was designed to distinguish civil war from other kinds of conflicts on the grounds of being both more formally organized and on a larger scale than other forms of irregular warfare. Yet in few recent civil wars have both sides controlled territory and possessed a "functioning government," let alone one that has been recognized internationally. The classification also conforms with a peculiar and rather rare instance of civil war, one involving armed forces more typical of interstate wars in the industrial era, the major example being the U.S. Civil War, which was hardly a model for most of the civil wars of the twentieth and twenty-first centuries. The utility of this definition is therefore rather limited for observers other than the

U.S. Army, and even for them it is not clear of what use it would be under the present conditions of asymmetrical warfare.

Patten judged that only one of this definition's five criteria—that the contestants possessed control of territory—had been satisfied in Iraq. When he deployed Melvin Small and David Singer's social-scientific definition of civil war, however, he found that "Iraq has suffered *seven* separate civil wars in the last forty-five years" alone, a total spectacularly at odds with the *five* civil wars Keegan and Bull discovered in the whole of modern history since the mid-seventeenth century or Taheri's *three* since the end of the Roman republic.[68]

All such attempts at precision are as doomed as they are illusory for the simple reason that civil war is an essentially contested concept. Indeed, even the separate ascriptions of both "civil" and "war" can be contested and, in most social-scientific analyses, change according to specific factors such as location, intensity, and duration. There is also no agreement about just which features of civil war take priority in its various definitions or even as to how they might be applied consistently to particular conflicts. Being precise, in the sense of using clear definitions, turns out to be inescapably political. The elements of those definitions as much as their application are always matters for principled dispute. This seems to be especially true of civil war—an essentially contested concept about the essential elements of contestation.

*

By the twentieth century, various conceptions of supranational community had generated dark fears and clear-eyed analyses of civil war as taking place on a regional, continental, and ultimately planetary scale. As the imaginative limits of civil war grew, they coincided with the knowledge that civil wars were themselves becoming more transnational in their form and global in their impact. The rueful cosmopolitanism of Fénelon was belatedly echoed by the Italian anti-Fascist writer Gaetano Salvemini, by the German painter Franz Marc, and by the economist John Maynard Keynes at either end of World War I. In September 1914, Salvemini warned his readers that they were now witnessing not a war among nations but a "global civil war" of peoples, classes, and parties in which no one could remain neutral; two months later, in November 1914, Marc called the Great War "a European civil war" for the first time.[69] After the war, in 1919, Keynes regretfully recalled the common civilization in which France, Germany, Italy, Austria, Holland, Russia, Romania, and Poland "flourished together, . . . rocked together in a war, and . . . may fall together" in the course of "the European Civil War."[70] That term appealed to liberals and Marxists alike across the century as a means of describing the continuities between the two "world" wars, in Europe at least.[71]

Intimations of enmity on the eve of World War II had raised the fear of an "international civil war" between "reds and blacks" that cut across Europe's countries.[72] After the conflict came, this "gigantic civil war on the international scale" presented an opportunity for national liberation, according to the Indian Marxist M. N. Roy, writing in

1941–42.[73] A similar idea occurred later in the century to the right-wing revisionist German historian Ernst Nolte, for whom the entire period from 1917 to 1945 was a "European Civil War" in the sense of a struggle within a single community torn between the opposed forces of Bolshevism and Fascism.[74] The characterization of the entire span of the world wars as a single internal conflict would also find purchase in unexpectedly prominent places, such as when the former U.S. secretary of state Dean Acheson wrote of 1914–45 as a "European Civil War"—in effect, a civilizational war—that had intersected with an "Asian Civil War" in East Asia.[75]

Such an expansion of the idea of civil war was fostered by the Cold War, a conflict that itself would be called "a global civil war [that] has divided and tormented mankind," as President John F. Kennedy put it in his second State of the Union address in January 1962.[76] Two months later, in March 1962, Carl Schmitt spoke in a lecture in Spain about "the global civil war of revolutionary class enmity" unleashed by Leninist socialism.[77] In Schmitt's case, the expansive idea of civil war was not of Cold War vintage; it had been something of a term of art for him and his followers since 1939, as a critique of the pretensions of all revolutionary universalisms, whether applied to the French Revolution, the Revolutions of 1848, or the "present global world civil war" (as he called it in 1950), for example.[78] More sympathetic to those legacies were the American Students for a Democratic Society, whose *Port Huron Statement* in June 1962 predicted that "the war which seems so close will not be fought between the United States and Russia, not externally between two national entities, but as an international civil war throughout the unrespected and unprotected *civitas* which spans the world."[79] Also sympathetic was Hannah Arendt, who argued in *On Revolution* the following year that the twentieth century had seen a new phenomenon arising from the interrelatedness of wars and revolutions: "A world war appears like the consequences of revolution, a kind of civil war raging all over the earth, as even the Second World War was considered by a sizeable portion of public opinion and with considerable justification."[80]

"Global civil war" has more recently been used to denote the struggle between transnational terrorists like the partisans of al-Qaeda against established state-actors like the United States and Great Britain. In the hands of some of its proponents, this post-9/11 usage refers to the globalization of an internal struggle, especially that within a divided Islam, split between Sunnis and Shi'ites, that has been projected onto a world scale. As a broader metaphor for terrorism, "global civil war" has also been used to imply an unbridled struggle between opposed parties without any of the constraints placed on conventional forms of warfare, a return to a state of nature in which there are no rules for a war of all against all, and a peculiar species of conflict in which the boundaries between "internal" and "external," intrastate and interstate, conflict are utterly blurred.[81] In this vein, the critical theorists Michael Hardt and Antonio Negri wrote in 2004 that "our contemporary world is characterized by a generalized, permanent global civil war, by the constant threat of violence that effectively suspends democracy."[82] This was civil war as what Schmitt had called the "state of exception": the state of emergency determined by an all-powerful sovereign, in which the rule of law can be replaced by discretionary rule or martial law. "Faced with the unstoppable progression of what has been called a 'global civil war,'" Giorgio Agamben observed in 2005, "the state of exception tends increasingly to appear as the dominant paradigm of government in contemporary politics."[83]

Such metaphorical expansions of the ambit of civil war carry with them recognizable features from past ideas of civil war—for example, that of a defined community, a struggle for dominance within it, and an aberration from any normal course of politics or "civilization." The idea of "global" civil war carries with it, additionally, an idea of universal humanity affirmed by discerning conflict within a single capacious community, that world city or cosmopolis peopled by hostile fellow citizens. In these regards, the recent language of global civil war appears as an intensification of long-standing, originally Roman ideas of civil war that were later broadened and intensified by cosmopolitanism's expansion of empathy and broadening of horizons. Such a "global" civil war may not be susceptible to analytical measurement, in the way that social scientists trust other forms of conflict might be. Nor is it subject to legal regulation or humanitarian amelioration, as international lawyers believe that other wars not of an international character might be. Yet the internal complexities the term encompasses, the ideological freight it carries from earlier in the twentieth century, and the anti-

Islamic connotations implied by some of its users, mark it, like "civil war" itself, as an essentially contested concept. In this regard, the recent discussion of "global civil war" can be seen as an intensification or a qualification of the competing conceptions of civil war that gave rise to it.

The idea of global civil war has gained added currency from the rise of transnational terrorism.[84] This terrifying phenomenon brings warlike violence into the domestic sphere, most wrenchingly into the streets of the world's cities—New York in 2001, Madrid in 2004, London in 2005, Mumbai in 2008, Sydney in 2014, Paris and San Bernardino in 2015, and Brussels in 2016, for example. The attackers are often demonized as alien to the societies they assault—even when they are natural-born or naturalized citizens of the country concerned—and hence they are not identified in the same manner as those who classically constituted the contending parties in "civil" wars or wars among fellow citizens. At the same time, the proliferation of various forms of irregular warfare and the more elastic conceptions of war devised to understand and combat them have helped to loosen and stretch the metaphorical reach of civil war. Finally, the long-term decline of wars between states accompanied by the rise of wars within them—at least proportionately to overall levels of organized violence—has encouraged the belief that there might be no wars but civil wars in the future.[85] In the twenty-first century, all wars may indeed be civil wars, but for very different reasons and in senses more slippery— and more chilling—than those imagined by Torres Bodet in 1949.

Civil Wars of Words

The stakes are now so high for applying or withholding the label "civil war" it is unlikely that politics can ever be eliminated from consideration. We should now be better equipped to see why. Once we know more of civil war's fractious history, we can see its birthmarks more clearly; we discern its accumulated scars; and we may see how sensitive the wounds of civil war remain. Our ideas of civil war transmit the pain of two thousand years. And that pain continues to unsettle our politics down to the present.

Like the term "genocide," "civil war" now has not only political connotations but also legal implications that can trigger action from the international community; indeed, to draw the boundary between genocide and civil war—two essentially contested concepts, each with legal effects—can be even more contentious.[1] Civil war conjures so many images and associations of horror and destruction that it is hard to imagine any good that might come of using it. This sense goes to the very heart of the term, which is a paradox, even an oxymoron. What could possibly be "civil" about a war? "Civil" is an adjective that qualifies otherwise benign forms of human activity, like civil society and civil disobedience, and even the civil service. Its nearest relatives, etymologically and linguistically, are "civility" and "civilization." War does not bring people together peacefully or direct their energies nonviolently; it hardly implies politeness or polish when it involves so much bloodshed and death. Surely the darkness of war blots out any brightness of what can be called civil.

Some might say that this is "merely" semantic or rhetorical, simple jousting with words and not matters of real life—or death. Another response is the approach I have taken throughout this book: to assume that such arguments reveal a great deal about the way we define our communities, how we identify our enemies, and how we encourage our allies. Words are the way we construct our world; they are not the only way, to be sure, but they are the means by which we build it in conversation with our fellow human beings as we try to persuade them of our own point of view, to justify our actions, and to sway outsiders or even posterity. But in speaking of wars, words themselves are wielded as weapons, whether the blood is hot or the battlefield has gone cold: "Words about war— even the names of war—can be contentious indeed."[2] And no form of war is more nominally contentious than civil war.

The application of the term "civil war" may depend on whether you are a ruler or a rebel, the victor or the vanquished, an established government or an interested third party. As one leading scholar of contemporary civil war has written, "The description of a conflict as a civil war carries symbolic and political weight since the term can confer or deny legitimacy. Indeed the very use (or not) of the term is part of the conflict itself."[3] Or, as Thomas De Quincey exclaimed more succinctly, "The casuistries of civil war— how vast!"[4] The battle over names can continue long after the conflict has ceased; for example, using the term "civil war" to describe the struggle between the Italian Resistance and the Fascist government during World War II has remained controversial because of the equivalence it seemed to imply between the two sides.[5]

More immediately during ongoing conflicts, the other powers of the earth may hedge their bets or decide that these wars are beyond their control because they are solely "civil," that is, internal, matters. The consequences of such decisions have been central to major conflicts across the centuries and around the world. For example, was the American Revolution a revolution only for the colonists in North America, or was it a civil war within the British Empire? Was the U.S. Civil War a war between equal opposing parties or a rebellion inside the boundaries of a single sovereign state? Did calling the conflicts in Rwanda and Bosnia in the 1990s "civil" wars allow the rest of the world to deny responsibility for what took place behind closed borders? And did naming what took place in Darfur after 2003 "genocide" rather than civil war render a fundamentally political conflict instead intractably ethnic, and hence beyond hope of reasonable resolution?[6]

The choice of category has moral as well as political consequences. It can be a matter of life or death for tens of thousands of people, usually those least able to control how their own destinies are shaped. Deciding whether what we see is indeed a civil war can have political, military, legal, and economic consequences for those outside the war-torn country as well as for those within it. As we have heard, the international community's motive for acknowledging the existence of such a conflict may be to avoid involvement: a civil war, it is sometimes assumed, is somebody else's business; outsiders should stay away. Conversely, the label can be applied to authorize intervention after a state has collapsed and a humanitarian crisis ensues.[7] These polarities both in motive and in response are also part of the concept's paradoxical nature.

The decision that a civil war is in progress may also determine which provisions of the laws of war and international humanitarian law can be applied while the fighting takes place as well as later, when the aggressors are judged and war criminals are potentially identified. The financial consequences are likewise momentous: millions of dollars of humanitarian aid from the UN and its agencies can also depend on the application or withholding of the label of civil war to a conflict in a member state. In all these situations, knowing civil war when you see it can be imprecise, dangerous, and expensive. Hence the great urgency of deciding on a definition and of applying it as rigorously as possible to particular cases. The pressure to define civil war is often inversely related to the political stakes for offering such a definition: the higher the pressure to be precise, the greater the chance that exactitude will itself be a source of political contention.

The very name "civil war" can bring legitimacy to forms of violence that would otherwise be suppressed or decried. At least since the nineteenth century, if violence within a state can be called a "war," rather than a rebellion or an insurrection, for example, then those waging it are liable for the protections of combatants (as well as the penalties for those who violate the laws of war). To have a conflict called a "war"—even if a "civil" war—can bring with it recognition from the international community, and in turn the possibility of various kinds of external support: economic, legal, even military. Recall, for example, the international recognition accorded in 2011–12 to the National Transitional Council in Libya during the Libyan civil war.[8] While the historical associations of the term "civil war" may be overwhelmingly negative, at certain times and in particular places its legal and political consequences have been positive.

Layered into current conceptions of civil war are its many meanings from the past, as well as from the surrounding discourses—of history, politics, law, and social science, for example—that have laid down their own strata of significance. From history, especially from Roman history, came the understanding of civil war as recurrent and sequential. From politics, civil war derived its links with civilization and sovereignty, rebellion and revolution. From law arose both the effort to constrain civil war within a precise definition and the attempt to regulate it according to legal protocols. And from the modern social sciences sprang the examination of civil war as a cumulative, global phenomenon, ripe for aggregation and susceptible to analysis as to its causes and consequences. These broad waves in the conceptual flow of civil war carried it across the centuries but also left choppiness in their wake. Civil war became so contested a concept because it could be used competitively and because it gradually gained prestige as a subject, particularly after legal thinkers such as Vattel and Lieber appointed it as a mark of belligerence, a signal for intervention, or a spur to humanitarian regulation. All these features remain contingently attached to civil war into the present, as evidence of its multiple, accumulated pasts and of the contestation over it, by now perhaps too precious ever to be settled.

Civil war is an inheritance humanity may not be able to escape. By this, I do not mean that humans are inherently competitive, greedy, and aggressive or that our lot will always be societal suicide—to drive swords into our own entrails, as Lucan might have put it. Instead, I mean that civil war is one of those indispensable concepts that, once invented, has proved to be surprisingly translatable. It moved from Rome into many major world languages without difficulty and lost none of its accumulated awkward baggage. That innovation that had eluded the Greeks became under the pithy oxymoron and compelling historical narrative devised by the Romans an unassailable idea until the nineteenth century. Even the utopian promise of revolutionary change could not dethrone civil war from the repertoire of political thought, if only because politics itself was always a form of civil war by other, less deadly means. In this way did the idea acquire the bewitching power of something not invented but discovered.

What can the historian do in the face of such a force? There are perhaps two ways to respond. One would be to try to recover some presumed essence of the term, to reduce somehow its profusion of meanings into something more manageable. The other would be to reconstruct it in all its complexity, to uncover just how it became so fraught with significance. As we have seen in recent debates about conflicts in Iraq and Syria, attempts to confine civil war within a single definition have led only to further complication and contestation. It would seem better, then, to work from the other direction and to excavate the various meanings of civil war as they have been laid down over the centuries. Abandoning the first approach's illusory promise of simplicity, one may yet be spared its inevitable result of perplexity.

Where a philosopher, a lawyer, or even a political scientist might find only confusion in disputes over the term "civil war," the historian scents opportunity. All definitions of civil war are necessarily contextual and conflictual. The historian's task is not to come up with a better one, on which all sides could agree, but to ask where such competing conceptions came from, what they have meant, and how they arose from the experience of those who lived through what was called by that name or who have attempted to understand it in the past.

Civil war is, first and foremost, a category of experience; the participants usually know they are in the midst of civil war long before international organizations declare it to be so. Yet it is an experience refracted through language and memory, via the record of past civil wars and the ways they were thought and argued about, often in distant times and far-flung places, and out of fears that the civil wars in one's own country's history might come again. It is an experience framed—some might say distorted—by the conceptual heritage of civil war. Once the concept had emerged, it became irrevocably available as a lens through which conflicts could be viewed and as a weapon with which the rhetorical battles over their significance would be waged. Civil war must still be understood in the realm of ideas that are both inherited and contested. Struggles over its meaning will ensure that its multiple futures will be as controversial and as transformative as its contentious past.

Afterword

There is a bitter Russian saying: the past is unpredictable. Every historian knows how true that can be. What we find historically important, what problems are worth scholarly investigation, what topics come to seem most urgent—all these change in light of current concerns. Sometimes only a coincidence, a moment when past and present illuminatingly intersect, can point the historian to the right question. This book began with just such a coincidence, as two battles over the meaning of civil war chimed across time.

Civil war was not a subject I ever expected, much less wanted, to spend my time on. And yet, in late 2006, I was working at the magnificent Huntington Library in San Marino, California. The library sits barely twenty miles from South Los Angeles, where the L.A. riots had taken place in 1992, but you would never guess it from the low-slung neoclassical buildings, its world-class gardens, or its renowned collection of British art. My theme arrived there during what turned out to be the most destructive period

of the Second Gulf War. At its bloody height, between
October 2006 and January 2007, an average of three thousand people a month—soldiers and civilians, Iraqis and
invaders—were dying in the hostilities in Iraq.[1]

At just that moment, I discovered that the papers of
Francis Lieber were among the Huntington's rich collec-
tions. Matters that Lieber had been among the earliest to
treat systematically, at least in the context of U.S. military
law—the status of enemy combatants, the treatment of
prisoners taken on the battlefield, and the rules of military justice—were becoming headline news in light of the
George W. Bush administration's pursuit of the "Global
War on Terror." As I worked through Lieber's letters and
the drafts, I found the past rhyming with the present in
insistent and troubling ways around the challenge of civil
war. Debate was beginning to flare in the United States,
in Iraq, and beyond about the character of the contemporaneous conflict in Mesopotamia. Lieber's perplexity in
the mid-nineteenth century about defining civil war and
the parallel complexity in the early twenty-first century of
applying the term in Iraq struck me as two stops along a
much longer historical journey that would go from ancient
Rome via the early modern period right up to the present.

A few weeks after my epiphany at the Huntington,
another chance encounter inspired me to work on civil
war. In February 2007, I launched my book, *The Declaration of Independence: A Global History*, at the John Carter
Brown Library in Providence, Rhode Island. The library's
director at the time, the historian and former presidential
speechwriter Ted Widmer, told me he was just completing

a work about the United States' mission to export freedom to the world.[2] Francis Lieber and the Iraq debates
were very much on my mind; I ungraciously told Ted that
instead of a story of the American export of liberty what
we needed was a much darker history, of civil war and its
meanings across time. Later that evening, a swift trawl of
the library catalogs convinced me that no one had ever
reconstructed that story. I decided I had to write a sequel
to my book on the Declaration of Independence and follow that study of *state making* with a history of *state breaking*. The result, many years, and many civil wars, later, is
Civil Wars: A History in Ideas.

*

Every book is collaborative; each is collaborative in its own
way. This one is the product of wide-ranging conversa-
tions, much good luck, and great gifts of friendship over
many years and in many places.

My main institutional debts are to the Huntington
Library, Queen's University Belfast, and Harvard University. I would have had no inkling of this project without
the Mellon Research Fellowship I held at the Huntington
in 2006–7. My first thanks therefore go to Roy Ritchie,
then the library's research director, for not asking too
many questions when the course of my work changed over
that year.

Two exhilarating events, in Belfast and in Cambridge,
Massachusetts, framed the writing of the book. In May
2010, I presented a very early version of my argument

as the Wiles Lectures at Queen's University. The charge to the Wiles lecturer is as intimidating as it is inspiring: to "relate the lecturer's researches to the general history of civilization" and to "bring out the results of reflection on the wider implications of more detailed historical studies." I am greatly indebted to the Wiles Trustees at the time— Sean Connolly, Robert Evans, David Hayton, and, above all, the late Chris Bayly—for the immense honor of their invitation and for a unique opportunity to place ideas of civil war within "the general history of civilization." I am also very grateful to Liz Cohen, then chair of my department, for relaxing my duties so that I could write and deliver the lectures at a particularly busy time.

Perhaps the greatest of the Wiles lecturer's many pleasures and privileges is the chance to invite a team of scholars to probe one's arguments in a series of bracing evening seminars tempered by fine Irish whiskey. Special gratitude goes to Duncan Bell, Richard Bourke, Mike Braddick, Michael Hopkinson, Colin Kidd, Jane Ohlmeyer, Josiah Osgood, Jennifer Pitts, and Adam Smith for coming to Belfast and offering their counsel, as well as to Richard English, Peter Gray, the late Keith Jeffery, David Livingstone, and Chris Marsh from the home team at Queen's. David Hayton, in his capacity as head of the School of History and Anthropology at the time, was an impeccable host for that memorable week.

Five years later, in April 2015, I presented a draft of the manuscript to a workshop sponsored by Harvard's Center for American Political Studies. Heartfelt thanks to Gabriella Blum, Darrin McMahon, Sam Moyn, Eric

Nelson, John Stauffer, and Richard Thomas, as well as to Peter Gordon, James Hankins, and Jim Kloppenberg, for their ruthless criticism and friendly advice, and to Joshua Ehrlich for keeping a record of the discussion. Dan Carpenter's generous support and Laura Donaldson's organizational skills were crucial to making the workshop such a success. Warm gratitude also goes to Michèle Lowrie and John McCormick for their responses during an equally invigorating seminar a few weeks later at the University of Chicago's Neubauer Collegium for Culture and Society and to the dedicated group who discussed the final manuscript at Universität Bielefeld in June 2016. Sabbatical support from Harvard's Weatherhead Center for International Affairs was indispensable to the completion of the book.

I have also been fortunate to present parts of my argument to acute and engaged audiences around the world. For welcome invitations to speak on civil war, I owe many thanks to Chris Bayly (Cambridge), Alastair Bellany (Rutgers), Kenzie Bok (Cambridge), Eva Botella Ordinas (Real Colegio Complutense), Richard Bourke (the Nicolai Rubinstein Lecture, Queen Mary), Nigel Bowles (the Sir John Elliott Lecture, Oxford), Charles Crouch (Savannah), Don Doyle (Charleston), Dan Edelstein (Stanford), Yasuo Endo (Tokyo), Laura Frader (Northeastern), Alison Games (Georgetown), Rebecca Goetz (the Ervin Frederick Kalb Lecture, Rice), Eva Marlene Hausteiner and Stefan Schlelein (Humboldt-Universität), Will Hay (Mississippi State), Russ Heller (Boise), Jakob Huber and Nimrod Kovner (LSE), Jun Iwai (Seigakuin), Paul Kennedy

(Yale), Christina Koulouri (Panteion), Alison LaCroix
(the Maurice and Muriel Fulton Lecture, Chicago Law
School), Jonathan Lear (Chicago), Sandy Levinson (the
Tom Sealy Lecture, University of Texas School of Law),
Matthijs Lok (Amsterdam), Dirk Moses (European Uni-
versity Institute), Panagiotis Roilos (Harvard), Helena
Rosenblatt (the John Patrick Diggins Memorial Lecture,
CUNY Graduate Center), Joan-Pau Rubiés and Neil
Safier (Huntington Library), Katherine Sawyer (Louisi-
ana State), Brian Schoen (the Costa Lecture, Ohio), Javier
Fernández Sebastián (Buenos Aires), Alex Semyonov (St.
Petersburg), Eric Slauter (Chicago), Glenda Sluga (Syd-
ney), Courtney Weiss Smith (Wesleyan), Peter Stacey
(UCLA), Simon Stern and Anna Su (the Katherine Baker
Memorial Lecture, Toronto Faculty of Law), Miles Tay-
lor (York), Spyridon Tegos (Rethymnon), Bruno Tribout
(London), Luciana Villas Bôas (Rio de Janeiro), Chris
Waters (Providence and Williams), Thomas Welskopp
(Bielefeld), Richard Whatmore (Sussex), Caroline Win-
terer (Stanford), and Ângela Xavier (Lisbon).

For many other informative exchanges over the years,
I am grateful to Cliff Ando, Charles Bartlett, Gary Bass,
David Bell, Peter Bol, Hannah Callaway, Elizabeth Cross,
Emma Dench, Ian Donaldson, Dan Edelstein, John Elli-
ott, Philip Fileri, Juan Francisco Fuentes, Michael Geyer,
Ninon Grangé, Jo Guldi, Bernard Harcourt, Jo Innes,
Maya Jasanoff, João Feres Júnior, Daniel Jütte, Shruti
Kapila, Ville Kari, Robin Kiera, Krishan Kumar, Carsten
Hjort Lange, Nicholas McDowell, Adam Mestyan, Sankar
Muthu, Louiza Odysseos, Anthony Pagden, Erika Pani,

John Pocock, Ingrid Purnell, Sophie Rosenfeld, Joan-Pau
Rubiés, Nick Sacco, Elaine Scarry, Rob Schneider, Mira
Siegelberg, Zoltan Simon, Emile Simpson, Giulia Sissa,
Lauri Tähtinen, Georgios Varouxakis, Ted Widmer, John
Witt, Susan Woodward, Philip Wynn, John Zammito, and
Andrew Zimmerman. I must also thank Jonathan Bate for
encouragement at a crucial point, Joshua Eaton for a per-
ceptive reading of an early draft of the manuscript, and,
above all, the incomparable staff of the Harvard History
Department, especially Janet Hatch, Ann Kaufman, Elena
Palladino, and Kimberly O'Hagan, for keeping me afloat
during my time as department chair.

The unwavering support of my agent, Andrew Wylie,
and of everyone at the Wylie Agency, particularly James
Pullen and Sarah Chalfant, has been sorely tried but
greatly appreciated, as has the patience of my publishers,
George Andreou, Heather McCallum, and Lilia Moritz
Schwarcz. Thank you all.

Finally, warmest thanks to those who cheered me on
over the long haul: Alison Bashford, Joyce Chaplin, the
three Ds, Graham Earles, Andrew Fitzmaurice, Stella
Ghervas, Eileen Gillooly, Peter Gordon, Jim Kloppenberg, Eric Nelson, and Quentin Skinner.

I dedicate this book to the memory of two steadfast
friends and inspirational historians who passed away as I
was finishing the manuscript. Their legacy endures.

Notes

INTRODUCTION
Confronting Civil War

1. John Lewis Gaddis, "The Long Peace: Elements of Security in the Postwar International System," in *Long Peace*, 214–45; Mueller, *Retreat from Doomsday*; Mandelbaum, *Dawn of Peace in Europe*; Howard, *The Invention of Peace and the Reinvention of War*; Sheehan, *Where Have All the Soldiers Gone?*
2. Allanson, Melander, and Themnér, "Organized Violence, 1989–2016"; Pettersson and Wallensteen, "Armed Conflicts, 1946–2014."
3. Braumoeller, "Is War Disappearing?"; Newman, "Conflict Research and the 'Decline' of Civil War"; Sarkees, "Patterns of Civil Wars in the Twentieth Century."
4. Ghervas, "La paix par le droit, ciment de la civilisation en Europe?"
5. Immanuel Kant, "Toward Perpetual Peace" (1795), in *Practical Philosophy*, trans. Gregor, 317, 351.
6. Goldstein, *Winning the War on War*; Pinker, *Better Angels of Our Nature*.
7. Hironaka, *Neverending Wars*, 4–5; Paul Collier, Lisa Chauvet, and Håvard Hagre, "The Security Challenge in Conflict-Prone

Countries," in *Global Crises, Global Solutions*, ed. Lomborg, 72, 99 (quoted); Skaperdas et al., *Costs of Violence*; World Bank, *World Development Report 2011*; Dunne, "Armed Conflicts"; Hoeffler, "Alternative Perspective."

8. Collier, *Wars, Guns, and Votes*, 139 (quoted); Collier, Hoeffler, and Söderbom, "On the Duration of Civil War"; Fearon, "Why Do Some Civil Wars Last So Much Longer Than Others?"; Walter, "Does Conflict Beget Conflict?"; Hironaka, *Neverending Wars*, 1, 50; World Bank, *World Development Report 2011*, 57.

9. Collier, *Bottom Billion*; Rice, Graff, and Lewis, *Poverty and Civil War*.

10. Mission statement, Centre for the Study of Civil War, Peace Research Institute Oslo, http://www.prio.org/Programmes /Extensions/Centre-for-the-Study-of-Civil-War/About/.

11. Enzensberger, *Civil War*, 12.

12. Agamben, *Stasis*, trans. Heron, 2. Compare Grangé, *Oublier la guerre civile?*, 7: "il est vrai que la guerre civile est occultée par les traités politiques"; Kissane, *Nations Torn Asunder*, 3: "There has been, in the history of political thought, no systematic treatise on civil war."

13. Mason, "Evolution of Theory on Civil War and Revolution," 63–66.

14. Allanson, Melander, and Wallensteen, "Organized Violence, 1989–2016," 576; Gleditsch, "Transnational Dimensions of Civil War"; Checkel, *Transnational Dynamics of Civil War*.

15. Mayer, *Furies*, 323 ("If war is hell, then civil war belongs to hell's deepest and most infernal regions"); Kalyvas, *Logic of Violence in Civil War*, 52–53.

16. Lucan, *Bellum civile* (1.31–32), in Lucan, *Civil War*, trans. Braund, 3–4; Michel de Montaigne, "Of Bad Meanes Emploied to a Good End" (*Essais*, 2.23), in *Essays Written in French by Michael Lord of Montaigne*, trans. Florio, 384; Frank Aiken, Aug. 3, 1922, quoted in Hopkinson, *Green Against Green*, 273.

17. Eliot, *Milton*, 3.

18. De Gaulle, quoted in Marañon Moya, "El general De Gaulle, en Toledo" ("Todas las guerras son malas . . . Pero las guerras

civiles, en las que en ambas trincheras hay hermanos, son imper-
donables, porque la paz no nace cuando la guerra termina").

19. Enzensberger, *Civil War*, trans. Spence and Chalmers, 11.

20. Girard, *Violence and the Sacred*; Giraldo Ramírez, *El rastro de Caín*;
Jacoby, *Bloodlust*; Esposito, *Terms of the Political*, 123–34. As Bill
Kissane notes, the term for civil war in modern Hebrew approxi-
mates to "war between brothers." Kissane, *Nations Torn Asunder*, 7.

21. Osgood, *Caesar's Legacy*, 3, citing Brunt, *Italian Manpower*,
225 *B.C.–A.D. 14*, 509–12.

22. Braddick, *God's Fury, England's Fire*, xii.

23. Faust, "'Numbers on Top of Numbers,'" 997; Faust, *This Republic of Suffering*, xi. Neely, *Civil War and the Limits of Destruction*, 208–16, criticized these figures, but Hacker, "Census-Based
Count of the Civil War Dead," has since persuasively revised
them upward from an estimated 620,000 to 750,000 dead

24. Kloppenberg, *Toward Democracy*, 21–60.

25. Clarendon, *The History of the Rebellion and Civil Wars in England,
Begun in the Year 1641*.

26. Schmitt, *Ex Captivitate Salus*, 56 ("Der Bürgerkrieg hat etwas
besonders Grausames. Er ist ein Bruderkrieg, weil er innerhalb
einer gemeinsamen . . . politischen Einheit . . . geführt wird, und
weil beide kämpfenden Seiten diese gemeinsame Einheit gleich-
zeitig absolut behaupten und absolut verneinen").

27. U.S. Department of War, *War of the Rebellion*.

28. Gingrich, quoted in Stauffer, "Civility, Civil Society, and Civil
Wars," 88.

29. "Pour Valls, le FN peut conduire à la 'guerre civile,'" *Le Monde*,
Dec. 11, 2015: "Il y a deux options pour notre pays. Il y a une
option qui est celle de l'extrême droite qui, au fond, prône la division. Cette division peut conduire à la guerre civile et il y a une
autre vision qui est celle de la République et des valeurs, qui est le
rassemblement."

30. Brass, *Theft of an Idol*, 3–20; Kalyvas, "Ontology of 'Political Violence'"; Kalyvas, "Promises and Pitfalls of an Emerging Research
Program"; Kissane and Sitter, "Ideas in Conflict."

31. Kaldor, *New and Old Wars;* Kalyvas, "'New' and 'Old' Civil Wars"; Münkler, *New Wars.*

32. Geuss, "Nietzsche and Genealogy"; Bevir, "What Is Genealogy?"

33. Skinner, "Genealogy of the Modern State," 325.

34. Nietzsche, *On the Genealogy of Morality,* 51.

35. Ibid., 53 (my emphasis).

36. Gallie, "Essentially Contested Concepts"; Collier, Hidalgo, and Maciuceanu, "Essentially Contested Concepts."

37. Gallie, preface to *Philosophy and the Historical Understanding,* 8–9.

38. Kalyvas, "Civil Wars," 417.

39. For helpful overviews, see Sambanis, "Review of Recent Advances and Future Directions in the Literature on Civil War"; Collier and Sambanis, *Understanding Civil War;* Blattman and Miguel, "Civil War."

40. Uppsala Conflict Data Program (1948–present), http://www.pcr.uu.se/research/UCDP/.

41. The Correlates of War Project, http://www.correlatesofwar.org/; Small and Singer, *Resort to Arms;* Gleditsch, "Revised List of Wars Between and Within Independent States, 1816–2002"; Sarkees and Wayman, *Resort to War;* Reiter, Stam, and Horowitz, "Revised Look at Interstate Wars, 1816–2007."

42. Dixon, "What Causes Civil Wars?," 730; Lounsbery and Pearson, *Civil Wars,* viii; Newman, *Understanding Civil Wars.*

43. Though for a recent exception, spanning the centuries from ancient Rome to Afghanistan, see Armitage et al., *"AHR Roundtable: Ending Civil Wars."*

44. Guldi and Armitage, *History Manifesto;* Armitage et al., "La longue durée en débat."

45. Armitage, "What's the Big Idea?"; McMahon, "Return of the History of Ideas?"; McMahon, *Divine Fury,* xiii.

46. McMahon, *Happiness;* McMahon, *Divine Fury;* Forst, *Toleration in Conflict;* Rosenfeld, *Common Sense;* Fitzmaurice, *Sovereignty, Property, and Empire, 1500–2000;* Kloppenberg, *Toward Democracy.*

47. Fitzmaurice, *Sovereignty, Property, and Empire, 1500–2000,* 20; Dubos, *Le mal extrême.*

48. DeRouen and Heo, *Civil Wars of the World*, is a more manageable compendium on the topic.

49. Manicas, "War, Stasis, and Greek Political Thought"; Berent, "*Stasis*, or the Greek Invention of Politics."

50. Gardet, "Fitna"; As-Sirri, *Religiös-politische Argumentation im frühen Islam (610–685)*; Ayalon, "From Fitna to Thawra"; Martinez-Gross and Tixier du Mesnil, eds., "La *fitna*: Le désordre politique dans l'Islam médiéval."

51. Similar terms for "internal war" are found in Finnish, Persian, and Turkish. Kissane, *Nations Torn Asunder*, 39.

52. Armitage, "Every Great Revolution Is a Civil War."

53. Armitage, "Cosmopolitanism and Civil War."

I

Inventing Civil War
The Roman Tradition

1. Loraux, *Divided City*, trans. Pache and Fort, 108.

2. Nicolet, *Demokratia et aristokratia*; Wiedemann, "Reflections of Roman Political Thought in Latin Historical Writing," 519.

3. "Aemulumque Thucydidis Sallustium": Velleius Paterculus, *Historiae* 2.36.2; Scanlon, *Influence of Thucydides on Sallust*; Pelling, "'Learning from That Violent Schoolmaster.'"

4. Botteri, "*Stásis.*"

5. Clavadetscher-Thürlemann, Πόλεμος δίκαιος *und bellum iustum*, 178–83; Wynn, *Augustine on War and Military Service*, 128–31.

6. Rosenberger, *Bella et expeditiones*.

7. Keenan, *Wars Without End*, 32.

8. Jal, *La guerre civile à Rome*, 19–21; Urbainczyk, *Slave Revolts in Antiquity*, 100–115; Schiavone, *Spartacus*.

9. Robert Brown, "The Terms *Bellum Sociale* and *Bellum Civile* in the Late Republic," 103.

10. On Roman understandings of the *civitas*, see Ando, *Roman Social Imaginaries*, 7–14.

11. Harvey, *Rebel Cities;* Hazan, *History of the Barricade.*

12. Brett, *Changes of State.*

13. Plato, *Republic* 462a–b, in *Collected Dialogues,* 701 (translation adapted).

14. Gehrke, *Stasis.*

15. Price, *Thucydides and Internal War,* 30–32.

16. Plato, *Republic* 470b–c, in *Collected Dialogues,* 709.

17. Plato, *Laws* 628b, 629d, in *Collected Dialogues,* 1229 (translation adapted), 1231; Price, *Thucydides and Internal War,* 67–70.

18. Stouratis, "Byzantine War Against Christians"; Kyriakidis, "Idea of Civil War in Thirteenth- and Fourteenth-Century Byzantium."

19. Panourgía, *Dangerous Citizens,* 81–86.

20. Loraux, *"Oikeios polemos."*

21. Plato, *Republic* 471e, in *Collected Dialogues,* 710.

22. Thucydides, *Eight Bookes of the Peloponnesian Warre* 3.81–83, trans. Hobbes, 187–90. The section immediately following this description of *stasis* (3.84) is now generally accepted to be a later interpolation. Fuks, "Thucydides and the Stasis in Corcyra."

23. Hobbes's was the first English translation of Thucydides from the Greek; an earlier English version, *The Hystory Writtone by Thucidides the Athenyan of the Warre, Whiche Was Betwene the Peloponesians and the Athenyans,* trans. Nicolls, was translated from the French version of Claude de Seysell. It, too, generally avoids "civil *war*" in favor of "civile dissention," "cyvill seditions," or "cyvill battailles," for example. On the political context of Hobbes's translation in the 1620s—therefore quite distinct from the civil wars of the 1640s—see Hoekstra, "Hobbes's Thucydides," 551–57; on the modern reception of Thucydides more generally, see Harloe and Morley, eds., *Thucydides and the Modern World.*

24. On Thucydides and contemporary medicine, see Price, *Thucydides and Internal War,* 14–18, and on the analogies between his description of *stasis* and his treatment of the plague at Athens (2.47–58), see Orwin, "Stasis and Plague."

25. Thucydides, *Eight Bookes of the Peloponnesian Warre,* trans. Hobbes, 198, 199 (i.e., pp. 188, 189). On the linguistic conse-

quences of *stasis*, see Loraux, "Thucydide et la sédition dans les mots."

26. Thucydides, *War of the Peloponnesians and the Athenians* 3.74, trans. Mynott, 208.

27. I am very grateful to Richard Thomas for stressing this important point about the spatial dimensions of civil war, as against *stasis*.

28. Thomas De Quincey, "['Greece Under the Romans,' draft]" (Jan.–March 1844), in *Works of Thomas De Quincey*, 15:539 (footnote). My thanks to Jennifer Pitts for alerting me to this passage.

29. Thucydides, *War of the Peloponnesians and the Athenians*, trans. Mynott, 212n1.

30. Thucydides, *Eight Bookes of the Peloponnesian Warre*, trans. Hobbes, 198 (i.e., 188).

31. Loraux, *Divided City*, 107–8, 197–213; Ando, *Law, Language, and Empire in the Roman Tradition*, 3–4.

32. Thucydides, *War of the Peloponnesians and the Athenians* 4.64, trans. Mynott, 273; Loraux, "Oikeios polemos."

33. Brunt, *Social Conflicts in the Roman Republic*; Lintott, *Violence in Republican Rome*.

34. On the distinction between tumults and civil war, see Jal, "'Tumultus' et 'bellum ciuile' dans les Philippiques de Cicéron"; Grangé, "*Tumultus* et *tumulto*."

35. Livy, *History of Rome* 1.7, in *Rise of Rome*, trans. Luce, 10–11; Wiseman, *Remus*.

36. Lucan, *Bellum civile* 1.95, in *Civil War*, trans. Braund, 5; also quoted in Augustine, *City of God Against the Pagans* 15.5, ed. and trans. Dyson, 640.

37. Beard, *SPQR*, 73–74.

38. On the meaning of *res publica*, see Lind, "Idea of the Republic and the Foundations of Roman Political Liberty."

39. Livy, *History of Rome* 2.1, in *Rise of Rome*, 71; Arena, *Libertas and the Practice of Politics in the Late Roman Republic*.

40. Raaflaub, *Social Struggles in Archaic Rome*.

41. See, for example, Draper, *Dictatorship of the Proletariat*, 11–27 (on "dictatorship"); Lekas, *Marx on Classical Antiquity*; Bonnell, "'A

Very Valuable Book': Karl Marx and Appian." Marx's use of the Roman language of internal conflict would merit much further research.

42. Plutarch, "Tiberius and Gaius Gracchus," in *Roman Lives*, trans. Waterfield, 98–99, 113–14.

43. Appian, *Civil Wars* 1.1–2, trans. Carter, 1; Price, "Thucydidean *Stasis* and the Roman Empire in Appian's Interpretation of History."

44. Ibid. 1.1–2, trans. Carter, 1–2 (translation amended).

45. Jal, "'Hostis (Publicus)' dans la littérature latine de la fin de la République."

46. Flower, "Rome's First Civil War and the Fragility of Republican Culture," 75–78.

47. Sherwin-White, *Roman Citizenship*, 40, 264–67.

48. Keaveney, *Sulla*, 45–50; Seager, "Sulla."

49. Raaflaub, "Caesar the Liberator?"

50. Appian, *Civil Wars* 1.59–60, trans. Carter, 32–33.

51. Ibid. 1.1, 1.55, trans. Carter, 1, 30.

2

Remembering Civil War
Roman Visions

1. At least according to the philosopher Seneca the Elder, who preserved his words: "Optima civilis belli defensio oblivio est." Seneca, *Controversiae* 10.3.5, quoted in Gowing, *Empire and Memory*, 82. The historian Josiah Osgood has recently suggested that for the Romans the "best defense was to half-forget." Osgood, "Ending Civil War at Rome," 1689. More generally, see Flower, *Art of Forgetting*.

2. Caesar, *Civil War* 2.29, 3.1, ed. and trans. Damon, 166, 192; Francis W. Kelsey, "Title of Caesar's Work on the Gallic and Civil Wars," 230; Batstone and Damon, *Caesar's "Civil War*," 8–9,

31–32; Brown, "The Terms *Bellum Sociale* and *Bellum Civile* in the Late Republic," 113–18.

3. Caesar, *Civil War* 1.22, ed. and trans. Damon, 35; Raaflaub, *Dignitatis contentio*.

4. On later representations of Caesar's crossing of the Rubicon, see Wyke, *Caesar*, 66–89, 263–66.

5. Appian, *Civil Wars* 2.35, trans. Carter, 88; Plutarch, *Caesar* 32, in *Roman Lives*, trans. Waterfield, 328–39. The line is usually quoted in Suetonius's Latin: "Iacta alea est." Suetonius, *The Deified Julius* 32, in *Suetonius*, trans. Rolfe, 1:76.

6. Suetonius, *Deified Julius* 31–32, in *Suetonius*, trans. Rolfe, 1:74–77; Lucan, *Bellum civile* (1.190–92, 225–27), in *Civil War*, trans. Braund, 8, 9.

7. Heuzé, "Comment peindre le passage du Rubicon?"

8. Caesar, *Civil War* 1.8, ed. and trans. Damon, 15.

9. Bonaparte, *Précis des guerres de Jules César*, 97–98 ("En passant le Rubicon, César avait déclaré la guerre civile et bravé les anathèmes prononcés contre les généraux qui passeraient en armes le Rubicon: ils étaient voués aux dieux infernaux"); Poignault, "Napoleon Ier et Napoleon III lecteurs de Jules César," 329–36.

10. Brown, "Terms *Bellum Sociale* and *Bellum Civile* in the Late Republic," 104.

11. Cicero, *De imperio Cn. Pompei* 28, in *Political Speeches*, trans. Berry, 119 (my emphasis).

12. Seager, *Pompey the Great*, 25–36, 43–48.

13. Lucan, *Bellum civile* 1.12, in *Civil War*, trans. Braund, 3; Schmitt, *Glossarium*, 32 ("Im Bürgerkrieg gibt es keinen Triumph"); Beard, *Roman Triumph*, 123–24, 303–4.

14. Valerius Maximus, *Memorable Deeds and Sayings* 2.8.7, quoted in Lange, "Triumph and Civil War in the Late Republic," 69–70.

15. Östenberg, "*Veni Vidi Vici* and Caesar's Triumph," 823.

16. Lange, "Triumph and Civil War in the Late Republic," 74, 76–78, 82–84. More generally, see Lange, *Triumphs in the Age of Civil War*.

17. Cicero, *De officiis* 1.85–86 ("apud Atheniensis magnae discordiae, in nostra re publica non solum seditiones sed etiam pestifera bella civilia"), in *On Duties*, 86–87, quoting Plato, *Republic* 420b (translation adapted).

18. Horace, *Odes* 2.1, in *Complete Odes and Epodes*, trans. West, 56; Mendell, "Epic of Asinius Pollio"; Henderson, *Fighting for Rome*, 108–59.

19. Tacitus, *Annals* 1.3, quoted in Harriet I. Flower, *Roman Republics* (Princeton, N.J.: Princeton University Press, 2010), 154 ("etiam senes plerique inter belli civilia nati: quotus quisque reliquus qui rem publicam vidisset"); Keitel, "Principate and Civil War in the *Annals* of Tacitus."

20. Gowing, "'Caesar Grabs My Pen,'" 250.

21. Masters, *Poetry and Civil War in Lucan's "Bellum Civile."*

22. On Lucan's reception history, see the relevant chapters in Asso, ed., *Brill's Companion to Lucan.*

23. Lucan, *In Cath Catharda;* Meyer, "Middle-Irish Version of the *Pharsalia* of Lucan."

24. *Rómverja Saga*, ed. Helgadóttir.

25. Dante, *Convivio* 4.28.13 ("quello grande poeta Lucano"); Geoffrey Chaucer, *The House of Fame* 3.1499, quoted in Susanna Braund, introduction to *Lucan*, ed. Tesoriero, Muecke, and Neal, 2–4.

26. Lucan, *M. Annaei Lvcani Pharsalia;* Grotius ("poeta phileleutheros"), quoted in Conte, *Latin Literature*, trans. Solodow, 451.

27. Petronius, *Satyricon* 118, in *Satyricon*, trans. Sullivan, 109 ("ingens opus"), 109–22 (Eumolpus's poem); Virgil, *Aeneid* 7.45 ("maius opus").

28. "But," Gibbon continued, "of what avail is tardy knowledge? Where error is irretrievable, repentance is useless." Note from winter 1790–91, in Gibbon, *History of the Decline and Fall of the Roman Empire*, British Library shelf mark C.60.m.1; Bowersock, "Gibbon on Civil War and Rebellion in the Decline of the Roman Empire."

29. Lucan, *Bellum civile* 1.223–24, in *Civil War*, trans. Braund, 27.

30. Florus, *Epitome* 1.intro., 1.47.14, 2.3.18, 2.8.20, 2.13.4–5, in *Epitome of Roman History*, trans. Foster, 5–7, 217, 233, 241, 267 (translations adapted).

31. Henderson, *Fighting for Rome*, pts. 1, 4; Breed, Damon, and Rossi, *Citizens of Discord*.

32. "Trina bella civilia, plura externa, ac plerumque permixta." Tacitus, *Histories* 1.2, in *Histories, Books I–III*, trans. Moore, 5 (translation adapted).

33. Florus, *Epitome* 2.13, in *Epitome of Roman History*, trans. Foster, 267 (translation adapted).

34. Lucan, *Bellum civile* 1.1–8, in *Civil War*, trans. Braund, 3.

35. Núñez González, "On the Meaning of *Bella Plus Quam Ciuilia* (Lucan 1, 1)."

36. Lucan, *Bellum civile* 1.682, in *Civil War*, trans. Braund, 21; Waller to Sir Ralph Hopton, June 16, 1643 (O.S.), in Coate, *Cornwall in the Great Civil War and Interregnum, 1642–1660*, 77.

37. Woodman, "Poems to Historians."

38. Augustine, *City of God Against the Pagans* 3.6, 15.5, ed. and trans. Dyson, 99, 639–40.

39. Horace, *Epodes* 7, in *Complete Odes and Epodes*, trans. West, 11.

40. Wiseman, *Remus*, 143.

41. Horace, *Epodes* 16, in *Complete Odes and Epodes*, trans. West, 18.

42. Sallust, *The War with Catiline* 16.4, in *Sallust*, trans. Rolfe, 17, 19, 27–28 ("civile bellum exoptabant") (translation adapted).

43. Sallust, fragments from *Histories*, bk. 1, frags. 8, 10, 12, in *Fragments of the Histories*, trans. Ramsey, 8–13.

44. Varro, *Di vita populi Romani*, frag. 114, quoted in Wiseman, "Two-Headed State," 26; see also Florus, *Epitome* 2.5.3, in *Epitome of Roman History*, trans. Foster, 228 ("iudiciaria lege Gracchi diviserant populum Romanum et bicipitem ex una fecerant civitatem").

45. Tacitus, *Histories* 2.38, in *Tacitus, Histories, Books I–III*, trans. Moore, 223 ("temptamenta civilium bellorum").

46. Cicero, *De officiis* 1.86, in Cicero, *On Duties*, 86–87.

47. Tacitus, *Histories* 1.50, in *Histories, Books I–III*, trans. Moore, 85 ("repetita bellorum civilium memoria") (translation adapted).

48. Braund, "Tale of Two Cities"; McNelis, *Statius' Thebaid and the Poetics of Civil War.*

49. Brown, *Augustine of Hippo*, 23–25.

50. Augustine, *City of God Against the Pagans*, 15.5, 2.19, 2.22, 2.25, 3.25, ed. Dyson, 640, 73, 81, 87, 134.

51. Ibid., 3.23 ("illa mala ... quae quanto interiora, tanto miseriora ... discordiae civiles vel potius inciviles ...; bella socialia, bella servilia, bella civilia quantum Romanum cruorem fuderunt, quantam Italiae vastationem desertionemque fecerunt!"), 3.28, 3.30, ed. Dyson, 132 (translation adapted), 137, 139.

52. Rohrbacher, *Historians of Late Antiquity*, 135–49.

53. Orosius, *Seven Books of History Against the Pagans* 2.18.1, 5.22.6, 8, trans. Fear, 105, 253.

54. Ibid., 23–24.

55. Augustine, *City of God Against the Pagans* 19.7, ed. Dyson, 929.

56. Appian, *Civil Wars* 1.6, trans. Carter, 4; Appian, *Auncient Historie and Exquisite Chronicle of the Romane Warres*, title page.

3
Uncivil Civil Wars
The Seventeenth Century

1. Hobbes, *On the Citizen*, ed. Tuck and Silverthorne, 4.

2. On Shakespeare's debt to the humanist curriculum, see Armitage, Condren, and Fitzmaurice, *Shakespeare and Early Modern Political Thought*; Skinner, *Forensic Shakespeare.*

3. Burke, "Survey of the Popularity of Ancient Historians, 1450–1700."

4. Jensen, "Reading Florus in Early Modern England"; Jensen, *Reading the Roman Republic in Early Modern England*, 56–73.

5. Schuhmann, "Hobbes's Concept of History," 3–4; Hobbes, *Behemoth; or, The Long Parliament*, 52.

6. Grafton, *What Was History?*, 194–95; see Wheare, *Method and Order of Reading Both Civil and Ecclesiastical Histories*, trans. Bohun, 77–78, on "the body of the Roman History … the Picture of which in Little is most Artfully drawn by our L. Annaeus Florus."

7. *Statutes of the University of Oxford Codified in the Year 1636 Under the Authority of Archbishop Laud*, 37.

8. Eutropius, *Eutropii historiæ romanæ breviarum*; Phillipson, *Adam Smith*, 18, plates 2–3.

9. MacCormack, *On the Wings of Time*, 15, 72, 76.

10. Garcilaso de la Vega, *Historia general del Peru trata el descubrimiento del; y como lo ganaron los Españoles*.

11. Montaigne, *Essays Written in French by Michael Lord of Montaigne*, trans. Florio, 547.

12. Hadfield, *Shakespeare and Republicanism*, 103–29, has called this tetralogy "Shakespeare's *Pharsalia*."

13. Bentley, *Shakespeare and Jonson*, 1:112; Donaldson, "Talking with Ghosts: Ben Jonson and the English Civil War."

14. *Shakespeare's Appian*; Logan, "Daniel's Civil Wars and Lucan's Pharsalia"; Logan, "Lucan—Daniel—Shakespeare."

15. Daniel, *The First Fowre Bookes of the Civile Wars Between the Two Houses of Lancaster and Yorke*, sig. B[1]r.

16. Norbrook, *Writing the English Republic*, 24.

17. Shapiro, "'Metre Meete to Furnish Lucans Style'"; Gibson, "Civil War in 1614"; Norbrook, "Lucan, Thomas May, and the Creation of a Republican Literary Culture"; Norbrook, *Writing the English Republic*, 43–50.

18. May, *History of the Parliament of England Which Began November the Third, MDCXL*, sig. A3v; Pocock, "Thomas May and the Narrative of Civil War."

19. Milton, *Paradise Lost*; Hale, *"Paradise Lost"*; Norbrook, *Writing the English Republic*, 438–67, 443.

20. McDowell, "Towards a Poetics of Civil War," 344.

21. Filmer, *Patriarcha*, title page, quoting Lucan, *Bellum civile* 3.145–46 ("Libertas . . . Populi, quem regna coercent / Libertate perit"); Hobbes, *Behemoth: The History of the Causes of the Civil-Wars of England*, title page, adapting Lucan, *Bellum civile* 1.1–2 ("Bella per Angliacos plusquam civilia campos, / Jusque datum sceleri loquiumur"); Hobbes, *Behemoth; or, The Long Parliament*, 90, 92.

22. Jean-Jacques Rousseau, *Extrait du projet de paix perpétuelle de monsieur l'abbé de Saint-Pierre*, title page (quoting Lucan, *Bellum civile* 4.4–5); Rousseau, *Discourse on the Origin and Foundations of Inequality Among Men*, in *Discourses and Other Early Political Writings*, trans. Gourevitch, 185 (quoting Lucan, *Bellum civile* 1.376–78).

23. Lucan, *Pharsale de M. A. Lucain*, trans. Chasles and Greslou, 1:xvii (quoting Lucan, *Bellum civile* 4.579).

24. See, for instance, Mason, ed., *The Darnton Debate*.

25. "Intestinae Simultates," in Whitney, *Choice of Emblemes and Other Devises*, 7.

26. Seaward, "Clarendon, Tacitism, and the Civil Wars of Europe."

27. Grotius, *De Rebus Belgicis*, 1.

28. Corbet, *Historicall Relation of the Military Government of Gloucester*, sig. A2v.

29. Biondi, "Civill Warrs of England," trans. Henry, Earl of Monmouth; Biondi, *History of the Civill Warres of England, Betweene the Two Houses of Lancaster and Yorke*, trans. Henry, Earl of Monmouth; Davila, *Historie of the Civill Warres of France*, trans. Cotterell and Aylesbury; Adams, *Discourses on Davila*.

30. Guarini, *Il Pastor Fido*, trans. Fanshawe, 303–12.

31. Sandoval, *Civil Wars of Spain in the Beginning of the Reign of Charls the 5t, Emperor of Germanie and King*.

32. Samuel Kem, *The Messengers Preparation for an Address to the King* (1644), quoted in Donagan, *War in England, 1642–1649*, 132; compare Robert Doughty, "Charge to the Tax Commissioners of South Erpingham, North Erpingham, North Greenhoe, and Hold Hundreds" (Feb. 1664), in *Notebook of Robert Doughty, 1662–1665*, 123: "our late uncivil civil wars."

33. Davila, *History of the Civil Wars of France*, trans. Cotterell and Aylesbury, sig. A2r.

34. Dugdale, *Short View of the Late Troubles in England*. Compare also Adamson, "Baronial Context of the English Civil War," with the more nuanced account in Adamson, *Noble Revolt*.

35. Larrère, "Grotius et la distinction entre guerre privé et guerre publique."

36. Grotius, *Commentary on the Law of Prize and Booty*, 50 ("aut civile in partem eiusdem reipublicae: aut externum, in alius, cuius species est quod sociali dicitur"). On Grotius's debt to Roman law, see Straumann, *Roman Law in the State of Nature*.

37. Grotius, *Commentary on the Law of Prize and Booty*, 80 ("bella Christianorum esse civilia, quasi vero totius Christianus Orbis una sit republica"), referring to Vázquez de Menchaca, *Controversiarum illustrium . . . libri tres*.

38. Grotius, *Rights of War and Peace* 1.3.1, 1:240.

39. Ibid., 1.4.19.1, 1:381, quoting Plutarch's *Life of Brutus* and Cicero's *Second Philippic*.

40. Rousseau, *The Social Contract* (1762), in *Social Contract and Other Later Political Writings*, 42–43, 44–45.

41. Hobbes, *Leviathan*, 3:850.

42. Thomas Hobbes, *De Corpore* 1.7, in *Elements of Law, Natural and Politic*, 190 ("causa igitur belli civilis est, quod bellorum ac pacis causa ignoratur"), 191.

43. Hobbes, *On the Citizen* 1.12, 29–30.

44. Ibid., 11–12.

45. Hobbes to Cavendish, July 1645, in Hobbes, *Correspondence*, 1:120.

46. Hobbes, *On the Citizen*, 82, 124 ("et bellum civile nascitur"), 149.

47. Ibid., 15.

48. On the background, see especially Kelsey, "Ordinance for the Trial of Charles I"; Kelsey, "Trial of Charles I"; Holmes, "Trial and Execution of Charles I."

49. Donagan, *War in England, 1642–1649*, 130.

50. Orr, "Juristic Foundation of Regicide."

51. "An Act of the Commons of England Assembled in Parliament for Erecting a High Court of Justice, for the Trying and Judging of Charles Stuart, King of England" (Jan. 6, 1649), in *Acts and Ordinances of the Interregnum, 1642–1660*, ed. Firth and Rait, 1:1253–54 (my emphasis). Heath, *Chronicle of the Late Intestine War in the Three Kingdomes of England, Scotland, and Ireland*, 194–95, and "The Act Erecting a High Court of Justice for the King's Trial" (Jan. 6, 1649), in Gardiner, *Constitutional Documents of the Puritan Revolution, 1625–1660*, 357, have "civil war" in place of "cruel War," but this is not attested in, for example, "An Ordinance of the Commons in England in Parliament Assembled with a List of the Commissioners & Officers of the Said Court by Them Elected" (Jan. 3, 1649), British Library E.536(35), fol. 1r, or in [John Nalson], *A True Copy of the Journal of the High Court of Justice, for the Tryal of K. Charles I*, 2.

52. *Journals of the House of Commons*, 6:107, 111, quoted in Orr, *Treason and the State*, 173.

53. Bauman, *Crimen Maiestatis in the Roman Republic and Augustan Principate*, 271–77; Orr, *Treason and the State*, 12, 44–45 (referring to 25 Edward III, st. 5, c. 3); *Digest* 48.4.3.

54. Hobbes, *Leviathan*, 2:192.

55. Ibid., 2:256, 274, 278, 282.

56. Hobbes, "Questions Relative to Hereditary Right" (1679), in *Writings on Common Law and Hereditary Right*, 177–78.

57. Locke, *Two Treatises of Government*, 137 ("The Preface").

58. Woolhouse, *Locke*, 11.

59. For example, Harrison and Laslett, *Library of John Locke*, items 2, 561–62, 927, 1146–48, 1818–19, 2792b, 3060.

60. Locke, *Two Treatises of Government*, 278 (2nd Treatise, § 16).

61. Ibid., 416–17 (2nd Treatise, §§ 227, 228).

62. Locke, "On Allegiance and the Revolution" (ca. April 1690), in *Political Essays*, 307.

63. Pocock, "Fourth English Civil War," 153, 159.

64. Sidney, *Discourses Concerning Government*, 198, 187–89.
65. Ibid., 193, 196–99.
66. Sidney, *Court Maxims*, 20.
67. Sidney, *Discourses Concerning Government*, 121.
68. Ibid., 198.
69. Filmer, *Patriarcha*, 54, 55–56, 57, 58.
70. Sidney, *Discourses Concerning Government*, 120.
71. Ibid., 172.
72. Montesquieu, *Reflections on the Causes of the Rise and Fall of the Roman Empire*, 61; Bates, *States of War*, 160–64.
73. Jouffroy, *Mélanges philosophiques par Théodore Jouffroy*, 140 ("Les guerres civiles de l'Europe sont finies").

4

Civil War in an Age of Revolutions
The Eighteenth Century

1. Abdul-Ahad, "'Syria Is Not a Revolution Any More.'"
2. Compare Viola, "Rivoluzione e guerra civile," 24: "In un certo senso la rivoluzione sprovincializza la guerra civile."
3. Arendt, *On Revolution*, 12.
4. Civil war is also not mentioned in the *Encyclopédie*'s major article on war: [Le Blond], "Guerre." The contemporaneous fourth edition of the *Dictionnaire de l'Académie Française* (1762) defines *"Guerre civile, & guerre intestine"* as "La guerre qui s'allume entre les peuples d'un même État": accessed via the ARTFL Project's "Dictionnaires d'autrefois," http://artfl-project.uchicago.edu/content/dictionnaires-dautrefois.
5. Koselleck, "Historical Criteria of the Modern Concept of Revolution," trans. Tribe, 47, 48, 49. On the conceptual continuities between "revolution" and "civil war," see Koselleck, *Critique and Crisis*, 160–61; Bulst et al., "Revolution, Rebellion, Aufruhr, Bürgerkrieg," esp. 712–14, 726–27, 778–80.

6. Momigliano, "Ancient History and the Antiquarian," 294; Goulemot, *Le règne de l'histoire*, 127–56.

7. Echard, *The Roman History from the Building of the City to the Perfect Settlement of the Empire by Augustus Cæsar.*

8. Vertot, *Histoire de la conjuration de Portugal*; Vertot, *Histoire des révolutions de Suède où l'on voit les changemens qui sont arrivez*; Vertot, *Histoire des révolutions de Portugal.*

9. Trakulhun, "Das Ende der Ming-Dynastie in China (1644)."

10. Sidney, *Discourses Concerning Government*, 195–96.

11. Vattel, *Law of Nations* (1758), 3.18.293, ed. Kapossy and Whatmore, 645.

12. "A Declaration by the Representatives of the United States of America, in General Congress Assembled" (July 4, 1776), in Armitage, *Declaration of Independence*, 165.

13. Vattel, *Law of Nations* 1.4.51, 3.1.1–2, ed. Kapossy and Whatmore, 105, 469.

14. Ibid., 3.18.287, 290, ed. Kapossy and Whatmore, 641, 642.

15. "Thomas Jefferson's 'Original Rough Draft' of the Declaration of Independence," in Armitage, *Declaration of Independence*, 161.

16. Vattel, *Law of Nations* 3.18.292, ed. Kapossy and Whatmore, 644–45. On Vattel's doctrine of civil war, see Rech, *Enemies of Mankind*, 209–13, 216–20.

17. Vattel, *Law of Nations* 3.18.293, ed. Kapossy and Whatmore, 645.

18. Ibid., 3.18.295, ed. Kapossy and Whatmore, 648–49.

19. Zurbuchen, "Vattel's 'Law of Nations' and the Principle of Nonintervention"; Pitts, "Intervention and Sovereign Equality."

20. Vattel, *Law of Nations* 2.4.56, ed. Kapossy and Whatmore, 290–91.

21. Braund, "Bernard Romans."

22. Romans, *To the Hon^e. Jno. Hancock Esqre.*; Romans, *Philadelphia, July 12. 1775.*

23. Romans, *Annals of the Troubles in the Netherlands.*

24. Belcher, *First American Civil War*, is the exception that proves the rule.

25. Paine, *Common Sense*, in *Collected Writings*, 25.

26. O'Shaughnessy, *Empire Divided*; more generally, see Armitage, "First Atlantic Crisis."

27. Lawson, "Anatomy of a Civil War"; Shy, *People Numerous and Armed*, 183–92; Wahrman, *Making of the Modern Self*, 223–37, 239–44; Simms, *Three Victories and a Defeat*, 593–600; Klooster, *Revolutions in the Atlantic World*, 11–44; Jasanoff, *Liberty's Exiles*, 21–53.

28. Elliott, *Empires of the Atlantic World*, 352.

29. Bollan, *The Freedom of Speech and Writing upon Public Affairs, Considered; with an Historical View of the Roman Imperial Laws Against Libels*, 158–59. On Bollan's use of Roman history, see York, "Defining and Defending Colonial American Rights," 213.

30. Price, *Observations on the Nature of Civil Liberty*, 91.

31. Smith, *An Inquiry into the Nature and Causes of the Wealth of Nations* 4.7.c, ed. Campbell and Skinner, 2:622.

32. Pocock, "Political Thought in the English-Speaking Atlantic, 1760–1790," 256–57.

33. *Newport Mercury*, April 24, 1775, quoted in Breen, *American Insurgents, American Patriots*, 281–82.

34. *Civil War; a Poem*; Hartley, *Substance of a Speech in Parliament, upon the State of the Nation and the Present Civil War with America*, 19; Roebuck, *Enquiry, Whether the Guilt of the Present Civil War in America, Ought to Be Imputed to Great Britain or America*.

35. [Jackson], *Emma Corbett*; Wahrman, *Making of the Modern Self*, 243–44.

36. Cooper, introduction (1831) to *Spy*, 13; Larkin, "What Is a Loyalist?"

37. Pocock, *Three British Revolutions, 1641, 1688, 1776*.

38. "A Declaration . . . Seting Forth the Causes and Necessity of Taking Up Arms" (July 6, 1775), in Hutson, *Decent Respect to the Opinions of Mankind*, 96, 97 (my emphasis).

39. Lord North to George III, July 26, 1775, quoted in Marshall, *Making and Unmaking of Empires*, 338.

40. Paine, *Common Sense*, in *Collected Writings*, 45–46.

41. Ibid., 18–19. Compare Howell, *Twelve Several Treatises, of the Late*

Revolutions in These Three Kingdomes, 118, where the total of "rebellions" since 1066 is given as "near upon a hundred."

42. On Paine and the "republican turn" in 1776, see Nelson, *Royalist Revolution*, 108–45.

43. "Declaration by the Representatives of the United States of America, in General Congress Assembled" (July 4, 1776), in Armitage, *Declaration of Independence*, 165, 170.

44. Beaulac, "Emer de Vattel and the Externalization of Sovereignty."

45. Franklin to C. G. F. Dumas, Dec. 9, 1775, in *Papers of Benjamin Franklin*, 22:287.

46. Armitage, *Declaration of Independence*, 165, 166.

47. Lempérière, "Revolución, guerra civil, guerra de independencia en el mundo hispánico, 1808–1825"; Adelman, "Age of Imperial Revolutions"; Pani, "Ties Unbound"; Lucena Giraldo, *Naciones de rebeldes*; Pérez Vejo, *Elegía criolla*.

48. José María Cos, "Plan de Guerra" (June 10, 1812), in Guedea, *Textos insurgentes (1808–1821)*, 52–55; San Martín to Tomás Godoy Cruz, April 12, 1816, quoted in John Lynch, *San Martín*, trans. Chaparro, 131.

49. Baker, "Revolution 1.0," 189; Baker, "Inventing the French Revolution," 203, 223.

50. Snow, "Concept of Revolution in Seventeenth-Century England"; Rachum, "Meaning of 'Revolution' in the English Revolution (London, 1648–1660)." For an alternative view, see Harris, "Did the English Have a Script for Revolution in the Seventeenth Century?"

51. Hobbes, *Behemoth; or, The Long Parliament*, 389.

52. Edelstein, "Do We Want a Revolution Without Revolution?"; compare Rey, *"Révolution"*; William H. Sewell Jr., "Historical Events as Transformations of Structures: Inventing Revolution at the Bastille," in *Logics of History*, 225–70.

53. Vlassopoulos, "Acquiring (a) Historicity," 166.

54. Furet, "The Revolutionary Catechism," in *Interpreting the French Revolution*, trans. Forster, 83.

55. Marx, *The Eighteenth Brumaire of Louis Bonaparte* (1851), in *Selected Writings*, 300.

56. Burke, *Reflections on the Revolution in France*, 26–27 (quoting Livy, *Histories* 9.1.10) (my emphasis).

57. Burke, *Letter from the Right Hon. Edmund Burke*, 41.

58. Vattel, *Law of Nations* 3.3.36, ed. Kapossy and Whatmore, 488. The fuller quotation reads, "Justum est bellum, quibus necessaria; et pia arma, quibus nulla nisi in armis relinquitur spes."

59. Burke, "Speech on the Seizure and Confiscation of Private Property in St. Eustatius" (May 14, 1781), in *Parliamentary History of England from the Earliest Period to 1803*, vol. 22, col. 231.

60. Burke, *Thoughts on French Affairs*, in *Further Reflections on the Revolution in France*, 207.

61. Vattel, *Law of Nations* 2.4.56, ed. Kapossy and Whatmore, 291; compare ibid., 3.16.253, ed. Kapossy and Whatmore, 627.

62. Kant, "Toward Perpetual Peace," in *Practical Philosophy*, trans. Gregor, 319–20; Hurrell, "Revisiting Kant and Intervention," 198.

63. Burke, "First Letter on a Regicide Peace" (Oct. 20, 1796), and Burke, "Second Letter on a Regicide Peace" (1796), in *Revolutionary War, 1794–1797*, 187, 267; Armitage, *Foundations of Modern International Thought*, 163–69.

64. See, for example, Martin, "Rivoluzione francese e guerra civile"; Martin, "La guerre civile"; Andress, *Terror*; Martin, *La Vendée et la Révolution*.

65. Mayer, *Furies*, 4–5.

66. Serna, "Toute révolution est guerre d'indépendance."

67. Drayton, *Charge, on the Rise of the American Empire*, 2, 8, 15.

68. Guizot, *Histoire de la révolution d'Angleterre, depuis l'avènement de Charles Ier jusqu'a la restauration*, 1:xvii: "Telle est enfin l'analogie des deux révolutions que la première n'eût jamais été bien comprise si la seconde n'eût éclaté."

69. Marx and Engels, *The Communist Manifesto* (1848), in Marx, *Selected Writings*, 230 ("den mehr oder minder versteckten Bürgerkrieg innerhalb der bestehenden Gesellschaft bis zu dem

Punkt, wo er in eine offene Revolution ausbricht"); Balibar, "On the Aporias of Marxian Politics."

70. Marx, *The Civil War in France*, in Marx and Engels, *Karl Marx, Friedrich Engels Gesamtausgabe (MEGA)*, 22:158 ("und der bei Seite fleigt, sobald der Klassenkampf Bürgerkrieg auflodert").

71. Lenin, *Clausewitz' Werk "Vom Kriege"*; Hahlweg, "Lenin und Clausewitz."

72. The description is Carl Schmitt's. Schmitt, *Theory of the Partisan*, trans. Ulmen, 93.

73. Lenin [and Grigorii Zinoviev], *The Military Programme of the Proletarian Revolution* (Sept. 1916), in *Collected Works*, 23:78. On the immediate context of Lenin and Zinoviev's pamphlet, see Nation, *War on War*, 80–83.

74. Stalin (1928), quoted in Rieber, "Civil Wars in the Soviet Union," 140.

75. Compare Eckstein, "On the Etiology of Internal Wars," 133; Canal, "Guerra civil y contrarrevolución en la Europa del sur en el siglo XIX," 46.

5
Civilizing Civil War
The Nineteenth Century

1. Lincoln, "Address Delivered at the Dedication of the Cemetery at Gettysburg" (Nov. 19, 1863), in *Collected Works of Abraham Lincoln*, 7:23.

2. See especially Wills, *Lincoln at Gettysburg*; Boritt, *Gettysburg Gospel*; and Johnson, *Writing the Gettysburg Address*, none of which treats the phrase "great civil war."

3. Cimbala and Miller, *Great Task Remaining Before Us*; Varon, *Appomattox*; Downs, *After Appomattox*.

4. Mably, *Des droits et des devoirs du citoyen* (1758), 62–63 ("la guerre civile est quelque foix un grand bien").

5. "La guerra civil es un don de cielo," quoted in Fuentes, "Guerra civil," 609; Fuentes, *"Belle époque,"* 84–93.

6. Chateaubriand, *Mémoires d'outre-tombe*, 1358; Caron, *Frères de sang*, 153–57.

7. Compare Ranzato, "Evidence et invisibilité des guerres civiles"; Grangé, *De la guerre civile*; Grangé, *Oublier la guerre civile?*; and, on the more general absence of war from social theory, Joas and Köbl, *War in Social Thought*, 2.

8. Rousseau, *Social Contract*, in *Social Contract and Other Later Political Writings* 1.4.9, ed. Gourevitch, 46–47. Rousseau's argument was, in part, an attack on Hugo Grotius's conception of a "private" war, on which see chapter 3 above.

9. Clausewitz, *On War*. Civil war also makes only fleeting appearances in Clausewitz's less well-known writings on "small war" (*kleiner Krieg*). Clausewitz, *Clausewitz on Small War*, trans. Daase and Davis, 121, 131, 163.

10. Mao and Guevara, *Guerrilla Warfare*.

11. "Vouloir donner des maximes pour ces sortes de guerres serait absurde": Jomini, *Précis de l'art de la guerre*, 1:85. For more recent accounts attempting to bring civil war within the pale of normative theory see Franco Restrepo, *Guerras civiles*; Fabre, *Cosmopolitan War*, 130–65.

12. Moynier, *Étude sur la Convention de Genève pour l'amélioration du sort des militaires blessés dans les armées en campagne (1864 et 1868)*, 304 ("Nous ne parlons pas, cela va sans dire, des guerres civiles; les lois internationales ne leur sont pas applicables.")

13. In volumes 4–8 of *Collected Works of Abraham Lincoln*, covering the period 1861–65, "rebellion" appears 340 times, "civil war" 64 times. http://quod.lib.umich.edu/l/lincoln/.

14. Gastineau, *Histoire de la souscription populaire à la médaille Lincoln*; Boritt, Neely, and Holzer, "European Image of Abraham Lincoln," 161; Doyle, *Cause of All Nations*, 295–97.

15. Hugo, *Les Misérables (The Wretched): A Novel*; *Providence Evening Bulletin*, May 25, 1885, quoted in Lebreton-Savigny, *Victor Hugo*

et les Américains (1825–1885), 31 (translation corrected). *Les Misérables* was published in French in Brussels in late March 1862 and in Paris in early April 1862.

16. Hugo, *Les Misérables: A Novel*, trans. Wilbour, 4:164–65.

17. Laurent, "'La guerre civile?'"; Caron, *Frères de sang*, 157–62.

18. Beckert, *Empire of Cotton*, 242–73.

19. Geyer and Bright, "Global Violence and Nationalizing Wars in Eurasia and America"; Bayly, *Birth of the Modern World, 1780–1914*, 148–65; Platt, *Autumn in the Heavenly Kingdom*.

20. Armitage et al., "Interchange."

21. Pavković, *Creating New States*, 65–94.

22. Wimmer and Min, "From Empire to Nation-State," 881 (quoted); Wimmer, Cederman, and Min, "Ethnic Politics and Armed Conflict"; Wimmer, *Waves of War*.

23. "Meeting of the Sub-committee [of the Société Publique for the Relief of Wounded Combatants], held on March 17, 1863," in International Committee of the Red Cross, "The Foundation of the Red Cross": 67.

24. Boissier, *Histoire du Comité international de la Croix-Rouge*, 391–94; Siordet, "The Geneva Conventions and Civil War"; Sivakumaran, *The Law of Non-international Armed Conflict*, 31–37 (to which I am indebted in this paragraph).

25. Mill, "A Few Words on Non-intervention," in *Collected Works of John Stuart Mill*, 21:120, 118, 121; Varouxakis, *Liberty Abroad*, 77–89.

26. Mill, "The Contest in America" (1862), in *Collected Works of John Stuart Mill*, 21:140, 142, 138; Varouxakis, "'Negrophilist' Crusader."

27. Pitts, "Intervention and Sovereign Equality."

28. "Declaration of the Immediate Causes Which Induce and Justify the Secession of South Carolina from the Federal Union" (Dec. 20, 1860), in *Journal of the Convention of the People of South Carolina, Held in 1860, 1861 and 1862*, 461–66 (my emphasis).

29. Lincoln, "Message to Congress in Special Session" (July 4, 1861),

in *Collected Works of Abraham Lincoln*, 4:426, 435, 436 (Lincoln's emphases).

30. Ibid., 4:433.

31. Lincoln, "First Inaugural Address" (March 4, 1861), in *Collected Works of Abraham Lincoln*, 4:265. Lincoln had originally written "Treasonable" in place of "revolutionary." Ibid., 4:265n16.

32. Pavković, *Creating New States*, 221–40.

33. Lincoln, "Address Delivered at the Dedication of the Cemetery at Gettysburg," in *Collected Works of Abraham Lincoln*, 7:23.

34. Wright, "American Civil War (1861–65)," 43.

35. Neff, *Justice in Blue and Gray*, 32–34.

36. The Prize Cases, 67 U.S. 635 (1863); McGinty, *Lincoln and the Court*, 118–43; Lee and Ramsey, "Story of the *Prize Cases*"; Neff, *Justice in Blue and Gray*, 20–29.

37. The Prize Cases, 67 U.S. 635 (1863), citing Vattel, *Law of Nations* 3.18.293, ed. Kapossy and Whatmore, 645.

38. Halleck, *International Law*, 73–75.

39. Halleck also derived the category of "wars of Islamism" from Jomini. Halleck later translated Jomini's *Life of Napoleon*.

40. Halleck, *International Law*, 332–33.

41. Carroll, *War Powers of the General Government*, 7–8, citing Vattel, *Law of Nations* 3.18.293.

42. Dyer, "Francis Lieber and the American Civil War"; Mack and Lesesne, *Francis Lieber and the Culture of the Mind*.

43. Baxter, "First Modern Codification of the Law of War"; Hartigan, *Military Rules, Regulations, and the Code of War*; Witt, *Lincoln's Code*; Finkelman, "Francis Lieber and the Modern Law of War."

44. Lieber to George Stillman Hillard, May 11, 1861, Lieber MSS, Henry E. Huntington Library, San Marino, Calif. (hereafter HEH), LI 2308.

45. Lieber, "[Notes on the] English and Ferench [*sic*] Revolutions" (ca. 1850), Lieber MSS, HEH LI 365.

46. Lieber, "Some Questions Answered—Secession—the Strength of Armies and Navys, &ca." (ca. 1851), Lieber MSS, HEH LI 369.

47. Lieber, "[Remarks Regarding the *Right of Secession*]" (ca. 1851), Lieber MSS, HEH LI 368.

48. Lieber, "Twenty-Seven Definitions and Elementary Positions Concerning the Laws and Usages of War" (1861) and "Laws and Usages of War" (Oct. 1861–Feb. 1862), Lieber MSS, Eisenhower Library, Johns Hopkins University, box 2, items 15, 16–18.

49. Lieber, "Laws and Usages of War," Lieber MSS, John Hopkins University, box 2, item 17. The reference to "contentio justa" comes from Alberico Gentili (1552–1608), cited in Kennedy, *Influence of Christianity on International Law*, 91.

50. Lieber, *"Civil War,"* Lieber MSS, John Hopkins University, box 2, item 18; Lieber, *Guerrilla Parties*, 21; Witt, *Lincoln's Code*, 193–96.

51. Halleck to Lieber, Aug. 6, 1862; Lieber to Halleck, Aug. 9, 1862, Lieber MSS, HEH, LI 1646, 1758.

52. Lieber to Bates, Nov. 9, 1862, Lieber MSS, HEH, LI 852.

53. Halleck, annotation to Lieber, *Code for the Government of Armies in the Field*, 25–[26], HEH, 243077.

54. Lieber to Halleck, March 4, 1863, Lieber MSS, HEH 1778; compare Lieber, [*U.S. Field Order 100.*] Section X.

55. Lieber, *Instructions for the Government of Armies of the United States in the Field*, 34.

56. Neff, *War and the Law of Nations*, 256–57.

57. U.S. Constitution, article I, secs. 8–9; Fourteenth Amendment (1868), sec. 3.

58. See also U.S. Naval War Records Office, *Official Records of the Union and Confederate Navies in the War of the Rebellion*.

59. Witt, *Lincoln's Code*, 340–45.

60. U.S. Department of War, *Instructions for the Government of Armies of the United States in the Field*.

61. Ramsey, *Masterpiece of Counterguerrilla Warfare*, 119–41.

62. For example, Davis, *Military Laws of the United States*, 798; U.S. Department of War, *Rules of Land Warfare*; U.S. Department of War, *Basic Field Manual*; U.S. Department of the Army, *Law of Land Warfare*, 9. More generally, see Kretchik, *U.S. Army Doctrine*.

63. Compare Fleche, *Revolution of 1861*.

64. Coulter, "Name for the American War of 1861–1865," 123, quoting Mildred Rutherford; Hoar, *South's Last Boys in Gray*, 524–25 (estimating 120 names for the war); Musick, "War by Any Other Name"; Coski, "War Between the Names"; Manning and Rothman, "Name of War."

65. Thomas M. Patterson, *Congressional Record* (Jan. 11, 1907), 944, in Record Group 94 (Office of the Adjutant General), Administrative Precedent File ("Frech File"), box 16, bundle 58, "Civil War," National Archives, Washington, D.C.

66. *Congressional Record* (Jan. 11, 1907), 944–49; clipping from unnamed Washington, D.C., newspaper, Jan. 12, 1907, "Frech File," National Archives, Washington, D.C.

67. Coulter, "Name for the American War of 1861–1865," 128–29; United Daughters of the Confederacy, *Minutes of the Twenty-First Annual Convention of the United Daughters of the Confederacy*, 298.

68. Blight, *Race and Reunion*, 15, 300–337.

69. Melville, "The Surrender at Appomattox (April, 1865)," in *Published Poems*, 100; Thomas, "'My Brother Got Killed in the War,'" 301–3.

70. Lucan, *Bellum civile* 1.128, in Lucan, *Civil War*, trans. Braund, 6; Jacob, *Testament to Union*, 169; Malamud, "*Auctoritas* of Antiquity," 310–11.

71. Engels to Marx, May 23, 1862, in Marx and Engels, *Collected Works*, trans. Dixon et al., 41:367.

6

Worlds of Civil War
The Twentieth Century

1. Torres Bodet, "Why We Fight." My thanks to Glenda Sluga for this reference.

2. Neumann, "International Civil War," 333, 350; Kunze, "Zweiter Dreißigjähriger Krieg."

3. Voltaire, *Le siècle de Louis XIV* (1756), quoted in Pagden, "Europe: Conceptualizing a Continent," in *The Idea of Europe: From Antiquity to the European Union*, ed. Pagden, 37.

4. Fénelon, *Fables and Dialogues of the Dead*, 183; Bell, *First Total War*, 59.

5. Lucan, *Bellum civile* 1.1–2: "*bella* per Emathios *plus quam civilia* campos, / . . . canimus" (my emphases).

6. Armitage, "Cosmopolitanism and Civil War."

7. Kant, "Toward Perpetual Peace," in *Practical Philosophy*, trans. Gregor, 330.

8. Rousseau, *Project for Perpetual Peace*, 9 ("presque la cruauté des guerres civiles").

9. Bourrienne, *Mémoires de M. de Bourrienne, ministre d'état*, 5:207: "La Turquie exceptée, l'Europe n'est qu'une province du monde; quand nous battons, nous ne faisons que de la guerre civile."

10. Martin, *La Russie et l'Europe*, 106: "Toutes les guerres entre Européens sont guerres civiles."

11. See, for example, G. K. Chesterton, in Hymans, Fort, and Rastoul, *Pax mundi*; Coudenhove-Kalergi, *Europe Must Unite*, title page.

12. Diplomatic Conference for the Establishment of International Conventions for the Protection of Victims of War, *Final Record of the Diplomatic Conference of Geneva of 1949*, 2B:325, 11; Sivakumaran, *Law of Non-international Armed Conflict*, 30–31, 40.

13. International Committee of the Red Cross, *Seventeenth International Red Cross Conference, Stockholm, August 1948: Report*, 71; Pictet, *Geneva Convention for the Amelioration of the Condition of the Wounded and Sick in Armed Forces in the Field*, 39–48. On the drafting of Common Article 3, see Moir, *Law of Internal Armed Conflict*, 23–29.

14. For guides to the legal background across the twentieth century, see Rougier, *Les guerres civiles et le droit des gens*; Siotis, *Le droit de la guerre et les conflits armés d'un caractère non-international*; Castrén, *Civil War*; La Haye, *War Crimes in Internal Armed Conflicts*; Solis, *Law of Armed Conflict*; Dinstein, *Non-international Armed Con-*

flicts in International Law; Moir, "Concept of Non-international Armed Conflict."

15. Geneva Convention, Common Article 3, in Pictet, *Geneva Convention for the Amelioration of the Condition of the Wounded and Sick in Armed Forces in the Field,* 37–38.

16. Sivakumaran, *Law of Non-international Armed Conflict,* 163; Diplomatic Conference for the Establishment of International Conventions for the Protection of Victims of War, *Final Record of the Diplomatic Conference of Geneva of 1949,* 1:351, quoted in ibid., 163. On the colonial determinants of the debate around the revised Geneva Conventions, see Klose, "Colonial Testing Ground," 108–11; Klose, *Human Rights in the Shadow of Colonial Violence,* trans. Geyer, 122–24.

17. Institut de Droit International, "Principle of Non-intervention in Civil Wars."

18. Moir, *Law of Internal Armed Conflict,* 89–132; Sivakumaran, *Law of Non-international Armed Conflict,* 49–92, 182–92.

19. Cullen, *Concept of Non-international Armed Conflict in International Humanitarian Law;* Vité, "Typology of Armed Conflicts in International Humanitarian Law," 75–83; David, "Internal (Non-international) Armed Conflict."

20. On the general question of classifying conflict, see Wilmshurst, *International Law and the Classification of Conflicts.*

21. Institut de Droit International, "Application of International Humanitarian Law and Fundamental Human Rights, in Armed Conflicts in Which Non-state Entities Are Parties."

22. Kolb, "Le droit international public et le concept de guerre civile depuis 1945"; Mattler, "Distinction Between Civil Wars and International Wars and Its Legal Implications."

23. International Criminal Tribunal for the Former Yugoslavia, *Prosecutor v. Tadić,* § 97.

24. For a summary and critique of these efforts, see Kreβ and Mégret, "The Regulation of Non-international Armed Conflicts."

25. U.K. Ministry of Defence, *Manual of the Law of Armed Conflict,* 381–408.

26. Sewall, introduction to *U.S. Army/Marine Corps Counterinsurgency Field Manual*, 352.

27. International Criminal Tribunal for the Former Yugoslavia, *Prosecutor v. Tadić*, §§ 126, 119.

28. U.S. Department of State, Office of Electronic Information, Bureau of Public Affairs, "Daily Press Briefing—December 2, 2011"; Pressman, "Why Deny Syria Is in a Civil War?"

29. Chenoweth, "Syrian Conflict Is Already a Civil War"; Murphy, "Why It's Time to Call Syria a Civil War."

30. "Syria Crisis: Death Toll Tops 17,000, Says Opposition Group," *Huffington Post*, July 9, 2012; "Syria in Civil War, Red Cross Says," *BBC News, Middle East*, July 15, 2012.

31. International Committee of the Red Cross, "Internal Conflicts or Other Situations of Violence."

32. Eckstein, "Introduction: Toward the Theoretical Study of Internal War," in *Internal War*, 1. On Eckstein, see Almond, "Harry Eckstein as Political Theorist."

33. Eckstein, "On the Etiology of Internal Wars." For recent overviews of the Cold War and the social sciences, see Engerman, "Social Science in the Cold War"; Gilman, "Cold War as Intellectual Force Field."

34. Orlansky, *State of Research on Internal War*, 3; compare Eckstein, *Internal War*, 32: "The crucial issues . . . are pre-theoretical issues."

35. U.S. Congress, Senate, Committee on Foreign Relations, *Nature of Revolution*, 155–56; Brinton, *Anatomy of Revolution*; McAlister, *Viet Nam*.

36. For the broader intellectual and political context within which Rawls gave his lectures, see Forrester, "Citizenship, War, and the Origins of International Ethics in American Political Philosophy, 1960–1975."

37. Rawls, "Moral Problems."

38. Compare, for example, Speier, *Revolutionary War*.

39. John Rawls, "Topic III: *Just War: Jus ad bellum*" (1969), Harvard

University Archives, Acs. 14990, box 12, file 4; Mill, "A Few Words on Non-intervention" (1859), in *Collected Works of John Stuart Mill*, 21:111–23.

40. Foucault, "La société punitive," Lecture 1 (Jan. 3, 1973), 16–17; Foucault, *La société punitive*, 14–15; Foucault, *Punitive Society*, trans. Burchell, 13.

41. Hoffman, "Foucault's Politics and Bellicosity as a Matrix for Power Relations."

42. Foisneau, "Farewell to Leviathan."

43. Foucault, "La société punitive," Lecture 2 (Jan. 10, 1973), 22–23, 28–29; Foucault, *La société punitive*, 26–31 ("la guerre civile se déroule sur le théâtre du pouvoir"), 34 ("la politique est la continuation de la guerre civile"); Foucault, *Punitive Society*, trans. Burchell, 24–32.

44. Wright, *Study of War*; Richardson, *Statistics of Deadly Quarrels*; Singer and Small, *Wages of War, 1816–1965*.

45. Small and Singer, *Resort to Arms*, 203–4.

46. Ibid., 210–20; Henderson and Singer, "Civil War in the Postcolonial World, 1946–92," 284–85.

47. Sambanis, "What Is Civil War?," 816.

48. For other discussions, see, for example, Duvall, "Appraisal of the Methodological and Statistical Procedures of the Correlates of War Project"; Cramer, *Civil War Is Not a Stupid Thing*, 57–86; Vasquez, *War Puzzle Revisited*, 27–29.

49. The metropole/periphery distinction was later dropped by the Correlates of War Project. Sarkees and Wayman, *Resort to War*, 43, 47.

50. This difficulty haunts even the more pragmatic definition of civil war offered by the Yale political scientist Stathis Kalyvas: "armed combat within the boundaries of *a recognized sovereign entity* between parties subject to a common authority at the outset of the hostilities." Kalyvas, *Logic of Violence in Civil War*, 17 (my emphasis).

51. Remak, *Very Civil War*, 157.

52. Hopkinson, *Green Against Green*, 272–73.

53. Sutton, *Index of Deaths from the Conflict in Ireland, 1969–1993*; Conflict Archive on the Internet, "Violence: Deaths During the Conflict."

54. Sambanis, "It's Official"; see also Toft, "Is It a Civil War, or Isn't It?"

55. Annan, quoted in Cordesmann, *Iraq's Insurgency and the Road to Civil Conflict*, 2:393.

56. Lando, "By the Numbers, It's Civil War."

57. Wong, "Matter of Definition."

58. Erdoğan, quoted in Cordesmann, *Iraq's Insurgency and the Road to Civil Conflict*, 2:393.

59. Keeter, "Civil War."

60. Stansfield, "Accepting Realities in Iraq."

61. Fearon, "Testimony to U.S. House of Representatives ... on 'Iraq: Democracy or Civil War?'"

62. Fearon, "Iraq's Civil War."

63. Zavis, "Maliki Challenges 'Civil War' Label."

64. Taheri, "There Is No Civil War in Iraq."

65. Keegan and Bull, "What Is a Civil War?"

66. Patten, "Is Iraq in a Civil War?": 32, 27.

67. *U.S. Army Field Manual 100–20: Military Operations in Low Intensity Conflict*, quoted in Patten, "Is Iraq in a Civil War?": 28

68. Patten, "Is Iraq in a Civil War?": 29 (my emphasis).

69. "Piú che ad una guerra fra nazioni, noi assistiamo ad una mondiale guerra civile": Salvemini, "Non abbiamo niente da dire" (Sept. 4, 1914), in *Come siamo andati in Libia e altri scritti dal 1900 al 1915*, 366; "... dieser Großkrieg ist ein *europäischer Bürgerkrieg, ein Krieg gegen der inneren, unsichtbaren Feind des europäischen Geistes*": Marc, "Das geheime Europa" (Nov. 1914), in Marc, *Schriften*, 165; Losurdo, *War and Revolution*, trans. Elliott, 82; Traverso, *A ferro e fuoco*, 29.

70. Keynes, *Economic Consequences of the Peace*, 5.

71. Rusconi, *Se cessiamo di essere una nazione*, 101–21; Traverso, *A ferro*

e fuoco; Traverso, "New Anti-Communism"; Cattani, "Europe as a Nation," 8–9.

72. Friedrich, "International Civil War," in *Foreign Policy in the Making,* 223–53; Losurdo, "Une catégorie centrale du révisionnisme."

73. Roy, *War and Revolution,* 46–54, 83–91, 96, 108–9; Manjapra, *M. N. Roy,* 128–29.

74. Nolte, *Der europäische Bürgerkrieg, 1917–1945;* Nipperdey, Doering-Manteuffel, and Thamer, *Weltbürgerkrieg der Ideologien;* Bonnet, "Réflexions et jeux d'échelles autour de la notion de 'guerre civile européenne.'" For a different approach, see Payne, *Civil War in Europe, 1904–1949.*

75. Acheson, *Present at the Creation,* 4–5.

76. John F. Kennedy, "State of the Union Address" (Jan. 11, 1962), in U.S. President (1961–1963: Kennedy), *Public Papers of the Presidents of the United States: John F. Kennedy,* 2.9, Miller, *Modernism and the Crisis of Sovereignty,* 15–16.

77. Schmitt, *Theory of the Partisan,* trans. Ulmen, 95.

78. Schmitt, *Donoso Cortés in gesamteuropäischer Interpretation,* 7 ("der europäische Bürgerkrieg von 1848 ... und der globale Weltbürgerkrieg der Gegenwart"), 18–19, 21, 85–86, 113–14; Schmitt, *La guerre civile mondiale;* Kesting, *Geschichtsphilosophie und Weltbürgerkrieg;* Schnur, *Revolution und Weltbürgerkrieg;* Portinaro, "L'epoca della guerra civile mondiale?"; Müller, *Dangerous Mind,* 104–15; Jouin, *Le retour de la guerre juste,* 269–90.

79. Students for a Democratic Society, *Port Huron Statement,* 27.

80. Arendt, *On Revolution,* 17; Bates, "On Revolutions in the Nuclear Age."

81. Galli, *Political Spaces and Global War* (2001–2), trans. Fay, 171–72; Härting, *Global Civil War and Post-colonial Studies;* Odysseos, "Violence *After* the State?"; Odysseos, "Liberalism's War, Liberalism's Order."

82. Hardt and Negri, *Multitude,* 341.

83. Agamben, *State of Exception,* trans. Attell, 2–3; see also Agamben, *Stasis,* trans. Heron, 24 ("The form that civil war has acquired

today in world history is 'terrorism'. . . . Terrorism is the 'global civil war' which time and again invests this or that zone of planetary space.").

84. On the congruences, empirical and definitional, between "civil war" and "terrorism," see Findley and Young, "Terrorism and Civil War."

85. Jung, "Introduction: Towards Global Civil War?"

CONCLUSION
Civil Wars of Words

1. Moses, "Civil War or Genocide?"; Rabinbach, "The Challenge of the Unprecedented."

2. Lepore, *Name of War*, xv.

3. Kalyvas, "Civil Wars," 416, where he notes it is "a phenomenon prone to serious semantic confusion, even contestation." See also Waldmann, "Guerra civil"; Angstrom, "Towards a Typology of Internal Armed Conflict"; Sambanis, "What Is Civil War?"; Mundy, "Deconstructing Civil Wars"; González Calleja, Arbusti, and Pinto, "Guerre civili," 34–42; González Calleja, *Las guerras civiles*, 34–78; Jackson, "Critical Perspectives," 81–83.

4. De Quincey, "[Fragments Relating to 'Casuistry']" (ca. 1839–43), in *Works of Thomas De Quincey*, 11:602.

5. Pavone, *Civil War*, 269–70.

6. Mamdani, "Politics of Naming"; Mamdani, *Saviors and Survivors*, 3–6.

7. Freedman, "What Makes a Civil War?"

8. Talmon, "Recognition of the Libyan National Transitional Council."

Afterword

1. http://www.iraqbodycount.org/database/; United Nations Assistance Mission for Iraq, "Human Rights Report, 1 September–31 October 2006," 4.
2. Ted Widmer, *Ark of the Liberties: America and the World* (New York: Hill and Wang, 2008).

Bibliography

PRIMARY SOURCES

Acheson, Dean. *Present at the Creation: My Years in the State Department.* New York: Norton, 1969.

Adams, John. *Discourses on Davila: A Series of Papers, on Political History.* Boston: Russell and Cutler, 1805.

Appian. *An Auncient Historie and Exquisite Chronicle of the Romane Warres, Both Civile and Foren.* London: Ralph Newbery and Henry Bynneman, 1578.

———. *The Civil Wars.* Translated by John Carter. London: Penguin Books, 1996.

———. *Shakespeare's Appian: A Selection from the Tudor Translation of Appian's Civil Wars.* Edited by Ernest Schanzer. Liverpool: Liverpool University Press, 1956.

Arendt, Hannah. *On Revolution.* London: Penguin, 1990.

ARTFL (Project for American and French Research on the Treasury of the French Language). "Dictionnaires d'autrefois." http://artfl -project.uchicago.edu/content/dictionnaires-dautrefois.

Astell, Mary. "An Impartial Enquiry into the Causes of the Rebellion and Civil War in This Kingdom." In *Political Writings,* edited by

Patricia Springborg, 135–97. Cambridge, U.K.: Cambridge University Press, 1996.

Augustine. *The City of God Against the Pagans*. Edited by R. W. Dyson. Cambridge, U.K.: Cambridge University Press, 1998.

Biondi, Giovanni Francesco. "Civill Warrs of England: In the Life of Henry the Sixth." Translated by Henry, Earl of Monmouth. f MS Eng 1055, Houghton Library, Harvard University.

———. *An History of the Civill Warres of England, Betweene the Two Houses of Lancaster and Yorke*. Translated by Henry, Earl of Monmouth. London: John Benson, 1641.

Bonaparte, Napoleon. *Précis des guerres de Jules César. Écrit à Sainte-Hélène par Marchand, sous la dictée de l'Empereur*. Bécherel: Perséides, 2009.

Bourrienne, Louis Antoine Fauvelet de. *Mémoires de M. de Bourrienne, ministre d'état; sur Napoléon, le directoire, le consulat, l'empire et la restauration*. 10 vols. Paris: L'Advocat, 1829–30.

Burke, Edmund. *Further Reflections on the Revolution in France*. Edited by Daniel E. Ritchie. Indianapolis: Liberty Fund, 1992.

———. *A Letter from the Right Hon. Edmund Burke . . . to Sir Hercules Langrishe . . . on the Subject of Roman Catholics of Ireland*. 2nd ed. London: J. Debrett, 1792.

———. *Reflections on the Revolution in France*. Edited by J. G. A. Pocock. Indianapolis: Hackett, 1987.

———. *The Revolutionary War, 1794–1797: Ireland*. Vol. 9 of *The Writings and Speeches of Edmund Burke*. Edited by R. B. McDowell. Oxford: Clarendon Press, 1991.

Caesar, Julius. *Civil War*. Edited and translated by Cynthia Damon. Cambridge, Mass.: Harvard University Press, 2016.

Carroll, Anna Ella. *The War Powers of the General Government*. Washington, D.C.: Henry Polkinhorn, 1861.

Chateaubriand, François-René. *Mémoires d'outre-tombe*. Edited by Pierre Clarac. Paris: Le Livre de Poche, 1973.

Cicero. *On Duties*. Translated by Walter Miller. Cambridge, Mass.: Harvard University Press, 1913.

———. *Political Speeches*. Translated by D. H. Berry. Oxford: Oxford University Press, 2006.

Civil War; a Poem. Written in the Year 1775. N.p.: n.d. [1776?].

Clarendon, Henry Hyde, Earl of. *The History of the Rebellion and Civil Wars in England, Begun in the Year 1641.* 2 vols. Oxford: At the Theatre, 1702–4.

Clausewitz, Carl von. *Clausewitz on Small War.* Edited and translated by Christopher Daase and James W. Davis. Oxford: Oxford University Press, 2015.

———. *On War.* Edited and translated by Michael Howard and Peter Paret. Princeton, N.J.: Princeton University Press, 1984.

Cooper, James Fenimore. *The Spy: A Tale of the Neutral Ground.* Edited by James P. Elliott, Lance Schachterle, and Jeffrey Walker. New York: AMS Press, 2002.

Corbet, John. *An Historicall Relation of the Military Government of Gloucester.* London: Robert Bostock, 1645.

Coudenhove-Kalergi, Richard Nicolaus. *Europe Must Unite.* Glarus: Paneuropa, 1939.

Davila, Arrigo Caterino. *The Historie of the Civill Warres of France.* Translated by Charles Cotterell and William Aylesbury. London: W. Lee, D. Pakeman, and G. Bedell, 1647–48.

———. *The History of the Civil Wars of France.* Translated by Charles Cotterell and William Aylesbury. London: Henry Herringman, 1678.

Davis, George B., ed. *The Military Laws of the United States.* Washington, D.C.: Government Printing Office, 1897.

De Quincey, Thomas. *The Works of Thomas De Quincey.* Edited by Grevel Lindop. 21 vols. London: Pickering & Chatto, 2000–3.

Diplomatic Conference for the Establishment of International Conventions for the Protection of Victims of War. *Final Record of the Diplomatic Conference of Geneva of 1949.* 3 vols. Bern: Federal Political Department, [1949].

Doughty, Robert. *The Notebook of Robert Doughty, 1662–1665.* Edited by James M. Rosenheim. Norwich, U.K.: Norfolk Record Society, 1989.

Drayton, William Henry. *A Charge, on the Rise of the American Empire.* Charleston, S.C.: David Bruce, 1776.

Dubos, Nicolas, ed. *Le mal extrême: La guerre civile vue par les philosophes*. Paris: CNRS, 2010.

Dugdale, William. *A Short View of the Late Troubles in England; Briefly Setting Forth Their Rise, Growth, and Tragical Conclusion. As Also, Some Parallel Thereof with the Barons Wars . . . but Chiefly with That in France, Called the Holy League*. Oxford: Moses Pitt, 1681.

Eutropius. *Eutropii historiæ romanæ breviarum*. 6th ed. Edinburgh: J. Paton, 1725.

Fénelon, François de Salignac de la Mothe. *Fables and Dialogues of the Dead. Written in French by the Late Archbishop of Cambray*. Translated by John Ozell. London: W. Chetwood and S. Chapman, 1722.

Filmer, Sir Robert. *Patriarcha; or, The Natural Power of Kings*. London: Walter Davis, 1680.

Florus. *Epitome of Roman History*. Translated by Edward Seymour Foster. Cambridge, Mass.: Harvard University Press, 1929.

Foucault, Michel. *The Punitive Society: Lectures at the Collège de France, 1972–1973*. Translated by Graham Burchell. Houndmills: Palgrave Macmillan, 2015.

———. *La société punitive: Cours au Collège de France, 1972–1973*. Edited by François Ewald, Alessandro Fontana, and Bernard Harcourt. Paris: EHESS, Gallimard, Seuil, 2013.

———. "La société punitive" (Jan. 3–March 28, 1973). Archives du Bibliothèque générale du Collège de France.

Franklin, Benjamin. *The Papers of Benjamin Franklin*. Edited by Leonard W. Labaree et al. 41 vols. New Haven, Conn.: Yale University Press, 1959–2011.

Friedrich, Carl Joachim. *Foreign Policy in the Making: The Search for a New Balance of Power*. New York: W. W. Norton, 1938.

Garcilaso de la Vega. *Historia general del Peru trata el descubrimiento del; y como lo ganaron los Españoles: Las guerras civiles que huvo entre Piçarros, y Almagros*. Córdoba: Andreas Barrera, 1617.

Gardiner, Samuel Rawson, ed. *The Constitutional Documents of the Pu-*

ritan Revolution, 1625–1660. 3rd ed. Oxford: Clarendon Press, 1903.

Gastineau, Benjamin. *Histoire de la souscription populaire à la médaille Lincoln*. Paris: A. Lacroix, Verbœckoven, [1865].

Gibbon, Edward. *The History of the Decline and Fall of the Roman Empire*. London: Andrew Strahan and Thomas Cadell, 1782–88.

Grotius, Hugo. *Commentary on the Law of Prize and Booty*. Edited by Martine Julia van Ittersum. Indianapolis: Liberty Fund, 2006.

———. *De Rebus Belgicis; or, The Annals and History of the Low-Countrey-Warrs*. London: Henry Twyford and Robert Paulet, 1665.

———. *The Rights of War and Peace*. Edited by Richard Tuck. 3 vols. Indianapolis: Liberty Fund, 2005.

Guarini, Baptista. *Il Pastor Fido: The Faithfull Shepheard with an Addition of Divers Other Poems Concluding with a Short Discourse of the Long Civill Warres of Rome*. Translated by Richard Fanshawe. London: Humphrey Moseley, 1648.

Guedea, Virginia, ed. *Textos insurgentes (1808–1821)*. Mexico, D.F.: Universidad Nacional Autónoma de México, 2007.

Guizot, François. *Histoire de la révolution d'Angleterre, depuis l'avènement de Charles Ier jusqu'a la restauration*. 2 vols. Paris: A. Leroux and C. Chantpie, 1826.

Halleck, H. W. *International Law; or, Rules Regulating the Intercourse of States in Peace and War*. San Francisco: H. H. Bancroft, 1861.

Harington, Sir John. *The Epigrams of Sir John Harington*. Edited by Gerard Kilroy. Farnham: Ashgate, 2009.

Hartley, David. *Substance of a Speech in Parliament, upon the State of the Nation and the Present Civil War with America*. London: John Almon, 1776.

Heath, James. *A Chronicle of the Late Intestine War in the Three Kingdomes of England, Scotland, and Ireland*. London: Thomas Basset, 1676.

Hobbes, Thomas. *Behemoth: The History of the Causes of the Civil-Wars of England*. London: William Crooke, 1682.

——. *Behemoth; or, The Long Parliament.* Edited by Paul Seaward. Oxford: Clarendon Press, 2010.

——. *The Correspondence.* Edited by Noel Malcolm. 2 vols. Oxford: Clarendon Press, 1994.

——. *The Elements of Law, Natural and Politic: Part I, Human Nature, Part II, De Corpore Politico; with Three Lives.* Edited by J. C. A. Gaskin. Oxford: Oxford University Press, 1994.

——. *Leviathan.* Edited by Noel Malcolm. 3 vols. Oxford: Clarendon Press, 2012.

——. *Writings on Common Law and Hereditary Right.* Edited by Alan Cromartie and Quentin Skinner. Oxford: Clarendon Press, 2005.

Horace. *The Complete Odes and Epodes.* Translated by David West. Oxford: Oxford University Press, 1997.

Howell, James. *Twelve Several Treatises, of the Late Revolutions in These Three Kingdomes.* London: J. Grismond, 1661.

Hugo, Victor. *Les Misérables: A Novel.* Translated by Charles Edward Wilbour. 5 vols. New York: Carleton, 1862.

——. *Les Misérables (The Wretched): A Novel.* Rev. trans. Richmond, Va.: West & Johnston, 1863–64.

Hutson, James H., ed. *A Decent Respect to the Opinions of Mankind: Congressional State Papers, 1774–1776.* Washington, D.C.: Library of Congress, 1976.

Hymans, Paul, Paul Fort, and Amand Rastoul, eds. *Pax mundi: Livre d'or de la paix.* Geneva: Société Paxunis, 1932.

Institut de Droit International. "The Application of International Humanitarian Law and Fundamental Human Rights, in Armed Conflicts in Which Non-state Entities Are Parties." *Annuaire de l'Institut de Droit International* 68 (1999): 386–99.

——. "The Principle of Non-intervention in Civil Wars." *Annuaire de l'Institut de Droit International* 56 (1975): 544–49.

International Committee of the Red Cross. "The Foundation of the Red Cross: Some Important Documents." Edited by Jean S. Pictet. *International Review of the Red Cross* 3 (1963): 60–75.

———. *Seventeenth International Red Cross Conference, Stockholm, August 1948: Report.* Stockholm: International Committee of the Red Cross, 1948.

International Criminal Tribunal for the Former Yugoslavia. *Prosecutor v. Tadić*, IT-94-1-AR72, Decision on Defence Motion for Interlocutory Appeal on Jurisdiction (Appeals Chamber), Oct. 2, 1995.

[Jackson, Samuel]. *Emma Corbett; or, The Miseries of Civil War. Founded on Some Recent Circumstances Which Happened in America.* 3 vols. Bath: Pratt and Clinch, 1780.

Jomini, Antoine Henri. *The Life of Napoleon.* Translated by Henry Wager Halleck. 4 vols. New York: D. Van Norstrand, 1864.

———. *Précis de l'art de la guerre; ou, Nouveau tableau analytique des principales combinaisons de la stratégie, de la grande tactique et de la politique militaire.* 2 vols. Paris. Anselin, 1838.

Jouffroy, Théodore Simon. *Mélanges philosophiques par Théodore Jouffroy.* Paris: Paulin, 1833.

Journal of the Convention of the People of South Carolina, Held in 1860, 1861, and 1862. Columbia, S.C.: R. W. Gibbes, 1862.

Kant, Immanuel. *Practical Philosophy.* Edited and translated by Mary J. Gregor. Cambridge, U.K.: Cambridge University Press, 1996.

Kennedy, C. M. *The Influence of Christianity on International Law.* Cambridge, U.K.: Macmillan, 1856.

Keynes, John Maynard. *The Economic Consequences of the Peace.* Harmondsworth: Penguin Books, 1988.

[Le Blond, Guillaume]. "Guerre." In *Encyclopédie; ou, Dictionnaire raisonné des sciences, des arts et des métiers,* edited by Denis Diderot and Jean le Rond d'Alembert, 7:985–98. 17 vols. Paris: Briasson, 1751–65.

Lenin, Vladimir Il'ich. *Clausewitz' Werk "Vom Kriege": Auszüge und Randglossen.* Berlin: Ministerium für nationale Verteidigung, 1957.

———. *Collected Works.* 45 vols. Moscow: Progress, 1960–72.

Lieber, Francis. *A Code for the Government of Armies in the Field, as*

Authorized by the Laws and Usages of War on Land. "Printed as Manuscript for the Board Appointed by the Secretary of War" (Washington, D.C., 1863), Henry E. Huntington Library, San Marino, Calif., HEH 243077.

————. *Guerrilla Parties: Considered with Reference to the Laws and Usages of War.* New York: D. Van Norstrand, 1862.

————. *Instructions for the Government of Armies of the United States in the Field.* New York: D. Van Nostrand, 1863.

————. "Twenty-Seven Definitions and Elementary Positions Concerning the Laws and Usages of War." 1861. Lieber MSS, Eisenhower Library, Johns Hopkins University, box 2, item 15.

————. [*U.S. Field Order 100.*] *Section X. Insurrection—Rebellion—Civil War—Foreign Invasion of the United States* [1863]. Henry E. Huntington Library, San Marino, HEH 240460.

Lincoln, Abraham. *The Collected Works of Abraham Lincoln.* Edited by Roy P. Basler. 11 vols. New Brunswick, N.J.: Rutgers University Press, 1953–55.

Livy. *The Rise of Rome: Books 1–5.* Translated by T. J. Luce. Oxford: Oxford University Press, 1998.

Locke, John. *Political Essays.* Edited by Mark Goldie. Cambridge, U.K.: Cambridge University Press, 1997.

————. *Two Treatises of Government.* Edited by Peter Laslett. Rev. ed. Cambridge, U.K.: Cambridge University Press, 1988.

Lucan. *Civil War.* Translated by Susan H. Braund. Oxford: Oxford University Press, 1992.

————. *In Cath Catharda: The Civil War of the Romans: An Irish Version of Lucan's Pharsalia.* Edited and translated by Whitley Stokes. Leipzig: Salomon Hirzel, 1909.

————. *M. Annaei Lvcani Pharsalia; sive, De bello civili Caesaris et Pompeii lib. X.* Edited by Hugo Grotius. Leiden: Frans Raphelengius, 1614.

————. *Pharsale de M. A. Lucain.* Translated by Philippe Chasles and M. Greslou. 2 vols. Paris: C. F. L. Panckoucke, 1835–36.

Mably, Gabriel Bonnot de. *Des droits et des devoirs du citoyen.* Edited by Jean-Louis Lecercle. Paris: Marcel Didier, 1972.

Mao Zedong and Che Guevara. *Guerrilla Warfare*. London: Cassell, 1962.

Marc, Franz. *Schriften*. Edited by Klaus Lankheit. Cologne: DuMont, 1978.

Marx, Karl. *Selected Writings*. Edited by David McLellan. Oxford: Oxford University Press, 1977.

Marx, Karl, and Friedrich Engels. *The Collected Works of Karl Marx and Frederick Engels*. Translated by Richard Dixon et al. 50 vols. London: Lawrence and Wishart, 1975–2004.

———. *Karl Marx, Friedrich Engels Gesamtausgabe (MEGA)*. Edited by Institut für Marxismus-Leninismus beim Zentralkomitee der Kommunistischen Partei der Sowjetunion und vom Institut für Marxismus-Leninsmus beim Zentralkomitee der Sozialistischen Einheitspartei Deutschlands. Berlin: Dietz, 1975–.

May, Thomas. *The History of the Parliament of England Which Began November the Third, MDCXL*. London: George Thomason, 1647.

Melville, Herman. *Published Poems*. Vol. 11 of *The Writings of Herman Melville*. Edited by Robert C. Ryan, Harrison Hayford, Alma MacDougall Reising, and G. Thomas Tanselle. Evanston, Ill.: Northwestern University Press, 2009.

Mill, John Stuart. *The Collected Works of John Stuart Mill*. Edited by John M. Robson. 33 vols. Toronto: University of Toronto Press, 1963–91.

Milton, John. *Paradise Lost: A Poem Written in Ten Books*. Edited by John T. Shawcross and Michael Lieb. 2 vols. Pittsburgh: Duquesne University Press, 2007.

Montaigne, Michel de. *Essays Written in French by Michael Lord of Montaigne*. Translated by John Florio. London: Edward Blount and William Barret, 1613.

Montesquieu, Charles de Secondat, baron de. *Reflections on the Causes of the Rise and Fall of the Roman Empire*. Edinburgh: Alexander Donaldson, 1775.

Moynier, Gustave. *Étude sur la Convention de Genève pour l'amélioration du sort des militaires blessés dans les armées en campagne (1864 et 1868)*. Paris: Librairie de Joël Cherbuliez, 1870.

[Nalson, John.] *A True Copy of the Journal of the High Court of Justice, for the Tryal of K. Charles I.* London: Thomas Dring, 1684.

Nietzsche, Friedrich. *On the Genealogy of Morality.* Edited by Keith Ansell-Pearson. Rev. ed. Cambridge, U.K.: Cambridge University Press, 2007.

"An Ordinance of the Commons in England in Parliament assembled with a List of the Commissioners & officers of the said Court by them elected" (January 3, 1649). British Library, London, shelfmark E.536(35).

Orléans, Pierre Joseph d'. *The History of the Revolutions in England Under the Family of the Stuarts, from the Year 1603, to 1690.* London: Edmund Curll, 1711.

Orosius. *Seven Books of History Against the Pagans.* Translated by A. T. Fear. Liverpool: Liverpool University Press, 2010.

Paine, Thomas. *Collected Writings.* Edited by Eric Foner. New York: Library of America, 1995.

The Parliamentary History of England from the Earliest Period to 1803. 36 vols. London: T. C. Hansard, 1806–20.

Petronius. *The Satyricon.* Translated by J. P. Sullivan. Rev. ed. London: Penguin, 2011.

Plato. *The Collected Dialogues of Plato Including the Letters.* Edited by Edith Hamilton and Huntington Cairns. Princeton, N.J.: Princeton University Press, 1961.

Plutarch. *Roman Lives.* Translated by Robin Waterfield. Oxford: Oxford University Press, 1999.

Price, Richard. *Observations on the Nature of Civil Liberty.* London: Thomas Cadell, 1776.

Rawls, John. "Moral Problems: Nations and War" (1969). Harvard University Archives, Acs. 14990, box 12, file 4.

Roebuck, John. *An Enquiry, Whether the Guilt of the Present Civil War in America, Ought to Be Imputed to Great Britain or America.* N.p., n.d. [1776?].

Romans, Bernard. *Annals of the Troubles in the Netherlands: . . . A Proper and Seasonable Mirror for the Present Americans.* 2 vols. Hartford, Conn.: Bernard Romans, 1778–82.

———. *Philadelphia, July 12. 1775. It Is Proposed to Print, a Complete and Elegant Map, from Boston to Worcester, Providence, and Salem. Shewing the Seat of the Present Unhappy Civil War in North-America.* Philadelphia: Robert Aitken, 1775.

———. *To the Hon^e. Jno. Hancock Esqre. President of the Continental Congress; This Map of the Seat of Civil War in America Is Respectfully Inscribed.* [Philadelphia: Nicholas Brooks?, 1775].

Rómverja saga. Edited by Þorbjörg Helgadóttir. 2 vols. Reykjavík: Stofnun Árna Magnússonar, 2010.

Rousseau, Jean-Jacques. *The Discourses and Other Early Political Writings.* Edited by Victor Gourevitch. Cambridge, U.K.: Cambridge University Press, 1997.

———. *A Project for Perpetual Peace.* London: M. Cooper, 1761.

———. *The Social Contract and Other Later Political Writings.* Edited by Victor Gourevitch. Cambridge, U.K.: Cambridge University Press, 1997.

Roy, M. N. *War and Revolution: International Civil War.* Madras: Radical Democratic Party, 1942.

Sallust. *Fragments of the Histories; Letters to Caesar.* Edited by John T. Ramsey. Cambridge, Mass.: Harvard University Press, 2015.

———. *Sallust.* Translated by J. C. Rolfe. Cambridge, Mass.: Harvard University Press, 1921.

Salvemini, Gaetano. *Come siamo andati in Libia e altri scritti dal 1900 al 1915.* Edited by Augusto Torre. Milan: Feltrinelli, 1963.

Sandoval, Prudencio de. *The Civil Wars of Spain in the Beginning of the Reign of Charls the 5t, Emperor of Germanie and King.* Translated by James Wadsworth. London: John Holden, 1652.

Schmitt, Carl. *Donoso Cortés in gesamteuropäischer Interpretation: Vier Aufsätze.* Cologne: Greven, 1950.

———. *Ex Captivitate Salus: Erfahrungen der Zeit 1945/47.* Cologne, Germany: Greven, 1950.

———. *Glossarium: Aufzeichnungen aus den Jahren 1947 bis 1958.*

Edited by Gerd Giesler and Martin Tielke. Berlin: Duncker & Humblot, 2015.

———. *La guerre civile mondiale: Essais (1943–1978)*. Translated by Céline Jouin. Maisons-Alfort: Ère, 2007.

———. *Theory of the Partisan: Intermediate Commentary on the Concept of the Political*. Translated by G. L. Ulmen. New York: Telos Press, 2007.

Sidney, Algernon. *Court Maxims*. Edited by Hans W. Blom, Eco Haitsma Mulier, and Ronald Janse. Cambridge, U.K.: Cambridge University Press, 1996.

———. *Discourses Concerning Government*. London: For the Booksellers of London and Westminster, 1698.

Smith, Adam. *An Inquiry into the Nature and Causes of the Wealth of Nations*. Edited by R. H. Campbell and A. S. Skinner. 2 vols. Oxford: Oxford University Press, 1976.

Statutes of the University of Oxford Codified in the Year 1636 Under the Authority of Archbishop Laud. Edited by John Griffiths. Oxford: Clarendon Press, 1888.

Students for a Democratic Society. *The Port Huron Statement*. New York: Students for a Democratic Society, 1964.

Suetonius. *Suetonius*. Translated by J. C. Rolfe. Rev. ed. 2 vols. Cambridge, Mass.: Harvard University Press, 1998.

Tacitus. *Histories, Books I–III*. Translated by Clifford H. Moore. Cambridge, Mass.: Harvard University Press, 1925.

Thucydides. *Eight Bookes of the Peloponnesian Warre*. Translated by Thomas Hobbes. London: Richard Mynne, 1629.

———. *The Hystory Writtone by Thucidides the Athenyan of the Warre, Whiche Was Betwene the Peloponesians and the Athenyans*. Translated by Thomas Nicolls. London: William Tylle, 1550.

———. *The War of the Peloponnesians and the Athenians*. Edited and translated by Jeremy Mynott. Cambridge, U.K.: Cambridge University Press, 2013.

Torres Bodet, Jaime. "Why We Fight." *UNESCO Courier*, Nov. 1, 1949, 12.

United Daughters of the Confederacy. *Minutes of the Twenty-First Annual Convention of the United Daughters of the Confederacy. Held in Savannah, Georgia, November 11–14, 1914.* Raleigh, N.C.: Edwards and Broughton, 1915.

U.S. Congress, Senate, Committee on Foreign Relations. *The Nature of Revolution: Hearings Before the Committee on Foreign Relations, United States Senate, Ninetieth Congress, Second Session (February 19, 21, 16, and March 7, 1968).* Washington, D.C.: U.S. Government Printing Office, 1968.

U.S. Continental Congress. *Observations on the American Revolution.* Philadelphia: s.n., 1779.

U.S. Department of the Army. *The Law of Land Warfare/Department of the Army, July 1956.* Washington, D.C.: Government Printing Office, 1976.

U.S. Department of War. *Basic Field Manual: Rules of Land Warfare.* Washington, D.C.: Government Printing Office, 1940.

———. *Instructions for the Government of Armies of the United States in the Field. Prepared by Francis Lieber, LL.D.* Washington, D.C.: U.S. Government Printing Office, 1898.

———. *Rules of Land Warfare.* Washington, D.C.: Government Printing Office, 1914.

———. *The War of the Rebellion: A Compilation of the Official Records of the Union and Confederate Armies.* 70 vols. Washington, D.C.: U.S. Government Printing Office, 1880–91.

U.S. Naval War Records Office. *Official Records of the Union and Confederate Navies in the War of the Rebellion.* 30 vols. Washington, D.C.: Government Printing Office, 1894–1922.

U.S. Office of the Adjutant General, Administrative Precedent File ("Frech File"). Record Group 94, box 16, bundle 58, "Civil War," National Archives, Washington, D.C.

U.S. President (1961–1963: Kennedy). *Public Papers of the Presidents of the United States: John F. Kennedy. Containing the Public Messages, Speeches, and Statements of the President, 1961–1963.* 3 vols. Washington, D.C.: U.S. Government Printing Office, 1962–63.

Vattel, Emer de. *The Law of Nations*. Edited by Béla Kapossy and Richard Whatmore. Indianapolis: Liberty Fund, 2008.

Vázquez de Menchaca, Fernando. *Controversiarum illustrium . . . libri tres*. Frankfurt: S. Feyerabend and G. Corvinus, 1572.

Vertot, René-Aubert de. *Histoire de la conjuration de Portugal*. Paris: La Veuve d'Edme Martin, 1689.

———. *Histoire des révolutions arrivées dans le gouvernement de la république romaine*. 3 vols. Paris: François Barois, 1719.

———. *Histoire des révolutions de Portugal*. Amsterdam: Aux Dépens d'Etienne Roger, 1712.

———. *Histoire des révolutions de Suède où l'on voit les changemens qui sont arrivez*. Paris: s.n., 1695.

Wheare, Degory. *The Method and Order of Reading Both Civil and Ecclesiastical Histories*. Translated by Edmund Bohun. London: Charles Brome, 1685.

Whitney, Geffrey. *A Choice of Emblemes and Other Devises*. Leiden: Christopher Plantin, 1586.

SECONDARY SOURCES

Abdul-Ahad, Ghaith. " 'Syria Is Not a Revolution Any More—This Is Civil War.' " *Guardian*, Nov. 18, 2013.

Adamson, John. "The Baronial Context of the English Civil War." *Transactions of the Royal Historical Society*, 5th ser., 40 (1990): 93–120.

———. *The Noble Revolt: The Overthrow of Charles I*. London: Weidenfeld & Nicolson, 2007.

Adelman, Jeremy. "An Age of Imperial Revolutions." *American Historical Review* 113, no. 2 (April 2008): 319–40.

Agamben, Giorgio. *Stasis: Civil War as a Political Paradigm*. Translated by Nicholas Heron. Stanford, Calif.: Stanford University Press, 2015.

———. *State of Exception*. Translated by Kevin Attell. Chicago: University of Chicago Press, 2005.

Allanson, Marie, Erik Melander, and Lotta Themnér. "Organized

Violence, 1989–2016." *Journal of Peace Research* 54, no. 4 (July 2017): 574–87.

Almond, Gabriel A. "Harry Eckstein as Political Theorist." *Comparative Political Studies* 31, no. 4 (Aug. 1998): 498–504.

Ando, Clifford. *Law, Language, and Empire in the Roman Tradition.* Philadelphia: University of Pennsylvania Press, 2011.

———. *Roman Social Imaginaries: Language and Thought in the Contexts of Empire.* Toronto: University of Toronto Press, 2015.

Andress, David. *The Terror: Civil War in the French Revolution.* London: Little, Brown, 2005.

Angstrom, Jan. "Towards a Typology of Internal Armed Conflict: Synthesising a Decade of Conceptual Turmoil." *Civil Wars* 4, no. 3 (Autumn 2001): 93–116.

Arena, Valentina. Libertas *and the Practice of Politics in the Late Roman Republic.* Cambridge, U.K.: Cambridge University Press, 2012.

Armitage, David. "Cosmopolitanism and Civil War." In *Cosmopolitanism and the Enlightenment,* edited by Joan-Pau Rubiés and Neil Safier. Cambridge, U.K.: Cambridge University Press, forthcoming.

———. *The Declaration of Independence: A Global History.* Cambridge, Mass.: Harvard University Press, 2007.

———. "Every Great Revolution Is a Civil War." In *Scripting Revolution: A Historical Approach to the Comparative Study of Revolutions,* edited by Keith Michael Baker and Dan Edelstein, 57–68. Stanford, Calif.: Stanford University Press, 2015.

———. "The First Atlantic Crisis: The American Revolution." In *Early North America in Global Perspective,* edited by Philip D. Morgan and Molly A. Warsh, 309–36. London: Routledge, 2014.

———. *Foundations of Modern International Thought.* Cambridge, U.K.: Cambridge University Press, 2013.

———. "Secession and Civil War." In *Secession as an International Phenomenon: From America's Civil War to Contemporary Separatist Movements,* edited by Don H. Doyle, 37–55. Athens: University of Georgia Press, 2010.

———. "What's the Big Idea? Intellectual History and the *Longue Durée.*" *History of European Ideas* 38, no. 4 (Dec. 2012): 493–507.

Armitage, David, et al. "*AHR Roundtable:* Ending Civil Wars." *American Historical Review* 120, no. 5 (Dec. 2015): 1682–1837.

———. "Interchange: Nationalism and Internationalism in the Era of the Civil War." *Journal of American History* 98, no. 2 (Sept. 2011): 455–89.

———. "La longue durée en débat." *Annales: Histoire, Sciences Sociales* 70, no. 2 (April–June 2015): 319–78.

Armitage, David, Conal Condren, and Andrew Fitzmaurice, eds. *Shakespeare and Early Modern Political Thought.* Cambridge, U.K.: Cambridge University Press, 2009.

Armitage, David, and Sanjay Subrahmanyam, eds. *The Age of Revolutions in Global Context, c. 1760–1840.* Basingstoke: Palgrave Macmillan, 2010.

As-Sirri, Ahmed. *Religiös-politische Argumentation im frühen Islam (610–685): Der Begriff Fitna: Bedeutung und Funktion.* Frankfurt: Peter Lang, 1990.

Asso, Paolo, ed. *Brill's Companion to Lucan.* Leiden: Brill, 2011.

Ayalon, Ami. "From Fitna to Thawra." *Studia Islamica* 66 (1987): 145–74.

Baker, Keith Michael. "Inventing the French Revolution." In *Inventing the French Revolution,* edited by Keith Michael Baker, 203–23. Cambridge, U.K.: Cambridge University Press, 1990.

———. "Revolution 1.0." *Journal of Modern European History* 11, no. 2 (May 2013): 187–219.

Balibar, Étienne. "On the Aporias of Marxian Politics: From Civil War to Class Struggle." *Diacritics* 39, no. 2 (Summer 2009): 59–73.

Bates, David. "On Revolutions in the Nuclear Age: The Eighteenth Century and the Postwar Global Imagination." *Qui Parle* 15, no. 2 (2005): 171–95.

———. *States of War: Enlightenment Origins of the Political.* New York: Columbia University Press, 2012.

Batstone, William W., and Cynthia Damon. *Caesar's "Civil War."* Oxford: Oxford University Press, 2006.

Bauman, Richard A. *The Crimen Maiestatis in the Roman Republic and*

Augustan Principate. Johannesburg: Witwatersrand University Press, 1967.

Baxter, R. R. "The First Modern Codification of the Law of War: Francis Lieber and General Orders No. 100." *International Review of the Red Cross* 3, nos. 25–26 (April–June 1963): 170–89, 234–50.

Bayly, C. A. *The Birth of the Modern World, 1780–1914*. Oxford: Blackwell, 2004.

BBC News, Middle East. "Syria in Civil War, Red Cross Says." July 15, 2012. http://www.bbc.com/news/world-middle-east-18849362.

Beard, Mary. *The Roman Triumph*. Cambridge, Mass.: Belknap Press of Harvard University Press, 2007.

———. *SPQR: A History of Ancient Rome*. London: Profile Books, 2015.

Beaulac, Stéphane. "Emer de Vattel and the Externalization of Sovereignty." *Journal of the History of International Law* 5, no. 2 (2003): 237–92.

Beckert, Sven. *Empire of Cotton: A Global History*. New York: Alfred A. Knopf, 2014.

Belcher, Henry. *The First American Civil War: First Period, 1775–1778*. 2 vols. London: Macmillan, 1911.

Bell, David A. *The First Total War: Napoleon's Europe and the Birth of Warfare as We Know It*. Boston: Houghton Mifflin, 2007.

Bentley, Gerald Eades. *Shakespeare and Jonson: Their Reputations in the Seventeenth Century Compared*. 2 vols. Chicago: University of Chicago Press, 1945.

Berent, Moshe. "*Stasis*, or the Greek Invention of Politics." *History of Political Thought* 19, no. 3 (Autumn 1998): 331–62.

Bevir, Mark. "What Is Genealogy?" *Journal of the Philosophy of History* 2, no. 3 (Fall 2008): 263–75.

Blattman, Christopher, and Edward Miguel. "Civil War." *Journal of Economic Literature* 48, no. 1 (March 2010): 3–57.

Blight, David W. *Race and Reunion: The Civil War in American Memory*. Cambridge, Mass.: Belknap Press of Harvard University Press, 2001.

Boissier, Pierre. *Histoire du Comité international de la Croix-Rouge. De Solférino à Tsoushima*. Paris: Plon, 1963.

Bonnell, Andrew G. "'A Very Valuable Book': Karl Marx and Appian." In *Appian's Roman History: Empire and Civil War*, edited by Kathryn Welch, 15–22. Swansea: The Classical Press of Wales, 2015.

Bonnet, Romain. "Réflexions et jeux d'échelles autour de la notion de 'guerre civile européenne.'" *Amnis* 14 (2015): http://amnis.revues.org/2282.

Boritt, Gabor. *The Gettysburg Gospel: The Lincoln Speech That Nobody Knows*. New York: Simon & Schuster, 2006.

Boritt, Gabor, Mark E. Neely Jr., and Harold Holzer. "The European Image of Abraham Lincoln." *Winterthur Portfolio* 21, no. 2/3 (Summer–Autumn 1986): 153–83.

Botteri, Paula. "*Stásis:* Le mot grec, la chose romaine." *Mêtis* 4, no. 1 (1989): 87–100.

Bowersock, G. W. "Gibbon on Civil War and Rebellion in the Decline of the Roman Empire." *Daedalus* 105, no. 3 (Summer 1976): 63–71.

Braddick, Michael. *God's Fury, England's Fire: A New History of the English Civil Wars*. London: Allen Lane, 2008.

Brass, Paul. *The Theft of an Idol: Text and Context in the Representation of Collective Violence*. Princeton, N.J.: Princeton University Press, 1997.

Braumoeller, Bear F. "Is War Disappearing?" Paper presented at the 109th American Political Science Association annual convention, Chicago, Aug. 28–Sept. 1, 2013. http://papers.ssrn.com/s013/papers.cfm?abstract_id=2317269.

Braund, Kathryn E. Holland. "Bernard Romans: His Life and Works." In *A Concise Natural History of East and West Florida*, by Bernard Romans, 1–41. Edited by Kathryn E. Holland Braund. Tuscaloosa: University of Alabama Press, 1999.

Braund, Susan. "A Tale of Two Cities: Statius, Thebes, and Rome." *Phoenix* 60, no. 3/4 (Fall–Winter 2006): 259–73.

Breed, Brian, Cynthia Damon, and Andreola Rossi, eds. *Citizens of*

Discord: Rome and Its Civil Wars. Oxford: Oxford University Press, 2010.

Breen, T. H. *American Insurgents, American Patriots: The Revolution of the People.* New York: Hill and Wang, 2010.

Brett, Annabel S. *Changes of State: Nature and the Limits of the City in Early Modern Natural Law.* Princeton, N.J.: Princeton University Press, 2011.

Brinton, Crane. *The Anatomy of Revolution.* Rev. ed. New York: Vintage Books, 1965.

Brown, Peter. *Augustine of Hippo: A Biography.* New ed. Berkeley: University of California Press, 2000.

Brown, Robert. "The Terms *Bellum Sociale* and *Bellum Civile* in the Late Republic." In *Studies in Latin Literature and Roman History 11*, edited by Carl Deroux, 94–120. Brussels: Latomus, 2003.

Brunt, P. A. *Italian Manpower, 225 B.C.–A.D. 14.* Oxford: Oxford University Press, 1971.

———. *Social Conflicts in the Roman Republic.* London: Chatto and Windus, 1971.

Bulst, Neithard, Jörg Fisch, Reinhart Koselleck, and Christian Meier. "Revolution, Rebellion, Aufruhr, Bürgerkrieg." In *Geschichtliche Grundbegriffe: Historisches Lexikon zur politisch-sozialen Sprache in Deutschland*, edited by Otto Brunner, Werner Conze, and Reinhart Koselleck, 653–788. 8 vols. Stuttgart: Ernst Klett, 1972–97.

Burke, Peter. "A Survey of the Popularity of Ancient Historians, 1450–1700." *History and Theory* 5, no. 2 (1966): 135–52.

Canal, Jordi. "Guerra civil y contrarrevolución en la Europa del sur en el siglo XIX: Reflexiones a partir del caso español." *Ayer* 55, no. 3 (2004): 37–60.

Caron, Jean-Claude. *Frères de sang: La guerre civile en France au XIXe siècle.* Seyssel: Champ Vallon, 2009.

Castrén, Erik. *Civil War.* Helsinki: Suomalainen Tiedeakatemia, 1966.

Cattani, Paola. "Europe as a Nation: Intellectuals and Debate on Europe in the Inter-war Period." *History of European Ideas* (30 June 2016): http://dx.doi.org/10.1080/01916599.2016.1202126.

Centre for the Study of Civil War, Peace Research Institute Oslo. http://www.prio.no/CSCW.

Checkel, Jeffrey T., ed. *Transnational Dynamics of Civil War*. Cambridge, U.K.: Cambridge University Press, 2013.

Chenoweth, Erica. "The Syrian Conflict Is Already a Civil War." *American Prospect*, Jan. 15, 2012.: http://prospect.org/article/syrian-conflict-already-civil-war.

Cimbala, Paul A., and Randall M. Miller, eds. *The Great Task Remaining Before Us: Reconstruction as America's Continuing Civil War*. New York: Fordham University Press, 2010.

Clavadetscher-Thürlemann, Silvia. *Πόλεμος δίκαιος und bellum iustum: Versuch einer Ideengeschichte*. Zurich: Juris, 1985.

Coate, Mary. *Cornwall in the Great Civil War and Interregnum, 1642–1660: A Social and Political Study*. Oxford: Clarendon Press, 1933.

Collier, David, Fernando Daniel Hidalgo, and Andra Olivia Maciuceanu. "Essentially Contested Concepts: Debates and Applications." *Journal of Political Ideologies* 11, no. 3 (Oct. 2006): 211–46.

Collier, Paul. *The Bottom Billion: Why the Poorest Countries Are Failing and What Can Be Done About It*. Oxford: Oxford University Press, 2007.

———. *Wars, Guns, and Votes: Democracy in Dangerous Places*. New York: Harper, 2009.

Collier, Paul, Anke Hoeffler, and Måns Söderbom. "On the Duration of Civil War." *Journal of Peace Research* 41, no. 3 (May 2004): 253–73.

Collier, Paul, and Nicholas Sambanis, eds. *Understanding Civil War: Evidence and Analysis*. 2 vols. Washington, D.C.: World Bank, 2005.

Conflict Archive on the Internet. "Violence: Deaths During the Conflict" (2001–). http://cain.ulst.ac.uk/issues/violence/deaths.htm.

Conte, Gian Biagio. *Latin Literature: A History*. Translated by Joseph B. Solodow. Baltimore: Johns Hopkins University Press, 1994.

Cordesmann, Anthony H. *Iraq's Insurgency and the Road to Civil Conflict*. With Emma R. Davies. 2 vols. Westport, Conn.: Praeger Security International, 2008.

Coski, John M. "The War Between the Names." *North and South* 8, no. 7 (Jan. 2006): 62–71.

Coulter, E. Merton. "A Name for the American War of 1861–1865." *Georgia Historical Quarterly* 36, no. 2 (June 1952): 109–31.

Cramer, Christopher. *Civil War Is Not a Stupid Thing: Accounting for Violence in Developing Countries.* London: Hurst, 2006.

Crenshaw, Martha. "Why Is America the Primary Target? Terrorism as Globalized Civil War." In *The New Global Terrorism: Characteristics, Causes, Controls,* edited by Charles W. Kegley Jr., 160–72. Upper Saddle River, N.J.: Prentice Hall, 2002.

Cullen, Anthony. *The Concept of Non-international Armed Conflict in International Humanitarian Law.* Cambridge, U.K.: Cambridge University Press, 2010.

David, Eric. "Internal (Non-international) Armed Conflict." In *The Oxford Handbook of International Law in Armed Conflict,* edited by Andrew Clapham and Paola Gaeta, 353–62. Oxford: Oxford University Press, 2014.

DeRouen, Karl, Jr., and Uk Heo, eds. *Civil Wars of the World: Major Conflicts Since World War II.* 2 vols. Santa Barbara, Calif.: ABC-CLIO, 2007.

Dinstein, Yoram. *Non-international Armed Conflicts in International Law.* Cambridge, U.K.: Cambridge University Press, 2014.

Dixon, Jeffrey. "What Causes Civil Wars? Integrating Quantitative Research Findings." *International Studies Review* 11, no. 4 (Dec. 2009): 707–35.

Donagan, Barbara. *War in England, 1642–1649.* Oxford: Oxford University Press, 2010.

Donaldson, Ian. "Talking with Ghosts: Ben Jonson and the English Civil War." *Ben Jonson Journal* 17, no. 1 (May 2010): 1–18.

Downs, Gregory P. *After Appomattox: Military Occupation and the Ends of War.* Cambridge, Mass.: Harvard University Press, 2015.

Doyle, Don. H. *The Cause of All Nations: An International History of the American Civil War.* New York: Basic Books, 2015.

Draper, Hal. *Karl Marx's Theory of Revolution.* Vol. 3, *The Dictatorship of the Proletariat.* New York: Monthly Review Press, 1977.

Dunne, J. Paul. "Armed Conflicts." In *Global Problems, Smart Solutions: Costs and Benefits*, edited by Bjørn Lomborg, 21–53. Cambridge, U.K.: Cambridge University Press, 2013.

Duvall, Raymond. "An Appraisal of the Methodological and Statistical Procedures of the Correlates of War Project." In *Quantitative International Politics: An Appraisal*, edited by Francis W. Hoole and Dina A. Zinnes, 67–98. New York: Praeger, 1976.

Dyer, Brainerd. "Francis Lieber and the American Civil War." *Huntington Library Quarterly* 2, no. 4 (July 1939): 449–65.

Eckstein, Harry. "On the Etiology of Internal Wars." *History and Theory* 4, no. 2 (1965): 133–63.

———, ed., *Internal War: Problems and Approaches*. New York: Free Press of Glencoe, 1963.

Edelstein, Dan. "Do We Want a Revolution Without Revolution? Reflections on Political Authority." *French Historical Studies* 35, no. 2 (Spring 2012): 269–89.

Eliot, T. S. *Milton: Annual Lecture on a Master Mind, Henriette Hertz Trust of the British Academy 1947*. London: Geoffrey Cumberlege, 1947.

Elliott, J. H. *Empires of the Atlantic World: Britain and Spain in America, 1492–1830*. New Haven, Conn.: Yale University Press, 2006.

Engerman, David C. "Social Science in the Cold War." *Isis* 101, no. 2 (June 2010): 393–400.

Enzensberger, Hans Magnus. *Civil War*. Translated by Piers Spence and Martin Chalmers. London: Granta Books, 1994.

Esposito, Roberto. *Terms of the Political: Community, Immunity, Biopolitics*. Translated by Rhiannon Noel Welch. New York: Fordham University Press, 2012.

Fabre, Cécile. *Cosmopolitan War*. Oxford: Oxford University Press, 2012.

Faust, Drew Gilpin. "'Numbers on Top of Numbers': Counting the Civil War Dead." *Journal of Military History* 70, no. 4 (Oct. 2006): 995–1009.

———. *This Republic of Suffering: Death and the American Civil War*. New York: Alfred A. Knopf, 2008.

Fearon, James D. "Iraq's Civil War." *Foreign Affairs* 86, no. 2 (March/April 2007): 2–16.

———. "Testimony to U.S. House of Representatives ... on 'Iraq: Democracy or Civil War?'" Sept. 15, 2006. https://web.stanford.edu/group/fearon-research/cgi-bin/wordpress/wp-content/uploads/2013/10/Testimony-before-the-U.S.-House-Subcommittee-on-National-Security-Emerging-Threats-and-International-Relations-September-15-2006.pdf.

———. "Why Do Some Civil Wars Last So Much Longer Than Others?" *Journal of Peace Research* 41, no. 3 (May 2004): 275–301.

Fearon, James D., and David Laitin. "Ethnicity, Insurgency, and Civil War." *American Political Science Review* 97, no. 1 (Feb. 2003): 91–106.

Findley, Michael G., and Joseph K. Young. "Terrorism and Civil War: A Spatial and Temporal Approach to a Conceptual Problem." *Perspectives on Politics* 10, no. 2 (June 2012): 285–305.

Finkelman, Paul. "Francis Lieber and the Modern Law of War." *University of Chicago Law Review* 80, no. 4 (Fall 2013): 2071–132.

Fitzmaurice, Andrew. *Sovereignty, Property, and Empire, 1500–2000.* Cambridge, U.K.: Cambridge University Press, 2014.

Fleche, Andre M. *The Revolution of 1861: The American Civil War in an Age of Nationalist Conflict.* Chapel Hill: University of North Carolina Press, 2012.

Flower, Harriet I. *The Art of Forgetting: Disgrace and Oblivion in Roman Political Culture.* Chapel Hill: University of North Carolina Press, 2006.

———. "Rome's First Civil War and the Fragility of Republican Culture." In *Citizens of Discord: Rome and Its Civil Wars*, edited by Brian W. Breed, Cynthia Damon, and Andreola Rossi, 73–86. New York: Oxford University Press, 2010.

Foisneau, Luc. "A Farewell to Leviathan: Foucault and Hobbes on Power, Sovereignty, and War." In *Insiders and Outsiders in Seventeenth-Century Philosophy*, edited by G. A. J. Rogers, Tom Sorell, and Jill Kraye, 207–22. London: Routledge, 2010.

Forrester, Katrina. "Citizenship, War, and the Origins of International

Ethics in American Political Philosophy, 1960–1975." *Historical Journal* 57, no. 3 (Sept. 2014): 773–801.

Forst, Rainer. *Toleration in Conflict: Past and Present*. Translated by Ciaran Cronin. Cambridge, U.K.: Cambridge University Press, 2013.

Franco Restrepo, Vilma Liliana. *Guerras civiles. Introducción al problema de su justificación*. Medellín: Editorial Universidad de Antioquia, 2008.

Freedman, Lawrence. "What Makes a Civil War?" *BBC News, Middle East*, April 20, 2006. http://news.bbc.co.uk./2/hi/middle_east /4902708.stm.

Fry, Douglas P. *Beyond War: The Human Potential for Peace*. Oxford: Oxford University Press, 2007.

Fuentes, Juan Francisco. "*Belle époque:* Mito y concepto de guerra civile en España (1898–1939)." *Revista de Occidente* 389 (Oct. 2013): 79–110.

———. "Guerra civil." In *Diccionario político y social del siglo XX español*, edited by Javier Fernández Sebastián and Juan Francisco Fuentes, 608–17. Madrid: Alianza, 2008.

Fuks, Alexander. "Thucydides and the Stasis in Corcyra: Thuc. III 82–3 versus [Thuc.] III 84." *American Journal of Philology* 92, no. 1 (Jan. 1971): 48–55.

Furet, François. *Interpreting the French Revolution*. Translated by Elborg Forster. Cambridge, U.K.: Cambridge University Press, 1981.

Gaddis, John Lewis. *The Long Peace: Inquiries into the History of the Cold War*. New York: Oxford University Press, 1987.

Galli, Carlo. *Political Spaces and Global War*. Translated by Elizabeth Fay. Minneapolis: University of Minnesota Press, 2010.

Gallie, W. B. "Essentially Contested Concepts." *Proceedings of the Aristotelian Society* 56 (1955–56): 167–98.

———. *Philosophy and the Historical Understanding*. 2nd ed. New York: Schocken Books, 1968.

Gardet, Louis. "Fitna." In *The Encyclopaedia of Islam*, edited by H. A. R. Gibb et al., 2:930. 2nd ed. 13 vols., Leiden: Brill, 1960–2009.

Gehrke, Hans-Joachim. *Stasis: Untersuchungen zu den inneren Kriegen in den griechischen Staaten des 5. und 4. Jahrhunderts v. Chr.* Munich: Beck, 1985.

Geuss, Raymond. "Nietzsche and Genealogy." In *Morality, Culture, and History,* 1–28. Cambridge, U.K.: Cambridge University Press, 1999.

Geyer, Michael, and Charles Bright. "Global Violence and Nationalizing Wars in Eurasia and America: The Geopolitics of War in the Mid-nineteenth Century." *Comparative Studies in Society and History* 38, no. 4 (Oct. 1996): 619–57.

Ghervas, Stella. "La paix par le droit, ciment de la civilisation en Europe? La perspective du Siècle des Lumières." In *Penser l'Europe au XVIIIe siècle: Commerce, civilisation, empire,* edited by Antoine Lilti and Céline Spector, 47–70. Oxford: Voltaire Foundation, 2014.

Gibson, Jonathan. "Civil War in 1614: Lucan, Gorges, and Prince Henry." In *The Crisis of 1614 and the Addled Parliament: Literary and Historical Perspectives,* edited by Stephen Clucas and Rosalind Davies, 161–76. Aldershot: Ashgate, 2002.

Gilman, Nils. "The Cold War as Intellectual Force Field." *Modern Intellectual History* 13, no. 2 (Aug. 2016): 507–23.

Giraldo Ramírez, Jorge. *El rastro de Caín: Una aproximación filosófica a los conceptos de guerra, paz y guerra civil.* Bogotá: Escuela Nacional Sindical, 2001.

Girard, René. *Violence and the Sacred.* Translated by Patrick Gregory. Baltimore: Johns Hopkins University Press, 1984.

Gleditsch, Kristian Skrede. "A Revised List of Wars Between and Within Independent States, 1816–2002." *International Interactions* 30, no. 3 (July–Sept. 2004): 231–62.

———. "Transnational Dimensions of Civil War." *Journal of Peace Research* 44, no. 3 (May 2007): 293–309.

Goldstein, Joshua S. *Winning the War on War: The Decline of Armed Conflict Worldwide.* New York: Dutton, 2011.

González Calleja, Eduardo. *Las guerras civiles: Perspectiva de análisis desde las ciencias sociales.* Madrid: Catarata, 2013.

González Calleja, Eduardo, Irene Arbusti, and Carmine Pinto. "Guerre civili: Un percorso teorico." *Meridiana* 76 (2013): 31–56.

Goulemot, Jean Marie. *Le règne de l'histoire: Discours historiques et révolutions XVIIe–XVIIIe siècles*. Paris: Albin Michel, 1996.

Gowing, Alain M. "'Caesar Grabs My Pen': Writing Civil War Under Tiberius." In *Citizens of Discord: Rome and Its Civil Wars*, edited by Brian W. Breed, Cynthia Damon, and Andreola Rossi, 249–60. New York: Oxford University Press, 2010.

———. *Empire and Memory: The Representation of the Roman Republic in Imperial Culture*. Cambridge, U.K.: Cambridge University Press, 2005.

Grafton, Anthony. *What Was History? The Art of History in Early Modern Europe*. Cambridge, U.K.: Cambridge University Press, 2007.

Grangé, Ninon. *De la guerre civile*. Paris: Armand Colin, 2009.

———. *Oublier la guerre civile? Stasis, chronique d'une disparition*. Paris: VRIN/EHESS, 2015.

———. "*Tumultus* et *tumulto:* Deux conceptions de la cité en guerre contre elle-même, Machiavel et Ciceron." *Historia Philosophica* 4 (2006): 11–31.

Guldi, Jo, and David Armitage. *The History Manifesto*. Cambridge, U.K.: Cambridge University Press, 2014.

Hacker, J. David. "A Census-Based Count of the Civil War Dead." *Civil War History* 57, no. 4 (Dec. 2011): 307–48.

Hadfield, Andrew. *Shakespeare and Republicanism*. Cambridge, U.K.: Cambridge University Press, 2005.

Hahlweg, Werner. "Lenin und Clausewitz: Ein Beitrag zur politischen Ideen-geschichte des 20. Jahrhunderts." *Archiv für Kulturge-schichte* 36 (1954): 20–59, 357–87.

Hale, John K. "*Paradise Lost:* A Poem in Twelve Books, or Ten?" *Philological Quarterly* 74, no. 2 (Spring 1995): 131–49.

Hardt, Michael, and Antonio Negri. *Multitude: War and Democracy in the Age of Empire*. New York: Penguin Press, 2004.

Harloe, Katherine, and Neville Morley, eds. *Thucydides and the Modern World*. Cambridge, U.K.: Cambridge University Press, 2012.

Harris, Tim. "Did the English Have a Script for Revolution in the

Seventeenth Century?" In *Scripting Revolution: A Historical Approach to the Comparative Study of Revolutions*, edited by Dan Edelstein and Keith Michael Baker, 25–40. Stanford, Calif.: Stanford University Press, 2015.

Harrison, John, and Peter Laslett. *The Library of John Locke.* Oxford: Oxford University Press for the Oxford Bibliographical Society, 1965.

Hartigan, Richard Shelly. *Military Rules, Regulations, and the Code of War: Francis Lieber and the Certification of Conflict.* New Brunswick, N.J.: Transaction, 2011.

Härting, Heike. *Global Civil War and Post-colonial Studies.* Globalization Working Papers 06/3. Institute on Globalization and the Human Condition, McMaster University, May 2006.

Harvey, David. *Rebel Cities: From the Right to the City to the Urban Revolution.* London: Verso, 2012.

Hazan, Éric. *A History of the Barricade.* Translated by David Fernbach. London: Verso, 2015.

Henderson, Errol A., and J. David Singer. "Civil War in the Post-colonial World, 1946–92." *Journal of Peace Research* 37, no. 3 (May 2000): 275–99.

Henderson, John. *Fighting for Rome: Poets and Caesars, History and Civil War.* Cambridge, U.K.: Cambridge University Press, 1998.

Heuzé, Philippe. "Comment peindre le passage du Rubicon?" In *Présence de César: Actes du Colloque de 9–11 Décembre 1983: Hommage au doyen Michel Rambaud*, edited by Raymond Chevallier, 57–65. Paris: Belles Lettres, 1985.

Hironaka, Ann. *Neverending Wars: The International Community, Weak States, and the Perpetuation of Civil War.* Cambridge, Mass.: Harvard University Press, 2005.

Hoar, Jay S. *The South's Last Boys in Gray: An Epic Prose Elegy.* Bowling Green, Ohio: Bowling Green State University Popular Press, 1986.

Hoeffler, Anke. "Alternative Perspective." In *Global Problems, Smart Solutions: Costs and Benefits*, edited by Bjørn Lomborg, 54–61. Cambridge, U.K.: Cambridge University Press, 2013.

Hoekstra, Kinch. "Hobbes's Thucydides." In *The Oxford Handbook of Hobbes*, edited by A. P. Martinich and Kinch Hoekstra, 547–74. Oxford: Oxford University Press, 2016.

Hoffman, Marcelo. "Foucault's Politics and Bellicosity as a Matrix for Power Relations." *Philosophy and Social Criticism* 33, no. 6 (Sept. 2007): 756–78.

Holmes, Clive. "The Trial and Execution of Charles I." *Historical Journal* 53, no. 2 (June 2010): 289–316.

Hopkinson, Michael. *Green Against Green: The Irish Civil War*. Dublin: Gill and Macmillan, 1988.

Howard, Michael. *The Invention of Peace and the Reinvention of War*. Rev. ed. London: Profile, 2002.

Huffington Post. "Syria Crisis: Death Toll Tops 17,000, Says Opposition Group." July 9, 2012. http://www.huffingtonpost.com/2012/07/09/syria-crisis-death-toll-17000_n_1658708.html.

Hurrell, Andrew. "Revisiting Kant and Intervention." In *Just and Unjust Military Intervention: European Thinkers from Vitoria to Mill*, edited by Stefano Recchia and Jennifer M. Welsh, 196–218. Cambridge, U.K.: Cambridge University Press, 2013.

International Committee of the Red Cross. "Internal Conflicts or Other Situations of Violence—What Is the Difference for Victims?" ICRC Resource Centre, Dec. 12, 2012. http://www.icrc.org/eng/resources/documents/interview/2012/12-10-niac-non-international-armed-conflict.htm.

Jackson, Richard. "Critical Perspectives." In *Routledge Handbook of Civil Wars*, edited by Edward Norman and Karl Derouen, 79–90. London: Routledge, 2014.

Jacob, Kathryn Allamong. *Testament to Union: Civil War Monuments in Washington, D.C.* Baltimore: Johns Hopkins University Press, 1998.

Jacoby, Russell. *Bloodlust: On the Roots of Violence from Cain and Abel to the Present*. New York: Free Press, 2011.

Jal, Paul. *La guerre civile à Rome: Étude littéraire et morale*. Paris: Presses Universitaires de France, 1963.

———. "'Hostis (Publicus)' dans la littérature latine de la fin de la République." *Revue des Études Anciennes* 65 (1963): 53–79.

———. " 'Tumultus' et 'bellum ciuile' dans les Philippiques de Cicéron." In *Hommages à Jean Bayet*, edited by Marcel Renard and Robert Schilling, 281–89. Brussels: Latomus, 1964.

Jasanoff, Maya. *Liberty's Exiles: American Loyalists in the Revolutionary World*. New York: Alfred A. Knopf, 2011.

Jensen, Freyja Cox. "Reading Florus in Early Modern England." *Renaissance Studies* 23, no. 5 (Nov. 2009): 659–77.

———. *Reading the Roman Republic in Early Modern England*. Leiden: Brill, 2012.

Joas, Hans, and Wolfgang Köbl. *War in Social Thought: Hobbes to the Present*. Translated by Alex Skinner. Princeton, N.J.: Princeton University Press, 2013.

Johnson, Martin P. *Writing the Gettysburg Address*. Lawrence: University Press of Kansas, 2013.

Jouin, Céline. *Le retour de la guerre juste: Droit international, épistémologie et idéologie chez Carl Schmitt*. Paris: J. Vrin, 2013.

Jung, Dietrich. "Introduction: Towards Global Civil War?" In *Shadow Globalization, Ethnic Conflicts and New Wars: A Political Economy of Intra-state War*, edited by Dietrich Jung, 1–6. London: Routledge, 2003.

Kaldor, Mary. *New and Old Wars*. 3rd ed. Cambridge, U.K.: Polity Press, 2012.

Kalyvas, Stathis N. "Civil Wars." In *The Oxford Handbook of Comparative Politics*, edited by Carles Boix and Susan C. Stokes, 416–34. Oxford: Oxford University Press, 2007.

———. *The Logic of Violence in Civil War*. Cambridge, U.K.: Cambridge University Press, 2006.

———. " 'New' and 'Old' Civil Wars: A Valid Distinction?" *World Politics* 54, no. 1 (Oct. 2001): 99–118.

———. "The Ontology of 'Political Violence': Action and Identity in Civil Wars." *Perspectives on Politics* 1, no. 3 (Sept. 2003): 475–94.

———. "Promises and Pitfalls of an Emerging Research Program: The Microdynamics of Civil War." In *Order, Conflict, and Violence*, edited by Stathis N. Kalyvas, Ian Shapiro, and Tarek Masoud, 397–421. Cambridge, U.K.: Cambridge University Press, 2008.

Keegan, John, and Bartle Bull. "What Is a Civil War? Are We Witnessing One in Iraq?" *Prospect* 129 (Dec. 2006): 18–19.

Keenan, Danny. *Wars Without End: The Land Wars in Nineteenth-Century New Zealand.* Rev. ed. Auckland: Penguin Books, 2009.

Keeter, Scott. "Civil War: What's in a Name?" Pew Research Center Publications, Dec. 6, 2006. http://pewresearch.org/pubs/104/civil-war-whats-in-a-name.

Keitel, Elizabeth. "Principate and Civil War in the *Annals* of Tacitus." *American Journal of Philology* 105, no. 3 (Autumn 1984): 306–25.

Kelsey, Francis W. "The Title of Caesar's Work on the Gallic and Civil Wars." *Transactions and Proceedings of the American Philological Association* 36 (1905): 211–38.

Kelsey, Sean. "The Ordinance for the Trial of Charles I." *Historical Research* 76, no. 193 (Aug. 2003): 310–31.

———. "The Trial of Charles I." *English Historical Review* 118, no. 477 (June 2003): 583–617.

Kesting, Hanno. *Geschichtsphilosophie und Weltbürgerkrieg: Deutungen der Geschichte von der französischen Revolution bis zum ost-west-konflikt.* Heidelberg: Carl Winter, 1959.

Kissane, Bill. *Nations Torn Asunder: The Challenge of Civil War.* Oxford: Oxford University Press, 2016.

Kissane, Bill, and Nick Sitter. "Ideas in Conflict: The Nationalism Literature and the Comparative Study of Civil War." *Nationalism and Ethnic Politics* 19, no. 1 (2013): 38–57.

Klooster, Wim. *Revolutions in the Atlantic World: A Comparative History.* New York: New York University Press, 2009.

Kloppenberg, James T. *Toward Democracy: The Struggle for Self-Rule in European and American Thought.* New York: Oxford University Press, 2016.

Klose, Fabian. "The Colonial Testing Ground: The International Committee of the Red Cross and the Violent End of Empire." *Humanity* 2, no. 1 (Spring 2011): 107–26.

———. *Human Rights in the Shadow of Colonial Violence: The Wars of Independence in Kenya and Algeria.* Translated by Dona Geyer. Philadelphia: University of Pennsylvania Press, 2013.

Kolb, Robert. "Le droit international public et le concept de guerre civile depuis 1945." *Relations Internationales* 105 (Spring 2001): 9–29.

Koselleck, Reinhart. *Critique and Crisis: Enlightenment and the Pathogenesis of Modern Society.* Oxford: Berg, 1988.

———. "Historical Criteria of the Modern Concept of Revolution." In Koselleck, *Futures Past: On the Semantics of Historical Time*, translated by Keith Tribe, 43–57. New York: Columbia University Press, 2004.

Kreß, Claus, and Frédéric Mégret. "The Regulation of Non-international Armed Conflicts: Can a Privilege of Belligerency Be Envisioned in the Law of Non-international Armed Conflict?" *International Review of the Red Cross* 96, no. 893 (March 2014): 29–66.

Kretchik, Walter E. *U.S. Army Doctrine: From the American Revolution to the War on Terror.* Lawrence: University Press of Kansas, 2011.

Kunze, Michael. "Zweiter Dreißigjähriger Krieg—internationaler Bürgerkrieg/Weltbürgerkrieg: Sigmund Neumanns Beitrag zu einer begriffsgeschichtlichen Kontroverse." In *Intellektuelle Emigration: Zur Aktualität eines historischen Phänoms*, edited by Frank Schale, Ellen Thümler, and Michael Vollmer, 127–53. Wiesbaden: Springer, 2012.

Kyriadis, Savvas. "The Idea of Civil War in Thirteenth- and Fourteenth-Century Byzantium." *Recueil des Travaux de l'Institut d'Études Byzantines* 49 (2012): 243–56.

La Haye, Eva. *War Crimes in Internal Armed Conflicts.* Cambridge, U.K.: Cambridge University Press, 2008.

Lando, Barry. "By the Numbers, It's Civil War." *Los Angeles Times*, Nov. 29, 2006. November 29, 2006: http://articles.latimes.com /2006/nov/29/opinion/oe-lando29.

Lange, Carsten Hjort. "Triumph and Civil War in the Late Republic." *Papers of the British School at Rome* 81 (2013): 67–90.

———. *Triumphs in the Age of Civil War: The Late Republic and the Adaptability of Triumphal Tradition.* London: Bloomsbury Publishing, 2016.

Larkin, Edward. "What Is a Loyalist? The American Revolution as Civil War." *Common-Place* 8, no. 1 (Oct. 2007). http://www.common-place.org/vol-08/no-01/larkin/.

Larrère, Catherine. "Grotius et la distinction entre guerre privé et guerre publique." In *Penser la guerre au XVIIe siècle*, edited by Ninon Grangé, 73–93. Saint-Denis: Presses Universitaires de Vincennes, 2012.

Laurent, Franck. "'La guerre civile? qu'est-ce à dire? Est-ce qu'il y a une guerre étrangère?'" In *Hugo et la guerre*, edited by Claude Millet, 133–56. Paris: Maisonneuve & Larose, 2002.

Lawson, Philip. "Anatomy of a Civil War: New Perspectives on England in the Age of the American Revolution, 1767–82." *Parliamentary History* 8, no. 1 (May 1989): 142–52.

Lebreton-Savigny, Monique. *Victor Hugo et les Américains (1825–1885)*. Paris: Klincksieck, 1971.

Lee, Thomas H., and Michael D. Ramsey. "The Story of the *Prize Cases:* Executive Action and Judicial Review in Wartime." In *Presidential Power Stories*, edited by Christopher H. Schroeder and Curtis A. Bradley, 53–92. New York: Foundation Press, 2009.

Lekas, Padelis. *Marx on Classical Antiquity: Problems in Historical Methodology*. Brighton, U.K.: Wheatsheaf Books, 1988.

Lempérière, Annick. "Revolución, guerra civil, guerra de independencia en el mundo hispánico, 1808–1825." *Ayer* 55, no. 3 (2004): 15–36.

Lepore, Jill. *The Name of War: King Philip's War and the Origins of American Identity*. New York: Alfred A. Knopf, 1998.

Lind, L. R. "The Idea of the Republic and the Foundations of Roman Political Liberty." In *Studies in Latin Literature and Roman History* 4, edited by Carl Deroux, 44–108. Brussels: Latomus, 1986.

Lintott, Andrew. *Violence in Republican Rome*. 2nd ed. Oxford: Oxford University Press, 1999.

Logan, George M. "Daniel's *Civil Wars* and Lucan's *Pharsalia*." *Studies in English Literature* 11 (1971): 53–68.

———. "Lucan—Daniel—Shakespeare: New Light on the Relation

between *The Civil Wars* and *Richard II*." *Shakespeare Studies* 9 (1976): 121–40.

Loraux, Nicole. *The Divided City: On Memory and Forgetting in Ancient Athens*. Translated by Corinne Pache and Jeff Fort. New York: Zone Books, 2002.

———. "*Oikeios polemos:* La guerra nella famiglia." *Studi Storici* 28, no. 1 (Jan.–March 1987): 5–35.

———. "Thucydide et la sédition dans les mots." *Quaderni di Storia* 23 (Jan.–June 1986): 95–134.

Losurdo, Domenico. "Une catégorie centrale du révisionnisme: le concept de guerre civile internationale." *Cités* 29 (2007): 13–23.

———. *War and Revolution: Rethinking the Twentieth Century*. Translated by Gregory Elliott. London: Verso, 2015.

Lounsberry, Marie Olson, and Frederic Pearson. *Civil Wars: Internal Struggles, Global Consequences*. Toronto: University of Toronto Press, 2009.

Lucena Giraldo, Manuel. *Naciones de rebeldes: Las revoluciones de independencia latinoamericanas*. Madrid: Taurus, 2010.

Lynch, Colum. "The U.N. War over Calling Syria a 'Civil War.'" *Foreign Policy*, June 13, 2012. http://turtlebay.foreignpolicy.com/posts/2012/06/13/the_un_war_over_calling_syria_a_civil_war.

Lynch, John. *San Martín: Soldado argentino, héroe americano*. Translated by Alejandra Chaparro. Barcelona: Critica, 2009.

MacCormack, Sabine. *On the Wings of Time: Rome, the Incas, Spain, and Peru*. Princeton, N.J.: Princeton University Press, 2007.

MacCormick, Neil. "Sovereignty and After." In *Sovereignty in Fragments: The Past, Present, and Future of a Contested Concept*, edited by Hent Kalmo and Quentin Skinner, 151–68. Cambridge, U.K.: Cambridge University Press, 2010.

Mack, Charles R., and Henry H. Lesesne, eds. *Francis Lieber and the Culture of the Mind*. Columbia: University of South Carolina Press, 2005.

Malamud, Margaret. "The *Auctoritas* of Antiquity: Debating Slavery Through Classical Exempla in the Antebellum USA." In *Ancient*

Slavery and Abolition: From Hobbes to Hollywood, edited by Edith Hall, Richard Alston, and Justine McConnell, 279–317. Oxford: Oxford University Press, 2011.

Mamdani, Mahmood. "The Politics of Naming: Genocide, Civil War, Insurgency." *London Review of Books,* March 8, 2007, 1–9.

———. *Saviors and Survivors: Darfur, Politics, and the War on Terror.* New York: Pantheon Books, 2009.

Mandelbaum, Michael. *The Dawn of Peace in Europe.* New York: Twentieth Century Fund Press, 1996.

Manicas, Peter T. "War, Stasis, and Greek Political Thought." *Comparative Studies in Society and History* 24, no. 4 (Oct. 1982): 673–88.

Manjapra, Kris. *M. N. Roy: Marxism and Colonial Cosmopolitanism.* New Delhi: Routledge, 2010.

Manning, Chandra, and Adam Rothman. "The Name of War." *Opinionator* (blog), *New York Times,* Aug. 17, 2013.: http://opinionator.blogs.nytimes.com//2013/08/17/the-name-of-war/.

Marañon Moya, Gregorio. "El general De Gaulle, en Toledo." *El País,* Aug. 8, 1981, 8.

Marshall, P. J. *The Making and Unmaking of Empires: Britain, India, and America, c. 1750–1783.* Oxford: Oxford University Press, 2005.

Martin, Jean-Clément. "La guerre civile: Une notion explicative en histoire?" *EspacesTemps* 71–73 (1999): 84–99.

———. "Rivoluzione francese e guerra civile." In *Guerre fratricide: Le guerre civili in età contemporanea,* edited by Gabriele Ranzato, 28–55. Turin: Bollati Boringhieri, 1994.

———. *La Vendée et la Révolution: Accepter la mémoire pour écrire l'histoire.* Paris: Perrin, 2007.

Martinez-Gross, Gabriel, and Emmanuelle Tixier du Mesnil, eds. "La *fitna:* Le désordre politique dans l'Islam médiéval." *Médiévales* 60 (Spring 2011): 5–127.

Mason, Haydn T., ed. *The Darnton Debate: Books and Revolution in the Eighteenth Century.* Oxford: Voltaire Foundation, 1998.

Mason, T. David. "The Evolution of Theory on Civil War and Revolution." In *Handbook of War Studies III: The Intrastate Dimension*, edited by Manus I. Midlarsky, 63–99. Ann Arbor: University of Michigan Press, 2009.

Masters, Jamie. *Poetry and Civil War in Lucan's "Bellum Civile."* Cambridge, U.K.: Cambridge University Press, 1992.

Mattler, Michael J. "The Distinction Between Civil Wars and International Wars and Its Legal Implications." *Journal of International Law and Politics* 26, no. 4 (Summer 1994): 655–700.

Mayer, Arno J. *The Furies: Violence and Terror in the French and Russian Revolutions.* Princeton, N.J.: Princeton University Press, 2000.

McAlister, John T. *Viet Nam: The Origins of Revolution.* Princeton, N.J.: Princeton University Press, 1969.

McDowell, Nicholas. "Towards a Poetics of Civil War." *Essays in Criticism* 65, no. 4 (Oct. 2015): 341–67.

McGinty, Brian. *Lincoln and the Court.* Cambridge, Mass.: Harvard University Press, 2008.

McMahon, Darrin M. *Divine Fury: A History of Genius.* New York: Basic Books, 2013.

———. *Happiness: A History.* New York: Atlantic Monthly Press, 2006.

———. "The Return of the History of Ideas?" In *Rethinking Modern European Intellectual History*, edited by Darrin McMahon and Samuel Moyn, 13–31. New York: Oxford University Press, 2014.

McNelis, Charles. *Statius' Thebaid and the Poetics of Civil War.* Cambridge, U.K.: Cambridge University Press, 2007.

Mendell, Charles W. "The Epic of Asinius Pollio." *Yale Classical Studies* 1 (1928): 195–207.

Meyer, Robert T. "The Middle-Irish Version of the *Pharsalia* of Lucan." *Papers of the Michigan Academy of Science, Arts, and Letters* 44, no. 3 (1959): 355–63.

Miller, Andrew John. *Modernism and the Crisis of Sovereignty.* New York: Routledge, 2008.

Moir, Lindsay. "The Concept of Non-international Armed Conflict." In *The 1949 Geneva Conventions: A Commentary*, edited by

Andrew Clapham, Paola Gaeta, and Marco Sassòli, 392–414. Oxford: Oxford University Press, 2015.

———. *The Law of Internal Armed Conflict*. Cambridge, U.K.: Cambridge University Press, 2002.

Momigliano, Arnaldo. "Ancient History and the Antiquarian." *Journal of the Warburg and Courtauld Institutes* 13, no. 3/4 (1950): 285–315.

Le Monde. "Pour Valls, le FN peut conduire à la 'guerre civile.'" Dec. 11, 2015. http://www.lemonde.fr/elections-regionales-2015/video/2015/12/11/pour-valls-le-fn-peut-conduire-a-la-guerre-civile_4829710_4640869.html.

Moses, Dirk. "Civil War or Genocide? Britain and the Secession of East Pakistan in 1971." In *Civil Wars in South Asia: State, Sovereignty, Development*, edited by Aparna Sundar and Nandini Sundar, 142–64. New Delhi: Sage India, 2014.

Mueller, John. *Retreat from Doomsday: The Obsolescence of Major War*. New York, Basic Books, 1989.

Müller, Jan-Werner. *A Dangerous Mind: Carl Schmitt in Post-war European Thought*. New Haven, Conn.: Yale University Press, 2003.

Mundy, Jacob. "Deconstructing Civil Wars: Beyond the New Wars Debate." *Security Dialogue* 42, 3 (June 2011): 279–95.

Münkler, Herfried. *The New Wars*. Translated by Patrick Camiller. Cambridge, U.K.: Polity, 2005.

Murphy, Dan. "Why It's Time to Call Syria a Civil War." *Christian Science Monitor*, June 5, 2012.: http://www.csmonitor.com/World/Backchannels/2012/0605/Why-it-s-time-to-call-Syria-a-civil-war.

Musick, Michael P. "A War by Any Other Name." *Prologue: The Journal of the National Archives* 27, no. 2 (Summer 1995): 149.

Nation, R. Craig. *War on War: Lenin, the Zimmerwald Left, and the Origins of Communist Internationalism*. Durham, N.C.: Duke University Press, 1989.

Neely, Mark A., Jr. *The Civil War and the Limits of Destruction*. Cambridge, Mass.: Harvard University Press, 2007.

Neff, Stephen C. *Justice in Blue and Gray: A Legal History of the Civil War.* Cambridge, Mass.: Harvard University Press, 2010.

———. *War and the Law of Nations: A General History.* Cambridge, U.K.: Cambridge University Press, 2005.

Nelson, Eric. *The Royalist Revolution: Monarchy and the American Founding.* Cambridge, Mass.: Harvard University Press, 2014.

Neumann, Sigmund. "The International Civil War." *World Politics* 1, no. 3 (April 1949): 333–50.

Newman, Edward. "Conflict Research and the 'Decline' of Civil War." *Civil Wars* 11, no. 3 (Sept. 2009): 255–78.

———. *Understanding Civil Wars: Continuity and Change in Intrastate Conflict.* London: Routledge, 2014.

Nicolet, Claude, ed. *Demokratia et aristokratia: À propos de Caius Gracchus: Mots grecs et réalités romaines.* Paris: Université de Paris I, 1983.

Nipperdey, Thomas, Anselm Doering-Manteuffel, and Hans-Ulrich Thamer, eds. *Weltbürgerkrieg der Ideologien: Antworten an Ernst Nolte: Festschrift zum 70. Geburtstag.* Berlin: Propyläen, 1993.

Nolte, Ernst. *Der europäische Bürgerkrieg, 1917–1945: Nationalsozialismus und Bolschewismus.* Berlin: Propyläen, 1987.

Norbrook, David. "Lucan, Thomas May, and the Creation of a Republican Literary Culture." In *Culture and Politics in Early Stuart England,* edited by Kevin Sharpe and Peter Lake, 45–66. Basingstoke: Palgrave, 1994.

———. *Writing the English Republic: Poetry, Rhetoric, and Politics, 1627–1660.* Cambridge, U.K.: Cambridge University Press, 1999.

Núñez González, Juan Maria. "On the Meaning of *Bella Plus Quam Ciuilia* (Lucan 1, 1): A Relevant Hyperbole." In *Studies in Latin Literature and Roman History 13,* edited by Carl Deroux, 380–89. Brussels: Latomus, 2006.

Odysseos, Louiza. "Liberalism's War, Liberalism's Order: Rethinking the Global Liberal Order as a 'Global Civil War.'" Paper presented at Liberal Internationalism, San Francisco, March 25, 2008.

———. "Violence *After* the State? A Preliminary Examination of the Concept of 'Global Civil War.'" Paper presented at Violence Beyond the State, Turin, Sept. 12–15, 2007.

Orlansky, Jesse. *The State of Research on Internal War.* Science and Technology Division, Research Paper P-565. Arlington, Va.: Institute for Defense Analyses, 1970.

Orr, D. Alan. "The Juristic Foundation of Regicide." In *The Regicides and the Execution of Charles I,* edited by Jason Peacey, 117–37. Basingstoke: Palgrave, 2001.

———. *Treason and the State: Law, Politics, and Ideology in the English Civil War.* Cambridge, U.K.: Cambridge University Press, 2002.

Orwin, Clifford. "Stasis and Plague: Thucydides on the Dissolution of Society." *Journal of Politics* 50, no. 4 (Nov. 1988): 831–47.

Osgood, Josiah. *Caesar's Legacy: Civil War and the Emergence of the Roman Empire.* Cambridge, U.K.: Cambridge University Press, 2006.

———. "Ending Civil War at Rome: Rhetoric and Reality, 88 B.C.E.– 197 C.E." *American Historical Review* 120, no. 5 (Dec. 2015): 1683–95.

O'Shaughnessy, Andrew. *An Empire Divided: The American Revolution and the British Caribbean.* Philadelphia: University of Pennsylvania Press, 2000.

Östenberg, Ida. "*Veni Vidi Vici* and Caesar's Triumph." *Classical Quarterly* 63, no. 2 (Dec. 2013): 813–27.

Pani, Erika. "Ties Unbound: Membership and Community During the Wars of Independence: The Thirteen North American Colonies (1776–1783) and New Spain (1808–1820)." In *Les empires atlantiques des Lumières au libéralisme, 1763–1865,* edited by Federica Morelli, Clément Thibaud, and Geneviève Verdo, 39–65. Rennes: Presses Universitaires de Rennes, 2009.

Panourgía, Neni. *Dangerous Citizens: The Greek Left and the Terror of the State.* New York: Fordham University Press, 2009.

Patten, David A. "Is Iraq in a Civil War?" *Middle East Quarterly* 14, no. 3 (Summer 2007): 27–32.

Pavković, Aleksandar. *Creating New States: Theory and Practice of Secession.* With Peter Radan. Aldershot: Ashgate, 2007.

Pavone, Claudio. *A Civil War: A History of the Italian Resistance.* Translated by Peter Levy and David Broder. London: Verso, 2013.

Payne, Stanley G. *Civil War in Europe, 1905–1949.* Cambridge, U.K.: Cambridge University Press, 2011.

Pelling, Christopher. "'Learning from That Violent Schoolmaster': Thucydidean Intertextuality and Some Greek Views of Roman Civil War." In *Citizens of Discord: Rome and Its Civil Wars*, edited by Brian W. Breed, Cynthia Damon, and Andreola Rossi, 105–18. New York: Oxford University Press, 2010.

Pérez Vejo, Tomás. *Elegía criolla: Una reinterpretación de las guerras de independencia hispanoamericanas*. Mexico, D.F.: Tusquets, 2010.

Phillipson, Nicholas. *Adam Smith: An Enlightened Life*. London: Allen Lane, 2010.

Pictet, Jean S. *Geneva Convention for the Amelioration of the Condition of the Wounded and Sick in Armed Forces in the Field: Commentary*. Geneva: International Committee of the Red Cross, 1952.

Pinker, Steven. *The Better Angels of Our Nature: Why Violence Has Declined*. New York: Viking, 2011.

Pitts, Jennifer. "Intervention and Sovereign Equality: Legacies of Vattel." In *Just and Unjust Military Intervention: European Thinkers from Vitoria to Mill*, edited by Stefano Recchia and Jennifer M. Welsh, 132–53. Cambridge, U.K.: Cambridge University Press, 2013.

Platt, Stephen R. *Autumn in the Heavenly Kingdom: China, the West, and the Epic Story of the Taiping Civil War*. New York: Alfred A. Knopf, 2012.

Pocock, J. G. A. "The Fourth English Civil War: Dissolution, Desertion, and Alternative Histories in the Glorious Revolution." *Government and Opposition* 23, no. 2 (April 1988): 151–66.

———. "Political Thought in the English-Speaking Atlantic, 1760–1790: I, The Imperial Crisis." In *The Varieties of British Political Thought, 1500–1800*, edited by J. G. A. Pocock, Gordon J. Schochet, and Lois G. Schwoerer, 246–82. Cambridge, U.K.: Cambridge University Press, 1993.

———. "Thomas May and the Narrative of Civil War." In *Writing and Political Engagement in Seventeenth-Century England*, edited by Derek Hirst and Richard Strier, 112–44. Cambridge, U.K.: Cambridge University Press, 1999.

———, ed. *Three British Revolutions, 1641, 1688, 1776*. Princeton, N.J.: Princeton University Press, 1980.

Poignault, Rémy. "Napoleon Ier et Napoleon III lecteurs de Jules César." In *Présence de César: Actes du Colloque de 9–11 Décembre 1983: Hommage au doyen Michel Rambaud*, edited by Raymond Chevallier, 329–45. Paris: Belles Lettres, 1985.

Portinaro, Pier Paolo. "L'epoca della guerra civile mondiale?" *Teoria Politica* 8, no. 1–2 (1992): 65–77.

Pressman, Jeremy. "Why Deny Syria Is in a Civil War?" *Mideast Matrix*, Jan. 16, 2012. http://mideastmatrix.wordpress.com/2012/01/16/syria-civil-war.

Price, Jonathan J. *Thucydides and Internal War*. Cambridge, U.K.: Cambridge University Press, 2001.

———. "Thucydidean *Stasis* and the Roman Empire in Appian's Interpretation of History." In *Appian's Roman History: Empire and Civil War*, edited by Kathryn Welch, 45–63. Swansea: The Classical Press of Wales, 2015.

Raaflaub, Kurt A. "Caesar the Liberator? Factional Politics, Civil War, and Ideology." In *Caesar Against Liberty? Perspectives on His Autocracy*, edited by Francis Cairns and Elaine Fantham, 35–67. Cambridge, U.K.: Francis Cairns, 2003.

———. *Dignitatis contentio: Studien z. Motivation u. polit. Taktik im Bürgerkrieg zwischen Caesar u. Pompeius*. Munich: Beck, 1974.

———, ed. *Social Struggles in Archaic Rome: New Perspectives on the Conflict of the Orders*. 2nd ed. Oxford: Blackwell, 2005.

Rabinbach, Anson. "The Challenge of the Unprecedented: Raphael Lemkin and the Concept of Genocide." *Simon Dubnow Institute Yearbook* 4 (2005): 397–420.

Rachum, Ilan. "The Meaning of 'Revolution' in the English Revolution (London, 1648–1660)." *Journal of the History of Ideas* 56, no. 2 (April 1995): 195–215.

Radan, Peter. "Lincoln, the Constitution, and Secession." In *Secession as an International Phenomenon: From America's Civil War to Contemporary Separatist Movements*, edited by Don H. Doyle, 56–75. Athens: University of Georgia Press, 2010.

Ramsey, Robert D., III. *A Masterpiece of Counterguerrilla Warfare:*

BG J. Franklin Bell in the Philippines, 1901–1902. Fort Leaven-worth, Kans.: Combat Studies Institute Press, 2007.

Ranzato, Gabriele. "Evidence et invisibilité des guerres civiles." In *La guerre civile entre histoire et mémoire*, edited by Jean-Clément Martin, 17–25. Nantes: Ouest, 1994.

Rech, Walter. *Enemies of Mankind: Vattel's Theory of Collective Security.* Leiden: Martinus Nijhoff, 2013.

Reiter, Dan, Allan C. Stam, and Michael C. Horowitz. "A Revised Look at Interstate Wars, 1816–2007." *Journal of Conflict Resolution* 60, no. 5 (Aug. 2016): 956–76.

Remak, Joachim. *A Very Civil War: The Swiss Sonderbund War of 1847.* Boulder, Colo.: Westview Press, 1993.

Rey, Alain. *"Révolution": Histoire d'un mot.* Paris: Gallimard, 1989.

Rice, Susan E., Corinne Graff, and Janet Lewis. *Poverty and Civil War: What Policymakers Need to Know.* Brookings Institution, Global Economy and Development Working Papers 02 (Dec. 2006).

Richardson, Lewis Fry. *Statistics of Deadly Quarrels.* Edited by Quincy Wright and C. C. Lienau. Pittsburgh: Boxwood Press, 1960.

Rieber, Alfred J. "Civil Wars in the Soviet Union." *Kritika: Explorations in Russian and Eurasian History* 4, no. 1 (Winter 2003): 129–62.

Rohrbacher, David. *The Historians of Late Antiquity.* London: Routledge, 2002.

Rosenberger, Veit. *Bella et expeditiones: Die antike Terminologie der Kriege Roms.* Stuttgart: Franz Steiner, 1992.

Rosenfeld, Sophia. *Common Sense: A Political History.* Cambridge, Mass.: Harvard University Press, 2011.

Rougier, Antoine. *Les guerres civiles et le droit des gens.* Paris: L. Larose, 1903.

Rusconi, Gian Enrico. *Se cessiamo di essere una nazione: Tra etnodemocrazie regionali e cittadinanza europea.* Bologna: Il Mulino, 1993.

Sambanis, Nicholas. "A Review of Recent Advances and Future Directions in the Literature on Civil War." *Defense and Peace Economics* 13, no. 2 (June 2002): 215–43.

———. "It's Official: There Is Now a Civil War in Iraq." *The New York Times*, July 23, 2006: http://www.nytimes.com/2006/07/23 /opinion/23sambanis.html.

———. "What Is Civil War? Conceptual and Empirical Complexities of an Operational Definition." *Journal of Conflict Resolution* 48, no. 6 (Dec. 2004): 814–58.

Sarkees, Meredith. "Patterns of Civil Wars in the Twentieth Century: The Decline of Civil War?" In *Routledge Handbook of Civil Wars*, edited by Edward Newman and Karl Derouen, 236–56. London: Routledge, 2014.

Sarkees, Meredith Reid, and Frank Whelon Wayman. *Resort to War: A Data Guide to Inter-state, Extra-state, Intra-state, and Non-state Wars, 1816–2007*. Washington, D.C.: CQ Press, 2010.

Scanlon, Thomas Francis. *The Influence of Thucydides on Sallust*. Heidelberg: Winter, 1980.

Schiavone, Aldo. *Spartacus*. Translated by Jeremy Carden. Cambridge, Mass.: Harvard University Press, 2013.

Schnur, Roman. *Revolution und Weltbürgerkrieg: Studien zur Ouverture nach 1789*. Berlin: Duncker & Humblot, 1983.

———. *Rivoluzione e guerra civile*. Edited by Pier Paolo Portinaro. Milan: Giuffrè, 1986.

Schuhmann, Karl. "Hobbes's Concept of History." In *Hobbes and History*, edited by G. A. J. Rogers and Tom Sorell, 3–24. London: Routledge, 2000.

Seager, Robin. *Pompey the Great: A Political Biography*. 2nd ed. Oxford: Blackwell, 2002.

———. "Sulla." In *The Cambridge Ancient History*. 2nd ed. Vol. 11, *The Last Age of the Roman Republic, 146–43 B.C.*, edited by J. A. Crook, Andrew Lintott, and Elizabeth Rawson, 165–207. Cambridge, U.K.: Cambridge University Press, 1994.

Seaward, Paul. "Clarendon, Tacitism, and the Civil Wars of Europe." In *The Uses of History in Early Modern England*, edited by Paulina Kewes, 285–306. San Marino, Calif.: Huntington Library, 2006.

Serna, Pierre. "Toute révolution est guerre d'indépendance." In *Pour quoi faire la Révolution,* edited by Jean-Luc Chappey, Bernard Gainot, Guillaume Mazeau, Frédéric Régent, and Pierre Serna, 19–49. Marseille: Agone, 2012.

Sewall, Sarah. Introduction to *The U.S. Army/Marine Corps Counterinsurgency Field Manual: U.S. Army Field Manual No. 3–24: Marine Corps Warfighting Publication No. 3–33.5.* Chicago: University of Chicago Press, 2007.

Sewell, William H., Jr. *Logics of History: Social Theory and Social Transformation.* Chicago: University of Chicago Press, 2005.

Shapiro, James. "'Metre Meete to Furnish Lucans Style': Reconsidering Marlowe's Lucan." In *"A Poet and a Filthy Playmaker": New Essays on Christopher Marlowe,* edited by Kenneth Friedenreich, Roma Gill, and Constance B. Kuriyama, 315–26. New York: AMS Press, 1988.

Sheehan, James J. *Where Have All the Soldiers Gone? The Transformation of Modern Europe.* Boston: Houghton Mifflin, 2008.

Sherwin-White, A. N. *The Roman Citizenship.* 2nd ed. Oxford: Clarendon Press, 1973.

Shy, John. *A People Numerous and Armed: Reflections on the Military Struggle for American Independence.* Rev. ed. Ann Arbor: University of Michigan Press, 1990.

Simms, Brendan. *Three Victories and a Defeat: The Rise and Fall of the First British Empire, 1714–1783.* London: Allen Lane, 2007.

Singer, J. David, and Melvin Small. *The Wages of War, 1816–1965: A Statistical Handbook.* New York: John Wiley & Sons, 1972.

Siordet, Frédéric. "The Geneva Conventions and Civil War." *Revue internationale de la Croix-Rouge. Supplement* 3, nos. 11–12 (Nov.–Dec. 1950): 132–44, 201–18.

Siotis, Jean. *Le droit de la guerre et les conflits armés d'un caractère non-international.* Paris: Librairie Générale de Droit et de Jurisprudence, 1958.

Sivakumaran, Sandesh. *The Law of Non-international Armed Conflict.* Oxford: Oxford University Press, 2012.

Skaperdas, Stergios, et al. *The Costs of Violence.* Washington, D.C.: World Bank, 2009.

Skinner, Quentin. *Forensic Shakespeare*. Oxford: Oxford University Press, 2014.

———. "A Genealogy of the Modern State." *Proceedings of the British Academy* 162 (2009): 325–70.

Small, Melvin, and J. David Singer. *Resort to Arms: International and Civil Wars, 1816–1980*. Beverly Hills, Calif.: Sage, 1982.

Snow, Vernon F. "The Concept of Revolution in Seventeenth-Century England." *Historical Journal* 5, no. 2 (1962): 167–74.

Solis, Gary D. *The Law of Armed Conflict: International Humanitarian Law in War*. Cambridge, U.K.: Cambridge University Press, 2010.

Speier, Hans. *Revolutionary War*. Santa Monica, Calif.: Rand, 1966.

Stansfield, Gareth. "Accepting Realities in Iraq." Chatham House Middle East Programme Briefing Paper 07/02 (May 2007). http://www.chathamhouse.org.uk/publications/papers/view/-/id/501/.

Stauffer, John. "Civility, Civil Society, and Civil Wars." In Center for Civil Discourse, *Civility and American Democracy: Nine Scholars Explore the History, Challenges, and Role of Civility in Public Discourse*, 88–99. Boston: University of Massachusetts, 2012.

Stouraitis, Ioannis. "Byzantine War Against Christians—an *Emphylios Polemos*?" *Byzantina Symmeikta* 20 (2010): 85–110.

Straumann, Benjamin. *Roman Law in the State of Nature: The Classical Foundations of Hugo Grotius's Natural Law*. Cambridge, U.K.: Cambridge University Press, 2015.

Suri, Jeremi. *Power and Protest: Global Revolution and the Rise of Détente*. Cambridge, Mass.: Harvard University Press, 2003.

Sutton, Malcolm. *An Index of Deaths from the Conflict in Ireland, 1969–1993*. Belfast: Beyond the Pale, 1994.

Taheri, Amir. "There Is No Civil War in Iraq: Here Is Why." *Asharq Al-Aswat*, March 31, 2006: http://www.aawsat.net/2006/03/article55267289.

Talmon, Stefan. "Recognition of the Libyan National Transitional Council." *ASIL Insights*, June 16, 2011. http://www.asil.org/insights/volume/15/issue/16/recognition-libyan-national-transitional-council.

Thomas, Richard. "'My Brother Got Killed in the War': Internecine Intertextuality." In *Citizens of Discord: Rome and Its Civil Wars*, edited by Brian W. Breed, Cynthia Damon, and Andreola Rossi, 293–308. New York: Oxford University Press, 2010.

Toft, Monica Duffy. "Is It a Civil War, or Isn't It?" *Nieman Watchdog*, July 28, 2006. www.niemanwatchdog.org/index.cfm?fuse action=ask_this.view&askthisid=220.

Tønnesson, Stein. "A 'Global Civil War'?" In *The Consequences of September 11: A Symposium on the Implications for the Study of International Relations*, edited by Bengt Sundelius, 103–11. Stockholm: Utrikespolitiska Institutet, 2002.

Trakulhun, Sven. "Das Ende der Ming-Dynastie in China (1644): Europäische Perspektiven auf eine 'große Revolution.'" In *Revolutionsmedien—Medienrevolutionen*, edited by Sven Grampp, Kay Kirchmann, Marcus Sandl, Rudolf Schlögl, and Eva Wiebe, 475–508. Constance: UVK, 2008.

Traverso, Enzo. *A ferro e fuoco: La guerra civile europea, 1914–1945*. Bologna: Il Mulino, 2007.

———. "The New Anti-Communism: Reading the Twentieth Century." In *History and Revolution: Refuting Revisionism*, edited by Mike Haynes and Jim Wolfreys, 138–55. London: Verso, 2007.

U.K. Ministry of Defence. *The Manual of the Law of Armed Conflict*. Oxford: Oxford University Press, 2004.

United Nations Assistance Mission for Iraq. "Human Rights Report, 1 September–31 October 2006." http://www.uniraq.org /documents/HR Report Sep Oct 2006 EN.pdf.

Uppsala Conflict Data Program. http://www.pcr.uu.se/research /UCDP/.

Urbainczyk, Theresa. *Slave Revolts in Antiquity*. Berkeley: University of California Press, 2008.

U.S. Army Field Manual 100-20: Military Operations in Low Intensity Conflict (Dec. 5, 1990). www.globalsecurity.org/military/library /policy/army/fm/100-20/10020gl.htm.

U.S. Department of State, Office of Electronic Information, Bureau of Public Affairs. "Daily Press Briefing—December 2, 2011." http://www.state.gov/r/pa/prs/dpb/2011/12/178090.htm.

Varon, Elizabeth R. *Appomattox: Victory, Defeat, and Freedom at the End of the Civil War.* New York: Oxford University Press, 2014.

Varouxakis, Georgios. *Liberty Abroad: J. S. Mill on International Relations.* Cambridge, U.K.: Cambridge University Press, 2013.

———. " 'Negrophilist' Crusader: John Stuart Mill on the American Civil War and Reconstruction." *History of European Ideas* 39, no. 5 (Sept. 2013): 729–54.

Vasquez, John A. *The War Puzzle Revisited.* Cambridge, U.K.: Cambridge University Press, 2009.

Viola, Paolo. "Rivoluzione e guerra civile." In *Guerre fratricide: Le guerre civili in età contemporanea,* edited by Gabriele Ranzato, 5–26. Turin: Bollati Boringhieri, 1994.

Vité, Sylvain. "Typology of Armed Conflicts in International Humanitarian Law: Legal Concepts and Actual Situations." *International Review of the Red Cross* 91, 873 (March 2009): 69–94.

Vlassopoulos, Kostas. "Acquiring (a) Historicity: Greek History, Temporalities, and Eurocentrism in the *Sattelzeit* (1750–1850)." In *The Western Time of Ancient History: Historiographical Encounters with the Greek and Roman Pasts,* edited by Alexandra Lianeri, 156–78. Cambridge, U.K.: Cambridge University Press, 2011.

Wahrman, Dror. *The Making of the Modern Self: Identity and Culture in Eighteenth-Century England.* New Haven, Conn.: Yale University Press, 2004.

Waldmann, Peter. "Guerra civil: Aproximación a un concepto difícil de formular." In *Sociedades en guerra civil: Conflictos violentos de Europa y América Latina,* edited by Peter Waldmann and Fernando Reinardes, 27–44. Barcelona: Paidós, 1999.

Walter, Barbara F. "Does Conflict Beget Conflict? Explaining Recurring Civil War." *Journal of Peace Research* 41, no. 3 (May 2004): 371–88.

Wellman, Christopher Heath. *A Theory of Secession: The Case for Political Self-Determination.* Cambridge, U.K.: Cambridge University Press, 2005.

Wiedemann, Thomas. "Reflections of Roman Political Thought in Latin Historical Writing." In *The Cambridge History of Greek and Roman Political Thought*, edited by Christopher Rowe and Malcolm Schofield, 517–31. Cambridge, U.K.: Cambridge University Press, 2000.

Wills, Garry. *Lincoln at Gettysburg: The Words That Remade America*. New York: Simon & Schuster, 1992.

Wilmshurst, Elizabeth, ed. *International Law and the Classification of Conflicts*. Oxford: Oxford University Press, 2012.

Wimmer, Andreas. *Waves of War: Nationalism, State Formation, and Ethnic Exclusion in the Modern World*. Cambridge, U.K.: Cambridge University Press, 2013.

Wimmer, Andreas, Lars-Erik Cederman, and Brian Min. "Ethnic Politics and Armed Conflict: A Configurational Analysis of a New Global Data Set." *American Sociological Review* 74, no. 2 (April 2009): 316–37.

Wimmer, Andreas, and Brian Min. "From Empire to Nation-State: Explaining Wars in the Modern World, 1816–2001." *American Sociological Review* 71, no. 6 (Dec. 2006): 867–97.

Wiseman, T. P. *Remus: A Roman Myth*. Cambridge, U.K.: Cambridge University Press, 1995.

———. "The Two-Headed State: How the Romans Explained Civil War." In *Citizens of Discord: Rome and Its Civil Wars*, edited by Brian W. Breed, Cynthia Damon, and Andreola Rossi, 25–44. New York: Oxford University Press, 2010.

Witt, John Fabian. *Lincoln's Code: The Laws of War in American History*. New York: Free Press, 2012.

Wong, Edward. "A Matter of Definition: What Makes a Civil War, and Who Declares It So?" *New York Times*, Nov. 26, 2006. http://www.nytimes.com/2006/11/26/world/middleeast/26war.html.

Woodman, A. J. "Poems to Historians: Catullus 1 and Horace, Odes 2.1." In *Myth, History, and Culture in Republican Rome: Studies in Honour of T. P. Wiseman*, edited by David Braund and Christopher Gill, 199–213. Exeter, U.K.: University of Exeter Press, 2003.

Woolhouse, Roger. *Locke: A Biography*. Cambridge, U.K.: Cambridge University Press, 2007.

World Bank. *World Development Report 2011: Conflict, Security, and Development*. Washington, D.C.: World Bank, 2011.

Wrangham, Richard, and Dale Peterson. *Demonic Males: Apes and the Origins of Human Violence*. Boston: Houghton Mifflin, 1996.

Wright, Quincy. "The American Civil War (1861–65)." In *The International Law of Civil War*, edited by Richard A. Falk, 30–108. Baltimore: Johns Hopkins Press, 1971.

———. *A Study of War*. 2 vols. Chicago: University of Chicago Press, 1942.

Wyke, Maria. *Caesar: A Life in Western Culture*. London: Granta Books, 2007.

Wynn, Philip. *Augustine on War and Military Service*. Minneapolis: Fortress Press, 2013.

York, Neil L. "Defining and Defending Colonial American Rights: William Bollan, Agent." *American Political Thought* 3, no. 2 (Fall 2014): 197–227.

Zavis, Alexandra. "Maliki Challenges 'Civil War' Label." *Los Angeles Times*, Dec. 5, 2006: http://articles.latimes.com/2006/dec/05/world/fg-iraq5.

Zurbuchen, Simone. "Vattel's 'Law of Nations' and the Principle of Non-intervention." *Grotiana* 31 (2012): 69–84.

Index